TEFL Lesson Plans

FOR DUMMIES

A Wiley Brand

TEFL Lesson Plans
FOR DUMMIES®
A Wiley Brand

by Michelle Maxom

FOR DUMMIES®
A Wiley Brand

TEFL Lesson Plans For Dummies®

Published by: **John Wiley & Sons, Ltd.,** The Atrium, Southern Gate, Chichester, www.wiley.com

This edition first published 2014

© 2014 John Wiley & Sons, Ltd, Chichester, West Sussex.

Registered office

John Wiley & Sons Ltd, The Atrium, Southern Gate, Chichester, West Sussex, PO19 8SQ, United Kingdom

For details of our global editorial offices, for customer services and for information about how to apply for permission to reuse the copyright material in this book please see our website at www.wiley.com.

For general information on our other products and services, please contact our Customer Care Department within the U.S. at 877-762-2974, outside the U.S. at (001) 317-572-3993, or fax 317-572-4002. For technical support, please visit www.wiley.com/techsupport.

For technical support, please visit www.wiley.com/techsupport.

A catalogue record for this book is available from the British Library.

ISBN 978-1-118-76427-5 (paperback) ISBN 978-1-118-72797-3 (ebk)

ISBN 978-1-118-76425-1 (ebk)

Printed in Great Britain by TJ International, Padstow, Cornwall.

10 9 8 7 6 5 4 3 2 1

Contents at a Glance

Table of Contents

Part II: Beginner and Elementary Classes 63

Introduction

Many people have undertaken some training in Teaching English as a Foreign Language (TEFL). Perhaps you did a distance learning course, or maybe you did a CELTA a while back and you're now ready to pack that suitcase and head abroad for your first teaching job. Or maybe you have teaching experience but need a bit of inspiration to try something different in the classroom. This book is for anyone wondering, 'How do I put a great TEFL lesson together?'

The book offers a choice: You can turn to one of my lessons and teach it yourself, straight off the page; or you can read through my ideas and then put your own spin on them, creating some sparkling lessons of your own. Either way, your students will benefit from a great deal of variety and fun, fast-paced activities, which will certainly motivate them to greater success.

About This Book

This book is for teachers who want an injection of new ideas. By reading the whole book through, you'll increase your repertoire of activities for all kinds of classes. Then again, you might keep it in your library for help with emergency cover lessons or spicing up a course you teach regularly. I've organised the book to make it easy for you to identify and prepare for many tricky teaching scenarios.

This book is also for teachers who are interested in moving with the times. After taking on many roles in my TEFL career, I decided to return to the classroom on a daily basis two years ago. To my delight, I found that advances in technology are continuing to enrich this field and provide teachers with fantastic educational tools. But, at the same time, English is taught the world over, sometimes in very basic conditions. So whether you have vast resources at your fingertips or barely any, in this book I show you ways to engage your students' minds.

Who is this book not for? Anyone who needs a single resource to teach an entire course. Course books are far better for that purpose. Also, although I have included scores of complete lesson plans, this doesn't mean that you can teach from this book without preparing. You need to understand the entire lesson plan before you start teaching it, and have your materials and classroom layout ready. This is vital in order for you to feel relaxed and comfortable enough to pass on your enjoyment of the lesson to your students. Of course, you may need to adapt some parts of the lesson too.

I don't believe that a set prescription exists for teaching English effectively. No doubt, I've left out some fantastic methodologies, approaches and activities. This doesn't mean that I've vetoed them in any way. I simply draw on my own experiences in this book and, like all good teachers, I'm still learning myself.

Here are some suggestions for how to use the plans in the book:

- ✔ I suggest the timing for each activity and try to give you enough variety within each lesson to keep it lively and diverse. However, do give the students more time for the activities they really seem to enjoy. On the other hand, you can shorten slightly an informative activity that doesn't seem to suit your class. Be adaptable.

- ✔ Most teachers are employed by a school or similar educational establishment. In this case, be sure to get the agreement of your course leader or academic manager before trying something previously unheard of there, or likely to cause controversy.

- ✔ Remember that cultures and teaching situations vary considerably. So, you must ensure that your lesson plan is suitable for your particular learners.

Finally, a note on photocopying. *TEFL Lesson Plans For Dummies* isn't a photocopiable resource, but you'll find online resources you can print on the books' own website (`http://www.dummies.com/extras/tefllessonplansuk`).

Conventions Used in This Book

I use various conventions in the book to make the text user friendly:

- ✔ I use the words *student* and *learner* interchangeably.

- ✔ I refer to the teacher as *T* and student(s) as *St(s)* in the lesson plans.

- ✔ For brevity, I refer to lesson *aims* and not objectives. However, in some teaching situations you may include both.

- ✔ *English* refers to whatever is normal in most English-speaking countries, though I draw on UK examples most of the time.

- ✔ Chapters alternate between using male and female pronouns in the interest of balance.

Although beginner teachers are taught to divide their lessons into quite specific stages – such as presentation, practice and production or engage, study, activate – I don't label the lessons in this way because each lesson follows a slightly different sequence, while covering all the stages. Though a lesson must have a variety of logical stages, what you call them and how you order them is by no means written in stone.

Finally, within this book, you may noticee that some Web addresses break across two lines of text. If you're reading this book in print and want to visit one of these Web pages, simply key in the Web address exactly as it's noted in the text, pretending as though the line break doesn't exist. If you're reading this as an e-book, you've got it easy – just click the Web address to be taken directly to the Web page.

Foolish Assumptions

This book helps people who have a basic knowledge of what TEFL involves but who lack experience, confidence or ideas when it comes to real live teaching. In writing, I have assumed that you, the reader

- Are a native speaker or proficient in speaking English

- Have an initial TEFL qualification or are undertaking one

- Understand references to English grammar and pronunciation (enough to be able to source further information rather than pull your hair out in surrender)

- Are concerned with your students' engagement in and enjoyment of your lessons

- Are open to using a wider range of methodology and resources in your lesson plans than those you've learnt and tried so far

- Are agreeable to teaching a range of classes in different situations

Icons Used in This Book

Throughout the book you'll see little pictures in the margins. Each kind of icon is designed to draw your attention to a different way.

When you see this icon you get detail that illustrates how you apply the point previously mentioned in a lesson.

This icon highlights helpful ideas for everything from websites to check out to ways to make your lessons run more smoothly.

Beware! This icon alerts you to common mistakes that newer teachers make and pointers that help you avoid problems.

The text beside this icon is well worth remembering.

This icon introduces an activity that I recommend you put into practise in class.

`T >> St`

`St >> St`

These micons indicate the participants in the activity and the nature of their participation. T stands for teacher, St for Student and Sts for Students, plural. So T-St indicates an activity led by the teacher with a single student, St-St an activity between two students, and so on.

Beyond the Book

In addition to the material in the print or e-book you're reading right now, this product also comes with some access-anywhere goodies on the Web. Check out the free Cheat Sheet at www.dummies.com/cheatsheet/tefllessonplansuk for helpful tips and pointers for putting together great lessons.

You can also find ideas and outlines for more than twenty additional lesson plans online at www.dummies.com/extras/tefllessonplansuk.

Where to Go from Here

If you aren't teaching at the moment, I recommend you begin with Part I. This helps you get an overview of planning styles and choose one that suits you as a starting point. Teachers who are working on a steady course at the moment may read the whole section on low-level students (Part I), low intermediate (Part II) or higher levels (Part III) according to their students' current proficiency. In this way you're with some lesson plans and ideas you can slot into the course at the appropriate time. I offer lessons that can span more than one level in Part IV.

You may also approach the chapters by topic area. Some teachers feel that they have a lack in one particular area, regardless of the level of course they're teaching. In this case, notice that in Parts II–V the same general themes appear in each part.

If you feel that you don't get students off to good start at the beginning of a course, read Chapters 4, 10, 16 and 22 on first day lessons. This should help to put a spring in your step so you begin the course with confidence and enthusiasm. The students themselves are often too timid to show their true language skills at first. The activities I present mix the classroom dynamics so that the students work in pairs, groups and as a class. In this way they get to know each other more quickly and are likely to find at least one learning situation they feel more relaxed in.

Go to Chapters 5, 11, 17 and 23 for back to basics lessons that feature lessons you do without much technology or many specialised teacher resources. I show you how to work with everyday items or a very basic classroom.

Turn to Chapters 6, 12, 18 and 24, the traditional resources lessons, to find out how to work with the kinds of resources most established language schools have on site. Even if they aren't all there now, suggesting that the school use them shouldn't cause much surprise or controversy.

Chapters 7, 13, 19 and 25 are for you if you're interested in technology. I include the use of classroom technologies such as a computer and Internet connection, as well as student technologies such as mobile phones. You learn to be more confident about using these as part of your lessons.

Culture is the theme of Chapters 8, 14, 20 and 26. I base lessons on topics that allow for inter-cultural comparisons and further knowledge of UK culture. Start with these chapters to give your classes an international perspective.

In Chapters 9, 15, 21 and 27 the teamwork lessons encourage close co-operation among students, which tends to improve the atmosphere and enjoyment in class. Begin your reading here if your students aren't quite gelling.

The bottom line is this: don't feel you have to start on the first page and read through to the last one. Skip about the content to best suit your needs, and dip in and out as you like.

Part I

Methodology in the Madness

Getting Started

with

TEFL Lesson Plans

In this part . . .

✔ Come to grips with the nitty-gritty of TEFL teaching, including an overview of what we've learned about English teaching down the years.

✔ Find out how to adapt recent advances and theories in TEFL to your work.

✔ Get the right fit between your lessons and the syllabus.

✔ Work out the anatomy of a great lesson plan.

✔ Put together a TEFL toolbox of worksheets, props and board activities.

Chapter 1

Grasping The Basics Of TEFL Teaching

*T*he Teaching English as Foreign Language (TEFL) industry has been in full flow for many years now. In this chapter, I give you an overview of workplace jargon, and various points that may be taken for granted in language schools but are still unclear for many new teachers. The chapter aims to help you understand the job of a modern-day teacher of English as a foreign language, which sets you up to dive into the lesson plans I provide in the later sections of the book.

Understanding TEFL Language Terminology

Understanding how sentences are put together is essential. Words have different classifications, and defining how these work in English provides the rules and patterns that help students learn. You, as the teacher, must know the terminology for describing language appropriately.

For a more detailed description of TEFL grammar, please refer to *Teaching English as a Foreign Language For Dummies* (Wiley, 2009).

Verbs and tenses

At primary school, pupils often learn that *verbs* are the 'doing words'. They tend to describe both actions and a state of being. For example, look at the following sentences in which the verbs are in italic:

> I *went* to the shop *to buy* a newspaper. I *was* happy *to find* that the *price had been reduced.*

Notice the verbs in their most basic form: 'to buy' and 'to find'. This is called the *infinitive* and it means that the verb hasn't been changed in at all. Take off the word 'to' and you can find the infinitive form in a dictionary.

On the other hand, 'went', 'was' and 'had been reduced' have been transformed into particular tenses. Often, extra verbs are added to the main one to create a tense. These extra parts are called *auxiliary verbs* (for example, '*have* seen'). When 'ing' is tacked on to the end of a verb it is called a *gerund* (for example 'listening').

Table 1-1 shows you the names of the various tenses. So, for example, 'I *have taught*' is called a present perfect sentence.

Table 1-1	Tenses in English			
	Simple	*Continuous*	*Perfect*	*Perfect Continuous*
Past	taught	was/were teaching	had taught	had been teaching
Present	teach(es)	am/is/are teaching	have/has taught	have/has been teaching
Future	will teach	will be teaching	will have taught	will have been teaching

Nouns and pronouns

You use nouns and pronouns to indicate a place, person, an animal, or a thing. They can also represent more abstract ideas. In the following sentence the nouns are in bold:

> I use a **diary** to write down my **thoughts**.

As you can see, nouns can be singular or plural. Nouns you can make plural are called *countable* nouns, but others are *uncountable* so they use words like 'some' or 'a little' instead of a specific number to define the quantity.

Use a little of my **money** to buy some **bread** at the supermarket.

Pronouns replace nouns so that sentences become less repetitive:

Florence needs water and Florence gets the water from the kitchen.

*Florence needs water and **she** gets **it** from the kitchen.*

Subjects and objects

The subject of a sentence is a noun, a pronoun or an entire phrase, and it tells you what the sentence is about. For example:

Florence needs water.

I went to the shop.

Reading books is fun.

After the subject of a sentence there is generally a verb. Then, sometimes there is another noun or pronoun that receives the action and this is called the *object*. For example:

I love **it**.

She reads **a book**.

They waved to **the boys**.

Prepositions

Prepositions introduce the object of a sentence. They include words such as 'with', 'through, and 'among'. For example:

You should walk **through** the park.

Mike lives **with** Jenna.

Adjectives

Adjectives give more information about nouns or pronouns. They may indicate size, colour, or quality. For example:

The **enormous** book lay on the **fabulous** desk.

Adverbs

Adverbs give more information about a verb, often showing how it is carried out:

The girl smiled **sweetly** and **timidly** as she stepped behind her sister.

Qualifiers

Qualifiers appear before adjectives and adverbs and show degree. For instance:

That meal was **rather** nice.

Gold is **quite** expensive.

Articles

Simply put, the articles in English are the *indefinite articles* 'a' or 'an', and the *definite article* 'the'. These words come before nouns and are types of adjective. However, the indefinite articles show that something is general, while the definite article indicates something more specific. For example:

A man arrived and **the** nurse greeted him.

Conjunctions

Conjunctions, sometimes called linking words, join parts of a sentence together and they include 'because', 'but' and 'although'. Note how they connect the words in this example:

I like plays **and** films, **although** I don't enjoy operas much.

Recognising the Different Types of English Course

It isn't enough to get a job a job teaching English. You really must know what kind of course it is and, in addition to its target age and level, how each course differs. Here's a breakdown of the main English courses available:

- ✔ **Academic English:** For students who want to undertake a course of higher education in the English language. On a course of this nature students learn how to express concepts, ideas, and theories using formal, impersonal language. Students also practise essay writing, giving formal presentations, listening, and note-taking for lectures.

- ✔ **Business English:** Tends to cover the same grammatical structures as general English. However, the context for using the language is always a business meeting, a negotiation, a formal letter, or another function of day-to-day business life. These courses may be sponsored by a company for its employees.

- ✔ **English for Speakers of Other Languages (ESOL):** For students who are now living in an English-speaking country where they want to settle. Practical skills such as speaking to employees at government offices and banks or visiting healthcare professionals are included in the course material.

- ✔ **English for Specific Purposes (ESP):** A branch of teaching whereby you analyse exactly what the student needs to do in English and gear the whole course towards that outcome. For example, you may teach English for nurses, or English for the banking industry.

- ✔ **Exam classes:** When students plan to take a particular exam, the preparatory course is entirely focused on this outcome. So you show students how to tackle the exam questions, breaking them down so that they understand what the examiners are looking for. Students analyse past papers and do practice tests.

- ✔ **General English:** Teaches students everyday language and usually comprises reading, writing, speaking, and listening, which are the four main skills of language learning.

- ✔ **One to one:** This might also be called a private lesson, although it could be arranged in the teacher's own time or as part of a job at a school. It basically means that there is one teacher and one student in the class, so you get to focus on the learner's individual needs.

✔ **Presessional and Insessional:** These courses are for students who have received an offer of a place on a degree course. A *presessional* course is generally run by the university that's offering the placement and is designed to acclimatise students to cultural differences and academic expectations. Successful completion of the course may be a requirement before the student can take up his place on the degree course. Then, *insessional* lessons are for international students who are already doing their degree course but require extra support in using academic English in order to succeed.

Determining the Common European Framework Levels

Most courses divide students into varying levels of proficiency. These days the Common European Framework of Reference for Languages (CEFR) descriptors are frequently used to specify a student's level in a particular language. The framework is based on what the student should be able to do in that tongue when a particular level is reached. Table 1-2 breaks down the levels.

Table 1-2	Classifications of proficiency levels in language teaching	
CEFR Level	**Everyday Level**	**Approximate Hours of Study**
A1	Basic English / beginner	Less than 100
A2	Basic English / elementary	200
B1	Independent user / low intermediate	400
B2	Independent user / high intermediate	600
C1	Advanced	800
C2	Proficiency	1,000+

Refer to the Cambridge English website for a set of descriptors for each CEFR level: www.cambridgeenglishteacher.org/what_is_this.

Getting to Grips with Lesson Planning Terms

As a teacher you're perfectly entitled to set out your lesson plans in the way you please . . . except, of course, if someone else needs to read them (such as another member of staff or an education inspector). In that case, you should follow certain conventions.

The traditional TEFL plan sets out the stages of the lesson and the different types of activities that you do with the students. It shows who is speaking to whom and may show what you intend to put on the board such as grammar and pronunciation features.

Organising a lesson

You can label major shifts of focus in your lesson according to the planning model you adopt. There are three main models:

- Engage / Study / Activate (ESA)
- Authentic use / Restricted use / Clarification and focus (ARC)
- Presentation / Practice / Production (PPP)

Refer to Chapter 3 of this book for guidance on using different styles of planning.

Look who's talking

TTT stands for Teacher Talking Time, whereas as when students speak it's *STT*. *T* usually represents the teacher throughout the plan and students are represented by *Sts* or *Ss*. Use any obvious abbreviation for pair or group work.

Noting aspects of pronunciation

Phonology and *phonemics* are terms related to the sounds that make up a particular language. One *phoneme* is a single unit of sound that you recognise in a language as part of a word. For example, the word 'fish' has three phonemes: f+ɪ+ʃ. You should write phonemes between forward slashes like this /fɪʃ/ (by the way /ʃ/ is the 'sh' sound).

If you compare /b/ and /p/ while touching your Adam's apple, you should feel the difference between *voiced* and *unvoiced* phonemes, because in the latter there isn't much vibration, just air forced from the mouth.

A *monothong* is a single vowel phoneme, but *dipthongs* are made by pushing two vowel sounds together as one; for example, /aɪ/ is the vowel sound in 'my'.

Minimal pairs refers to two words that are pronounced in almost the same way except for one different phoneme, such as 'pill' and 'pull'.

Homophones such as 'ate' and 'eight' sound exactly the same but with different spellings, whilst *homographs* 'bow' /bəʊ/(one you tie) and 'bow' /baʊ/ (lower the top half of your body out of respect) are written in the same way.

You can put *stress* on one syllable in a word, or particular words in a sentence, by pronouncing that part more strongly. *Intonation*, meanwhile, refers to the way you make your voice go up or down to show your attitude, or whether you're asking a question instead of making a statement.

See Chapter 12 of *Teaching English as a Foreign Language For Dummies* (Wiley, 2009) for more information about teaching pronunciation and a list of all the phonemes.

Fathoming the Business of Language Schools

When you first enter the teachers' room and hear the everyday banter of your colleagues, you'll doubtless find a tremendous amount of jargon to get through. Here's a brief explanation of teachers' room chatter.

Equipment

Authentic material is borrowed from the real world (such as a newspaper) rather than something specifically designed for TEFL, and if you bring in some props to help you explain a point (such as a pair of socks to teach the word 'socks') that's called *realia*.

Key books for learning typically include the students' *course book* for everyday use in the classroom, the *workbook*, which contains homework exercises for students, and the *teacher's book*, which contains all the answers as well as lesson plans and extra activities. Many of these publications are accompanied by a

CD/DVD/CD rom. There should also be *learners' dictionaries* in the classroom, which feature the most commonly used words in the language and useful information on grammar. Finally, you need *readers*, which are very slim novels written to match a particular level of English.

Technical equipment in the best-equipped classrooms include an *interactive whiteboard* (IWB), which is a board connected to a computer and projector, and a *visualiser* for showing printed documents from hard copy on a computer screen. Of course, you ought to have a TV and PC, but if you're using older resources on a cassette you might have a professional-standard cassette player such as those manufactured by Coomber.

Student exams

A range of widely recognised examining bodies exist for the UK and for the general international market.

- The **Cambridge** suite of exams is particularly well known and wide-ranging. For young learners, you have Starters, Movers, and Flyers tests, which are progressively more difficult. The general English exams are KET (Key English Test), PET (PreliminaryEnglish Test), FCE (First Certificate in English) CAE (Certificate in Advanced English), CPE (Cambridge Proficiency Exam) and ESOL(English for Speakers of Other Languages) Skills for Life, which cover all the stages of learning from elementary to proficiency. Cambridge BEC (Business English Certificate) and BULATS (Business Language Testing Service) are tailored towards business English. For more information see www.cambridgeenglish.org/exams-and-qualifications.

- **Pearson** tests of English, or PTE, in general English, academic English and younger learners categories are also available. See pearsonpte.com/Pages/Home.aspx.

- **IELTS** is an exam students can take in a general or academic English format. It is recognised by government immigration departments, employers, and educational establishments. Find out more at takeielts.britishcouncil.org.

- **TOEFL** serves a similar purpose as IELTS, and many institutions accept a set score in either. **TOEIC,** on the hand, is used by employers. The website for these two exams is www.ets.org.

- The **London Chamber of Commerce and Industry** (LCCI) offers a range of ESP exams in English for tourism, speaking in business settings and accounting. Check out www.lcci.org.uk for more information.

Teacher qualifications

Generally speaking, it's best to have a degree and a TEFL qualification that includes real live teaching practice observed by a tutor, if you want to be accepted in a broad range of teaching establishments.

The most recognised initial qualifications in the UK are CELTA and TrinityCert-Tesol. However, if you want to move forward in the job and be eligible for higher positions, you need a diploma such as the DELTA or Trinity DipTESOL. Masters degrees in TEFL/TESOL tend to be for new teachers, but serving teachers sometimes go on to do a master's in applied linguistics.

For the UK ESOL sector, new teachers need to do a course leading to an award in Preparing to Teach in the Lifelong Learning Sector (PTLLS).

For more information about EFL teacher training courses, see Chapter three of Teaching English as Foreign Language For Dummies (Wiley 2009)

TEFL organisations

Here are some organisations you'll likely come across:

- ✔ The **British Council** works to share aspects of British arts, education and the English language with other cultures around the world, and English as a Foreign Language organisations in the UK generally seek to be accredited by the council. You can apply to it for teaching work abroad, but if you're in the UK, be aware that when your colleagues are talking about this organisation it's usually because the inspectors are coming to visit the school. That means a thorough review of the school's practices, including your teaching. The British Council website also provides teaching materials and advice. Visit www.britishcouncil.org/learning-teaching-english-gateway.

- ✔ **English UK** is the national association of accredited English language centres and it runs fairs, conferences and training days for the TEFL industry.

- ✔ **UKBA** is the border agency for the UK and its rules and policies about visas influence who can study in the UK. The agency influences the number of hours visa holders can study (Tier 4 visa students are mentioned most) and how teachers record student attendance in class.

Chapter 2

Adapting Recent Approaches and Methodologies to Your Work

In This Chapter

▶ Finding out why TEFL courses are so varied

▶ Identifying great sources for professional development

▶ Considering different views on course planning

▶ Getting lots of ideas for dynamic lessons

*I*t's likely that throughout your teaching career you'll work for schools that have varying approaches and methodologies. You may even develop a few of your own. Still, as a TEFL teacher you needn't consider any particular approach or methodology as being exclusively right or wrong. Keeping an open mind helps you to be adaptable and to select the best points from various sources, which you can then bring into your classroom.

In this chapter, I introduce you to a selection of approaches and methodologies in TEFL that are likely to influence your course design and teaching practice on a daily basis. The list is by no means exhaustive, but helps you to understand the thinking behind the current view of 'best practice' in English language teaching.

The insight gained from studying a bit of the theoretical stuff also helps you to start supporting your own ideas and instincts about teaching within an academic foundation. If you can explain why you're following a particular procedure in your lessons, your managers and others who observe you, such as inspectors, are more likely to accept that you've prepared well and should be allowed to try new things. So I provide references for further reading too, to help you investigate the approaches and methodologies that appeal to you most.

Think of this chapter as developing an armoury. Some pieces are new and some old, but no matter what problem arises in the 'battle', you'll have equipment to help you deal with it. First I explain some of the beliefs about language learning that course planners consider before deciding on the precise content of a course and the order it should be presented in, and then I move on to discussing actual classroom practice. The most exciting courses contain an eclectic mix of a few approaches, methodologies and hypotheses based on the observations of educators, and in this way teachers can meet a whole range of student needs (not to mention that the mix keeps the job interesting).

Approaches and Methods in Language Teaching by Jack Richards and Theodore Rodgers (Cambridge Language Teaching Library, 2001) gives you lots more useful information on this topic than I have space for here.

Knowing How People Learn, and How to Help Them Learn

Over the last century or so linguists such as Chomsky, Bruner and Piaget have put forward various theories about how humans learn their first language and how this knowledge should help us teach additional languages. Here I summarise the most common beliefs about language development without getting too technical.

Comparing the learning of a first language and a second one

To grasp a language you need to recognise its individual sounds, whole words, and then the grammar that makes sentences. Amazingly, it seems that almost all children everywhere are born ready to learn these things. So infants realise that if they make certain sounds, they get the same response over and over again, and they imitate those around them. Their caregivers reinforce learning of the language by encouraging the infant and by simplifying communication for them. Very young children can also decipher basic principles of grammar and structure as long as they receive lots of input from adults. To a large extent, then, imitation and conditioning are involved, but also there is an innate ability to develop language skills.

The aim of EFL teachers is to harness some of this knowledge so that we can use similar processes in the classroom. Teachers become like the caregivers, drilling language, grading the information to suit the student's level, and egging the learners on. However, we rarely produce a student as successful as the infant. Our students may well progress but few reach native speaker-like proficiency. Why is this?

✔ The student's first language is so embedded that the learner can't help but refer back to it as 'the right way'. This is how mother tongue interference arises, meaning that students somehow use rules and vocabulary from the mother tongue and transfer them to the new language. This, of course, creates errors.

✔ Learners become self-conscious and nervous, which slows them down.

✔ The stresses of life are far greater than when the learners were infants, so the mind is occupied with other things. The very struggle to learn can be demotivating in itself.

Helping successful language learning

First-language acquisition gives many clues as to how to assist learners with their second language.

In the classroom

Use principles from the infant and caregiver situation to enhance your teaching by following this guidance:

✔ Make new language relevant to learners.

✔ Ensure students feel relaxed.

✔ Grade lessons to become progressively more challenging.

✔ Give students encouragement and motivation.

✔ Repeat language items several times so that they're truly learnt.

✔ Use non-verbal communication, such as mime and facial expressions, to reinforce meaning.

✔ Employ rictures and realia to clarify meaning and create interest.

✔ Set new language within a clear context.

✔ Follow this order for students: listen, speak, read and then write.

✔ Don't correct every single mistake, which inhibits communication, but correct select ones to help students improve.

✔ Make sure students know the grammatical principles of the language in order to construct sentences.

✔ Teach culture and language together.

Outside the classroom

Like the growing child, students have to be motivated enough to develop their own skills rather than just relying on a teacher. Language students should endeavour to

✔ Get some good learning materials, such as a dictionary and a grammar book.

✔ Practise frequently.

✔ Read sentences or at least individual words aloud to get used to pronouncing the language.

✔ Try some of the same enjoyable activities in English as in their own mother tongue.

✔ Use memory aids such as flashcards.

✔ Set short-term and long-term learning goals.

✔ Be willing to make mistakes.

Inspiring success

As a teacher, your role is to facilitate learning by developing your personal and professional qualities:

✔ Training and experience put you in a position to prepare lessons well. Also, it's best to maintain your own desire to learn so that you continually find new information to refresh and update your lessons.

✔ Your lessons must be well-organised, stimulating, and tailored to your particular students.

✔ A good level of commitment to your employer and your students means that you're reliable and true to your word. So, for example, if you set homework, students should reasonably expect to get it back within a short time, marked, and with constructive comments.

✔ In your general interaction with the learners, do your best to be patient, positive and in possession of a sense humour!

Looking at Approaches and Methodologies for Course Planning

Have you noticed that every course book claims to offer something a little different to the competition? Then again, every language school believes that the way it teaches English is far better than other establishments. These notions of superiority are often based on the underlying approach or methodology that the school or author adopts and consequently applies to a syllabus.

Learning from past developments in TEFL

Here, for your interest, are some of the phases that language teaching has passed through, leading to the approaches and methodologies that are more common in the 21st century.

- **Grammar-translation Method** (19th century onwards): This method started as a means of teaching languages that were not going to be spoken by the learners (typically Latin). Teachers used reading texts, direct translation, and grammar rules with a focus on accuracy and comprehension of literature. The teacher generally spoke in the students' native language.

- **Direct Method** (1900 onwards): This method began as a backlash against grammar-translation. So in direct method classes, lessons are taught entirely in the new language without the use of translation. They feature everyday lexis and the emphasis is on getting students to speak and understand. Students are required to repeat language and respond to the teachers' questions without formal teaching of grammatical rules. Instead, like young children do, learners should decipher the rules by simply using them.

- **Audio-lingual method** (mainly since the 1950s): Audio-lingual classes mainly differ from previous methods in that they make liberal use of recorded or teacher-read dialogues that are repeated line by line by the class. Lots of drilling is done with the idea that learning a language is all about forming good habits, so errors are bad.

- **Cognitive theory** (since the 1960s): A range of educational approaches are in use these days that take into account the individual's mind, prior experiences and the personal meanings humans create. So learners actively participate in the process, learning rather than just being in the learning environment to receive information. For this reason some lessons are designed to emphasise the learning process rather than a definite final outcome.

- **Communicative approach** (mainly since the 1980s): This approach moved away from the earlier teacher-led methods and gets students communicating with each other in a meaningful way through role-plays and pair-work tasks (during which simple errors are expected and permissible). Teachers use authentic materials and try to link classroom activities to real-world situations.

As a newer teacher, course planning in a school is often taken out of your hands. It's quite normal to simply follow the syllabus in the chosen course book. It is not unheard of, though, for an organisation to give you a group of students, something approximating a classroom, and expect you to get on with planning and delivering the course. And you'll certainly receive private requests for one-to one-lessons in which students puts their faith in you to give their learning real structure.

Use this section to help you understand course planning and work out how to adapt a syllabus.

Killing two birds with one stone: Content and language integrated learning

Content and language integrated learning, or CLIL, is a way of designing a curriculum in which students in mainstream education learn about another subject in English. So instead of having a truly language-based lesson about English adverbs or prepositions, they learn about biology, for example, in English.

The principles of CLIL include

- ✔ Pupils should use language to study a school subject as well as discover how to use the language.
- ✔ It is normal for bilingual speakers to *code switch*, meaning that they use both languages in the same sentence or conversation.
- ✔ Exposure to different cultures helps learners develop deeper perspectives.

Considering the advantages and disadvantages

The strengths are many. Schools that use this type of course design generally promote bilingualism and create a higher level of motivation in their students. They believe in students picking up language in natural settings, which is a good long-term strategy for retaining it. Also, the English teacher's work isn't repetitive because you have the potential to cover many subjects (I can't tell you how many times I've taught the tenses, and it can get a little dull!)

The approach has weaknesses too, though. As you can imagine, such an approach requires a great deal of co-operation between subject teachers and language teachers. However, in some circumstances an educator may see CLIL as an infringement on her specialist role. You also need to be willing to learn more about the other subject in order to teach it, so success depends on the language teacher being highly motivated. In addition, as yet few TEFL courses prepare you for this kind of work.

Applying CLIL to your course

Something you can learn from CLIL that benefits all courses is that students don't always want to focus on language itself. For instance, higher level learners get tired of studying the present perfect tense or the difference between all the conditional structures. Just because they can't get it right in practice doesn't mean that they want to study it again and again relentlessly.

Here are some tips for using CLIL:

✔ Leave space in the syllabus for you to join the students in learning about a topic they're interested in; it can be a really refreshing way to approach English language studies. I did a session on Paul Weller's music recently and the students were really engaged in the culture.

✔ Encourage the students to talk about their first language (or L1, as it's known). Bilingual people don't block out one language, they just choose when and how to use it. So, allow students to tell you about the structure, vocabulary and idioms of their mother tongue and use this information to make interesting comparisons.

✔ When students speak to you in their first language, answer their questions in English. Bilingual families tend to operate like that when the parents want to keep their mother tongue to the fore.

Focusing on frequently used expressions: The Lexical Approach

The Lexical Approach: The State of ELT and the Way Forward by Michael Lewis (Language Teaching Publications, 1993) presents an approach that looks at chunks of language that students could learn as little set phrases rather than just trying to memorise individual words. Lewis asserts that fluency is based on knowing lots of 'lexical chunks' rather than simply mastering grammar. So, using this approach you teach a complete string of words, because that is how people make conversations and it would be inefficient for students to put each of those words into a sentence one by one. Here's an example of a question I've divided into three chunks of lexis for students to learn.

By the way, have you ever been on a cruise?

[By the way] + [have you ever] + been + [on a cruise]

Considering the advantages and disadvantages

There is a great deal to be said for this approach. We all use English this way, rattling off clichés, idioms and collocations in everyday speech, and when you begin to learn a foreign language you normally learn how to ask for what you need using a whole chunk from your phrase book. A focus on native-speaker-like fluency and authentic usage is often more attractive to students than grammar.

However, the problem is that nobody knows the order in which you should teach all the chunks in the English language, whereas already a well-recognised order exists for teaching grammar right from beginner to advanced level. For that reason, planning a course based entirely on this approach is a challenging task.

Applying the Lexical Approach to your course

The general consensus is that using some of Lewis's principles is beneficial.

Here are six practical ideas:

- ✔ Introduce your students to authentic materials (not materials written especially for TEFL but taken from real life) as early in their learning as possible so that they can see vocabulary in its natural context.

- ✔ Highlight commonly used chunks of language in set reading or listening texts.

- ✔ From the beginning of a course, make sure you train your students to record whole chunks, not individual words, in their notebooks.

- ✔ Make English–English dictionaries available in the classroom and use them frequently for information about collocations, not just meaning.

- ✔ Build songs into the course so that whole phrases stick in the students' minds in a fun way.

- ✔ Encourage students to guess the meaning of vocabulary from the context.

Types of activities typical of a lexical course include matching, deleting and categorising of vocabulary.

Even if you don't have a syllabus based on the Lexical Approach, you can use principles and techniques from this approach to handle vocabulary more effectively in lessons.

Being a counsellor for your students: Community language learning

Not to be confused with CLIL above, you could say that community language learning (CLL) courses are designed by the students themselves in the sense that the teacher, called the *knower*, only translates and transcribes the things the students have decided to discuss. CLL is generally used with monolingual groups who all sit in a circle, rather like a group counselling session. The process is something like this for lower levels:

1. **The learners decide what to discuss. You sit nearby but slightly out of the circle.**

2. **Someone calls you over and whispers to you in their first language explaining what she wants to say.**

3. **You whisper back the translation.**

4. You record the utterances and a whole discussion builds up.

5. You transcribe the discussion using the recording.

6. You analyse the discussion with the group in another session.

7. The class reflects on the session and what they have accomplished.

The methodology here is that students gradually learn to increase their independence. Eventually, they don't need much help from the teacher/knower and another learner can take the role of the knower by assisting weaker members of the group.

Considering the advantages and disadvantages

One of the good things about counselling learning, as it is sometimes called, is that the students take more responsibility for their learning and also build up a strong team spirit. They provide the content themselves so it's highly relevant to the group. Practitioners consider this kind of course to be more holistic in its approach because the knower doesn't dominate the group or force anyone to speak.

The downside is that the knower needs a good knowledge of the students' first language and it's difficult to translate constantly without preparation of the topic. Even for a bilingual knower, the session can be very draining. Then there's that annoying tendency we teachers have of wanting to actually teach! Of course, with this approach you have to avoid butting into the discussion.

When it comes to the students, CLL doesn't suit all ages because the students need a sufficient level of maturity and patience to handle the counselling style. The first few sessions can be painfully slow too, until students get the hang of it.

Applying CLL to your course

Occasional use of CLL can help you reassess your role as teacher and show your students that you value their input. You can use it to help your class to become more active participants if they're inclined to leave it all up to you.

Here are some suggestions to consider:

- ✔ If your class has a range of different skills and backgrounds, set up smaller groups with one student acting as the knower who'll help the others learn about their own particular specialism. So, for instance, the graduate in fashion design may be the one to help the others learn about clothing expressions.

- ✔ Because many students have recording devices built into their mobile phones, you could integrate recording and analysis of classroom discussions into your course as a way of recycling language.

✔ At the beginning of each week, ask your students to come up with a topic for a ten-minute discussion. Help them prepare the necessary vocabulary. Record the discussion session, making sure to stay out of it (except for the odd whispered bit of assistance). Then get the students to transcribe the discussion as you play it back (the whole thing or just the good bits depending on how much time you have). Finally, they can offer each other correction on their respective errors.

Deciding between global English and other varieties

Global English and English as a lingua franca are expressions that are becoming more common. These days there is a move afoot in the TEFL world to banish something called *linguistic imperialism* in which 'good English' traditionally means the kind used by educated native speakers in countries such as the UK, the USA, Canada, New Zealand and Australia, giving them a rather unfair advantage in the world (which we TEFL teachers tend to exploit shamelessly, of course). The supporters of ELF (English as a lingua franca) and Global English propose that TEFL teachers adjust their view of correctness.

In our first language varieties of English plenty of linguistic idiosyncrasies exist that learners find totally frustrating and not entirely necessary for effective communication. In reality the majority of people in the world who speak English aren't native speakers at all. They've learnt it as a second or third language, or are life-long bilinguals, and a great many of them use the language very fluently and effectively. This is despite the fact that they don't apply all the rules the academics of the native-speaker community insist on.

So those in favour of ELF may say that if most non-native and bilingual speakers drop the third person 's' anyway ('He speak', for example), why insist on teaching and correcting it? A good number of native speakers do it too, so ELF advocates argue that TEFL teachers should recognise this as a variant, not a grammatical error. After all, in the global village it is communication that matters and everyone can understand the simpler ELF version, so there should be no problem.

Questions therefore arise about the future of the English language and which form of it teachers should be teaching in the classroom. So when designing a TEFL course, considering what your group of students need is important. Is it British English, American English, or perhaps something else?

Considering the advantages and disadvantages

Using ELF is a very modern take on English language teaching and the debate surrounding it forces reflection on your beliefs as a teacher and 'guardian' of the language. This new form of English is simpler, logical in structure and yet easy for every speaker of the language to understand. As it develops it can accommodate the input of educators and speakers all over the world in establishing the core language. Surely this is better than having rules dictated by a seemingly elite minority? Moreover, students could achieve proficiency much more quickly than with current models of English.

But publishers haven't yet latched on to ELF in a big way, so it's rather difficult to find course books that support using it. In fact, some academics don't even recognise that this variant form of English exists! Furthermore, although ELF speakers can communicate, they may find that they're disadvantaged in situations where native speaker varieties are held in higher esteem. Whether you like it or not, your clients, the students, often like the prestige that certain varieties of English seem to offer, and business is business, so you just have to give the customers what they want.

Applying ELF or global English to your course

Follow these pointers:

- ✔ Whatever your beliefs about linguistic imperialism, make sure the materials you use fit the kind of English your students actually need or specifically request.

- ✔ Remember that many people around the world resent having to learn English and blame the language for undermining local culture. Be sensitive to this in the classroom and adapt as necessary.

- ✔ Promote bilingualism instead of always setting native speaker-like competence as the ultimate goal.

- ✔ Encourage some translation rather than thinking in English.

- ✔ Don't teach British English (or some other high status version) as the best; put it on a par with Standard Jamaican English, Indian English or any other effective and well-used variety.

Exploring a notional functional approach

The traditional way to structure English language courses is to start with the easy grammar and vocabulary and then get progressively more difficult with each lesson, but this isn't the case with a notional functional syllabus. With this kind of approach the course designer has to consider what the students actually need to do using the English language. You analyse social contexts and organise the courses based on these. So if today's lesson is about shopping, it's at this point that the students learn: *How much is that? Could I have . . .?* And so on. The fact that grammatically speaking 'could' is a modal verb and is followed by an infinitive is rather less important here than the students' need to say these particular words when they want to buy something.

Considering the advantages and disadvantages

A course syllabus organised in this way can be highly motivating for students. This is because they feel that they can actually go out and do something in the real world using their English. What they learn has a communicative purpose.

Then again, what happens if the student doesn't want to perform that function? Perhaps your course features a whole lesson on shopping but you have a class of teenage geeks who only ever order things online? One of the main problems then is that course designers tend to use their own intuition about the notions and functions students will need and they're not always right.

And what if beginner students seem to require some very complex grammar and vocabulary in English that they're not yet ready to learn? There are obviously issues of grading language if you don't start from easy and progress to the difficult parts.

Life isn't just about social functions. Where other goals are important, such as taking exams for access to academic courses, this kind of syllabus may not prepare students adequately. So educators' needs can be different to the students' view of their needs.

Keep in mind that men and women perform different social functions in many cultures and so this syllabus may not have the equal gender appeal of a grammatical one.

Finding a framework

The Common European Framework of Reference for Languages is a set of guidelines compiled by the Council of Europe in a notional functional way. This document includes a detailed list of all the things students should be able to do at each level of language proficiency and it influences most modern language teaching in the EU. It shapes course book design as well as student expectations, so it's good to become familiar with it if you're teaching in this part of the world.

Applying a notional/functional approach to your course

Here are some ideas to try:

✔ When you write your lesson plan, include this sentence and add a particular function or notion: *By the end of this lesson my students will be able to . . .* If, after every lesson your students are able to say 'I know how to do x in English now', their motivation will be higher.

✔ When you plan your lessons, think about notions and functions so that you don't end up teaching abstract pieces of grammar, even if your syllabus wasn't designed in this way. For example, when it's time to teach the third conditional, tell your students that they're going to learn about expressing their regrets. This makes the grammar more approachable; after all, everyone has an 'If only . . .'

✔ Use this approach to question your choice of vocabulary to teach. You may have some interesting words you'd love to tell students about but ask yourself in what context they could ever use them. If you can't come up with a realistic context, don't bother teaching the vocab!

Face to face meets online tuition with blended learning

At the name suggests, *blended learning* is a mixture of media for course delivery. Modern technology affords course providers the opportunity to vary the way they give instruction so that some content is provided online, outside of the classroom lesson, and some is delivered in a more traditional way by a teacher.

Blended learning has much in common with Computer Assisted Language Learning (CALL), when students use computers in the classroom. *The International Teaching English as a Second Language Journal* has a vast array of CALL links on its website: iteslj.org/links/TESL/CALL/.

Considering the advantages and disadvantages

Computerised media allows students to access documents such as resources, syllabi, learning objectives, and marking criteria with ease online. The resources they access reflect their own pace of learning and encourage learner independence. In addition, students can set up their own discussion forum for mutual support or field questions and comments back to the teacher online, which can bring greater focus to the face-face sessions.

Using computerised media is eco-friendly because it reduces photocopying drastically and effectively means that the language school is open all hours (or at least its online library is). The computer will happily let you repeat an exercise again and again if needs be, without getting frustrated or being subject to the time constraints a teacher has.

Where the technology falls down is that some students are demotivated by being forced to stare at a screen. Others don't have access to reliable Internet connections so find themselves at a disadvantage having to spend hours in the library rather than with a simple course book at home.

That brings me to the advantages of the classroom component of blended learning courses. Students want personalised commendation and correction. Teachers can give positive reinforcement with a simple smile, nod or pat on the back. Also, students generally enjoy the friendship and spontaneity of classmates they can see, and this stimulates further progress. Access to a teacher is vital because you cannot possibly predict all the questions students will need to ask and store the answers online.

So, taking all that into account, blending makes sense. It requires language schools to invest in technology and in the initial preparation time for the teacher to place all the documents and links online. The blended course may not be quite as spontaneous as a purely teacher-led one in the sense that after the syllabus and materials have been posted online, you can't so easily shift to suit your particular learners. However, because most 21st-century students seem to spend a great deal of time on the Internet anyway, why not harness that for the students' good?

Applying blended learning to your course

Taking both forms of course delivery into consideration, the blended approach seems to be the way forward wherever the technology to do so is available. If your school hasn't designed the course this way, you can still mimic some of the principles that blended learning embodies.

Try these ideas:

✔ Give students plenty of opportunity to learn independently by supplying references for further study whether in print or online.

✔ Even if the Internet isn't available in your school, students may well have access to it privately. Set some homework based on Internet research every now and then.

✔ Apply a level of differentiation to your course by having extra but non-essential activities on hand.

Assessing Approaches and Methodologies for Classroom Delivery

This section helps you to develop your own personal flair in the classroom. Even when your syllabus is set in stone, you often get to choose how exactly you deliver the information to the students. Finding out about different ways to deliver your lesson makes you less predictable and more dynamic.

Using principles from the Silent Way

Silent Way teaching has been around since the 1970s. As the name suggests, the teacher doesn't say much, but actually uses props, gestures, and charts to elicit all the responses from students and prompt further utterances.

I recommend that you find a video to show you the method in operation because no written description can do it justice. For example, search for Silent Way ESL Class on YouTube. It's worth a look!

The main principles behind the Silent Way are:

- You help students to learn through discovery and creating instead of memorising and repetition.

- Actual physical objects do much to aid learning. Typical props are:

  - *Cuisenaire rods:* wooden sticks of different colours and lengths that you can use to represent something different; for example, parts of a sentence or characters in a story.

  - A chart with all the sounds of English represented in colourful blocks. When you point to the appropriate place on the chart the student makes that sound and pronounces the word correctly.

  What's good about these props is that when students try to remember what they've learnt, they recall the colours and shapes as well as, or instead of, just words.

- Problem-solving activities related to the material the learners are focusing on are very effective.

Considering the advantages and disadvantages

There are no intimidating course books to put students off. Students don't take a back seat and let the teacher do all the work; they have to get stuck in from the outset. On the whole students in the Silent Way classroom take more responsibility for their learning and become quite independent.

This way of teaching has not taken off everywhere, which can only mean drawbacks exist. One is that students don't tend to communicate with each other as much as with other methods; they speak aloud in response to what you're doing. In addition, teachers don't give the students any examples to start them off, nor offer correction. Also, many teachers find the Silent Way less effective with larger classes. Finally, although the props are useful you can't teach everything in the language using them. That's why I particularly recommend using the principles of this approach with lower-level students.

Applying the Silent Way to your course

Here are elements of the approach you may want to incorporate in your teaching:

- ✔ Limit teacher talking time. Don't always jump in when your students need a little thinking time.

- ✔ Use visual prompts in the classroom including colour and shape. Mime and gestures are great too.

- ✔ Have useful charts on the wall – for example, a coloured phonology one – to remind the students of points they need.

- ✔ Engage your students' curiosity.

- ✔ Don't simply offer the answers. Let the students work things out because problem-solving engages more of the brain.

- ✔ Don't be totally reliant on the course book.

- ✔ Remain silent while the students are working so that you can observe more. Then you'll know their strengths and weaknesses.

Allowing students to acquire, not learn, with the natural approach

Before considering the natural approach you need to know the difference between learning a language and acquiring one, because this is at its core.

Learning is very much a conscious process. You sit with a teacher and pay attention to the rules, structure and vocabulary. However, *acquisition* is basically picking up language, allowing the brain to do what it did naturally when you were an infant.

With that differentiation in mind, the natural approach is designed to recognise the limited, but necessary, value of learning.

Typically, you speak to the class about a given topic, or play an audio recording, while the students listen. Then the students do an activity based on what they've heard, such as filling in a gapped text or labelling a diagram. You correct the students according to the meaning they've conveyed, not their grammar. Then you set a more challenging communicative activity on the topic.

These are some of the basic principles:

- ✔ The main focus is communicative ability.

- ✔ Vocabulary is the most important part of the language, not grammar.

- ✔ Taking in the language by listening and reading should come first and speaking and writing later.

- ✔ Language is all about meaningful messages.

- ✔ Learning the rules of a new language only helps you correct yourself following acquisition.

Considering the advantages and disadvantages

A great aspect of the natural approach is that motivation, self-confidence and low anxiety are very important considerations, so the classroom allows the student to acquire English in a relaxed environment. Learners don't speak until they feel ready to do so because comprehension takes priority over producing language. Another positive aspect is that most language learners dread grammar, but the natural approach has no grammatical syllabus. Finally, the input provided is well graded so that students are given a slightly harder challenge each time.

On the other hand, some would argue that if learners 'emerge' and begin speaking when they feel ready to, this may happen at too many different stages among the students in one class and make activities difficult to manage. In addition, the natural approach places a great deal of emphasis on graded reading texts, whereas some learners would prefer to just read about things they're interested in, even if the level is much higher than their current stage. Finally, many teachers feel that producing language (speaking and writing), helps to solidify learning or acquisition, but this approach stresses receiving language (reading and listening).

Applying the natural approach to your course

See how the natural approach can inspire your teaching:

- ✔ Get students responding to a listening text by following a map, filling in a grid, or putting information in order.

- ✔ Recognise that controlled teacher talking time can be valuable. If you have periods of speaking about a chosen topic, students can acquire expressions in English very naturally from you.

✔ Don't over-correct students. Allow them to continue during a communicative activity for as long as they're able to convey the right meaning (despite dodgy grammar).

✔ Use closed questions before open ones. For example, give students multiple choice or yes/no questions before expecting them to be comfortable enough with the vocabulary to express an opinion.

Teaching playfully with Suggestopaedia

Practitioners of *Suggestopaedia* (sometimes called Desuggestopaedia or spelled Suggestopedia) believe in the power of both conscious and non-conscious influences on the mind. The method uses carefully selected music, art, decorations, and furniture in the classroom. It's quite teacher-centred because you provide all the information, but you do so in a playful manner.

Here are the key principles:

✔ Learning happens on two levels – through linguistic messages given by the teacher and another message suggested by the rich sensory environment of the classroom.

✔ Students must be relaxed and have an expectation of success.

✔ Teachers should employ a range of activities such as acting things out, singing and playing games.

Lessons taught in this way attempt to follow a typical pattern:

1. **The introduction stage:** The teacher imparts the material playfully but doesn't analyse the new grammar or lexis.

2. **The concert session:** You play classical or baroque music quietly enough so that you can read a text over it with special intonation. The text contains the new information for the students to learn. The music provides a sense of relaxation, as well as structure and pace due to its regular beat.

3. **Practice time:** The teacher uses games or activities to practise and help students remember.

4. **Discussion time:** The class can engage in freer discussion in English.

Considering the advantages and disadvantages

Some of the principles of this method are very easy to adapt. For example, a newer teacher may know that students need to relax in the classroom but be unsure of how to make that happen. Suggestopaedia teaches you the value of music, not just as a recreational tool but as a learning tool. It encourages a positive self-image for the learner because the environment is relaxing but the course promotes confident, independent learning using the materials posted around the room. Suggestopaedia claims to produce results far more quickly than other methods and approaches.

Unfortunately, it's not all good news, because only a limited number of teachers can create a cosy classroom with comfortable furniture and baroque music. The resources aren't always available. Also, Suggestopaedia may place a little too much emphasis on memorisation rather than students working things out for themselves and communicating meaningfully with others in the class.

Applying Suggestopaedia to your course

Give Suggestopaedia principles a try:

- ✔ Use carefully chosen background music during your lessons. Apparently music in 4/4 time is the most effective for learning.

- ✔ Make sure your classroom is a relaxing place for your students.

- ✔ Use the tone and rhythm of your voice more deliberately when you read. Doing so adds meaning.

- ✔ Embed new vocabulary into stories for the class to listen to.

Making movement part of your plan: Total physical response

Total physical response, or TPR, describes a way of delivering language lessons that mimics the way very young children learn – that is, they respond to what others say by their actions even before they can speak. Here's the idea:

- ✔ Adults can learn languages better than children do (with the exception of pronunciation) but they need particular circumstances.

- ✔ TPR instructors mimic the behaviour of parents by giving direct commands.

- ✔ Speaking and comprehension happen in different parts of the brain, so students can suffer from brain overload, meaning slow learning, if they are forced to do both at the same time. Students don't have to speak in a TPR activity but they perform actions instead, which is less demanding on the brain.

In the TPR classroom the teacher gives commands, usually accompanied by an action that helps demonstrate meaning, and then the students perform the action. When they know the action, students can try repeating the command and later give each other commands.

Considering the advantages and disadvantages

A particular advantage of TPR is that students feel less stressed when they don't have to speak. TPR is called a 'brain compatible tool for learning', and that means that students effectively retain language in the short and long terms. Anyone can enjoy this kind of lesson, from small children upwards, and you can adapt it for all levels. Another positive point is that students don't need to be gifted language learners or have an academic mind. Kinaesthetic students especially, who learn best through movement, love TPR. Conveniently for you, there is no photocopying or lengthy preparation of materials. Finally, research shows that students achieve comprehension very quickly.

On the other hand, TPR doesn't work so well when classroom space is restricted because it limits the commands that you can give. For instance, if you have a small classroom, you can't instruct students to walk up and down. And while it's great to begin the course in this way, your class may eventually get bored, so after a while you need to mix in other kinds of activities. TPR also makes it tricky to express some of the abstract ideas or higher level grammar as a command.

Applying TPR to your course

Some ideas for employing TPR:

- ✔ Use a TPR activity as an icebreaker on the first day or when you need to lift the mood.

- ✔ Teach students a recipe or how to fix something in this way. No doubt you can bring in all kinds of verbs and vocabulary.

- ✔ Give groups of students some new vocabulary and then get them to perform the actions to each other using TPR routines.

Helping students bond with NLP

Neuro-Linguistic Programming is all about understanding processes in the mind and how you can train your brain to improve your life. It takes into account personal identity and positive environments. These are a few of the basic principles:

- ✔ Each individual learner is important.

- ✔ You must take into account and accommodate visual, auditory, and kinaesthetic (VAK) styles of learning.

✔ Students have personal filters that affect the way they learn, namely what they remember, value, believe, and decide.

✔ You should teach both verbal and non-verbal communication in the classroom.

NLP involves encouraging students to create a comfortable new identity for themselves in the new language. They must observe the things others do well and try to imitate, or mirror, them thereby creating a good rapport. You need to be aware that faced with new language the students will delete from their minds whatever they can't handle.

Considering the advantages and disadvantages

Many people advocate the use of NLP in second language acquisition because it helps students to feel positive and successful without stress. Understanding more about how the mind works helps teachers to chunk ideas and vocabulary together, making it easier to store. Also, NLP is about *how* you learn more than *what* you learn, so students who've been exposed to English for a long time but haven't achieved the desired results may find it refreshing to undo negative thinking about their learning and renew their thoughts using NLP

The main obstacle is that many people believe NLP is a pseudo-science, lacking in scientific evidence. It has also failed to produce the results it claimed in some areas. Without a truly positive attitude from instructors and learners, NLP can't be wholly effective in the classroom.

Applying NLP to your course

You can take the following ideas and see how they benefit your students:

✔ Use mind maps on the board and encourage students to make notes in this way.

✔ Maintain flow in lessons by varying the activities and not sticking to your own preferences.

✔ Allow students to learn from the successes of others in the class and emphasise good tactics.

✔ Don't focus on errors.

✔ Establish a good rapport by being supportive and showing empathy.

✔ Get students to question themselves about when, where, and how they acquire language best by means of questionnaires and discussion.

For a general background on the use of NLP check out *Neuro-Linguistic Programming For Dummies* by Romilla Ready and Kate Burton, (Wiley, 2nd edition 2010).

Keeping everyone interested using multiple intelligences theory

Multiple intelligences (MI) theory recognises different kinds of intelligences rather than just the conventional academic view of one overall intelligence such as the kind of intelligence measured by an IQ test. Developed by Howard Gardner, a Harvard professor, MI theory tells educators to acknowledge these eight types of intelligence which are each related to the ability of an individual to solve problems in a particular social or cultural setting:

- Verbal/linguistic – using words
- Visual spatial – using pictures and images
- Bodily kinaesthetic – using movements and the body
- Interpersonal – using co-operation with others
- Intrapersonal – using self-awareness
- Musical – using music or rhythm
- Logical mathematical – using a mathematical formula or a form of logic
- Environmental – using the natural world

Academics traditionally recognise only the verbal/linguistic and logical mathematical intelligences.

Considering the advantages and disadvantages

The best thing about MI theory, is that TEFL teachers use it to move out of their comfort zone (which is likely to be standing up and speaking) and think instead about how to give students a more rounded experience through varied activities. Students are more likely to become proficient in the second language because they have used a variety of skills and maintained interest in learning.

 Sometimes students hit a plateau at about intermediate level because they are simply bored. So, test their intelligences and see which are strongest. You may be able to re-ignite a student's enthusiasm if you present activities which match her main intelligence.

Unfortunately, some educators are put off this theory by the lack of scientific data to support it. In addition, some teachers feel that the categories are too broad to realistically be applied in the classroom. For example, they find it unnecessary to consider an application of grammar to the natural world for the benefit of environmentally intelligent students. Added to that, from the student's perspective there might be some resistance to a non-traditional approach.

Applying MI to your course

If MI appeals, try these tips:

- ✔ Use a questionnaire to establish the intelligences of your students and then plan your lessons according to what will suit them.

- ✔ Help students to be aware of their own strengths and weaknesses; this will help them in setting goals.

- ✔ Give your learners the opportunity to present their work in different ways. For example, some prefer writing an essay and others prefer an oral presentation.

- ✔ Set a project. Each student in the group can perform a task that suits her intelligence.

Choosing a deductive or inductive approach to lesson plans

As I show you in Chapter 3, several well-recognised models exist for lesson planning. They basically cover two approaches: deductive and inductive reasoning:

- ✔ A **deductive** approach might also be called 'top down'. You start off with the rule and then continue to practise it. Anyone on a TEFL course learns this kind of lesson planning as the traditional PPP (Presentation, Practice, Production).

- ✔ An **inductive** approach is 'bottom up' or 'guided discovery'. So this time you start with examples of language use in context and then you use these to work out the rules.

Considering the advantages and disadvantages

A deductive lesson has certain advantages. It's clearly structured, and because most educators in the world take this approach, the students have a sense of the familiar. They understand how the lesson works, which in turn builds trust. The guided examples you provide build confidence before the students try using the new language input for themselves. Finally, deductive lessons are quicker to teach than inductive ones. The only issue is that students get bored after decades of these kinds of lessons in the education system.

The inductive way has advantages too. It encourages students to use their own observations to establish probabilities, so they make explorations that engage the mind. Inductive thinkers use their natural ability to decipher language, and when your learners do finally work it out they're more likely to remember the information. However, it takes longer to prepare an inductive lesson because you cannot be sure what your students will say or how long they need to reach the right conclusion. Therefore, you have to be ready for different outcomes.

Be careful that students don't over-generalise, though, trying to make rules that don't exist (drink/drank/drunk, `think/thank/thunk`).

Applying the deductive and inductive approaches to your course

Students can be highly sceptical of inductive lessons at first because they may not fit their image of real learning. Use both approaches until the students relax and show some faith in you.

Here are some suggestions:

- ✔ For an inductive approach, find several texts that provide examples of the point you're teaching and see whether students can spot the similarities.

- ✔ Use an inductive approach when students seem tired of studying in general.

- ✔ Use a deductive approach when lesson time is very limited and when students are not used to studying, for example with adult students who have been out of the education system for some time.

There is often a 'clever clogs' in the class who'll blurt out the answers at the beginning of an inductive lesson. You don't have to confirm or deny what that student says at the outset. Let the class continue and test out the student's theory.

Taking a task-based approach to language learning

The idea behind *task-based learning* (TBL) is that students should undertake a task in English that mimics something they may do in their own language. The focus is on fluency, and the class learns the particular vocabulary and grammar required for the task rather than having a structured syllabus. The lessons follow this type of structure:

1. **Pre-task stage:** You introduce the task and allow for preparation of the language that students will need to complete it.

2. **Task:** You run a problem-solving activity that's tackled in small groups.

3. **Plan report:** The groups prepare a report about how the task went.

4. **Deliver report:** Each group delivers their report by speaking or writing.

5. **Analysis:** You help the class to correct some language points that came up during the lesson.

Considering the advantages and disadvantages

In a TBL lesson one of the main advantages is that the students are freer in their use of language because they say whatever they can to complete the task. The students can see the relevance of the language as it is contextualised and generated by them, which is more natural than a course book syllabus. On the whole they enjoy themselves because they communicate for a larger proportion of the lesson and this is very motivating.

One of the criticisms of TBL is that it may not be appropriate for beginner students because they're unable to produce enough language to complete tasks. They need input. Another problem is that it takes a considerable amount of time to get through the tasks and their success depends on the students' abilities to undertake team work effectively. Also, you need to control the noise and discipline when the students are working independently in many groups.

Applying TBL to your course

Give these ideas a go:

- ✔ Even if you have a fixed syllabus, use TBL from time to time for extra speaking practice.

- ✔ Make sure the activities you set for your students are linked to things they (will) do in the real world.

- ✔ Sometimes students lose interest while other students are speaking. Use a reporting stage by getting the students to make notes about what others say and then compile a report about whose ideas they preferred.

Chapter 3

Getting Down to Planning

- -

In This Chapter

▶ Knowing what to keep in mind before you start to plan

▶ Making a plan to cover a week's material

▶ Incorporating the most important elements of a lesson plan

▶ Seeking inspiration from different approaches to lesson planning

- -

*W*hen it comes to actually teaching a class, you've many considerations to ensure you do a good job. Even when you think you some have great lesson content in mind, you need to ask yourself

✔ Why am I teaching this language point?

✔ How does it fit into the course?

✔ What should my lesson planning include?

✔ In what order do I present what I want to teach?

Before you start your teaching you need to do some decent paperwork to make sure that your lessons are thorough and organised. A weekly plan and a lesson plan, as explained in this chapter, helps both you and your students see that you're covering all the necessary elements, ultimately benefitting both you and your students.

In this chapter, I take you through the nuts and bolts of organising your lessons, from working with the syllabus to establishing weekly plans and individual lesson plans. I also take you through several approaches to lesson planning that can inspire your own organisation.

Establishing and Sticking to the Syllabus

A *syllabus* is a document outlining the things that are going to be taught during a course, in what order and over what period of time (the duration of the course). The syllabus helps to ensure that the course has set aims. Usually, academic managers and experienced teachers prepare it based on the contents of a chosen course book or the specific needs of a group of students.

Great TEFL teachers know what their students need to accomplish and they lead their students to success step by step, using the syllabus as the foundation. The syllabus is like a learning roadmap that guides everyone involved.

Sometimes, you may be tempted to deviate from the syllabus because you have good ideas about lessons you want to teach which are not included in it.

So why stick to the syllabus? Here are three good reasons:

- ✔ You make sure that your classes cover the breath of material required; no gaps or repetition.

- ✔ Your course content is specifically organised so that the class learns X before they can Y. So if a student whines 'Why can't we learn about . . . ?' you can explain that that point belongs to a different course or level.

- ✔ If you happen to be off sick or on holiday, another teacher can fill in for you by following the syllabus structure.

True, a syllabus might sometimes feel like a constraint if it's a poor fit, but at least you have a framework to negotiate with.

But what do you do if you'd prefer a different syllabus? Well, if you are working for a school, you can inform the school's managers so that they can adapt the syllabus for next time, or if the syllabus is based on a course book then you can suggest a different one.

Departures from the syllabus should be fairly brief and have a specific reason so that the course remains well organised.

Designing Weekly Plans

After you know your syllabus, the next step is to divide it into manageable parts. Now you know what you have to teach, you need to work out how much time to spend on each topic. You do this by making a weekly plan first, and then individual lesson plans (see the next section).

A weekly plan is very much like a mini syllabus. In some schools, teachers have to post their weekly plans on the classroom wall for the students and managers to see. School authorities and inspectors usually consider this to be best practice.

The weekly plan works for classes you teach more than once a week (a monthly plan is effective if your lessons are more widely spaced). Consider some of the benefits of the plan:

- ✔ The plan assures students that you are organised enough to think ahead about their learning.

✔ Students are reminded that the course has structure and that they need to keep up with the pace of learning because they can see when you are going to teach the next topic which is likely more challenging than the present one.

✔ Your plan can include a space for students' to request topics they want you to teach them about or questions they want you to answer. For example, they might write a request for another lesson on the present continuous tense because they are not clear how it differs from present simple tense. If students ask ahead of time, you can then prepare well to answer questions they write on the plan and allot an appropriate amount of time to dealing with them.

✔ It helps you to avoid going off piste too much, because it's easy to be so distracted by questions and topics that arise in the lesson that you spend too much time dealing with them and forget that you need time to teach other important things. The syllabus reminds you of all the things you ought to cover and that helps to put you back on track.

✔ You can use it as a revision tool at the end of the week. Look at the things in the syllabus you have covered and test the students to see what they can remember.

✔ You can see how well you are balancing out the skills focus (reading, writing, speaking, listening) because it is all set out in the syllabus making it easier to allocate appropriate time to each one.

✔ The plan makes it easier to determine when to set homework and collect it in, So you spread longer, more detailed homework assignments evenly across the course and indicate these on your syllabus. In between these, you set easier tasks so that you have enough time to mark written work and so that your students are not overloaded

If you're worried that by having a weekly plan your lessons will lack spontaneity, just don't fill your plan up too much. Make it a general guide for each day rather than a detailed list. In that way you can still tweak your daily lesson plans. Figure 3-1 gives you an idea of how a weekly plan may look.

Figure 3-1:
An example of a typical weekly plan on display in my classroom.

	__Topic__	__Student Requests__
Monday	Grammar review: Narrative tenses – past simple, past continuous, past perfect (HW: worksheet)	*Can we watch a film about Princess Diana?*
Tuesday	Reading and understanding biographies – extracts from famous memoirs	*What's the difference between the past simple and present perfect?*
Wednesday	Relating personal experiences – speaking practice	
Thursday	Recording personal experiences – writing Making your text more descriptive (HW: essay)	
Friday	Reviewing a biographical movie – clips from *Gandhiz*	*I want to go on a trip to the museum!*

Set a writing homework task on Thursday. The students have time to ask additional questions about it on Friday and you can provide examples to help them succeed. They hand in the homework on Monday, and while they're concentrating on the reading task or group activity you've set them, you get to sit quietly and start reviewing their written work during the lesson (a bit of learner autonomy is good for students). This is an efficient use of your time. Even if you don't have daily lessons with the same class, you can spread the work out in a similar way.

Making Effective Lesson Plans

Your weekly plan (see the preceding section) gives you an idea of what you want to teach each day. Now it's time to get down to the nitty gritty and put together lesson plans.

If you fail to plan, you plan to fail. But, conversely, if you plan your lesson carefully, you're already off on the right foot. If your lesson is being observed by your manager, even if it goes badly on the day, you'll be forgiven as long as your plan was solid.

At the beginning of your teaching career, and when you're being observed by another professional, your lesson plans need to be very clear and detailed. At times planning can take you hours! However, it's easy to get nervous and forget your excellent ideas when you're actually up there in front of the class, so good notes are invaluable. As you mature as a teacher, you develop your own shorthand for putting lessons together. I must admit, though, even after many years in TEFL, I still get to the board on a bad day and wonder what I'm doing there, or simply draw a blank on how to spell the word I want to teach. Embarrassing! That's why lesson plans are an excellent support.

The following sections outline what you need to include in your lesson plans (for more information on lesson plans, take a look at my book *Teaching English as a Foreign Language For Dummies*, published by Wiley).

Setting out aims and objectives

The topic of aims and objectives comes up a lot in the field of education. So the first question is, what's the difference between the two?

- ✔ An **aim** is an overall idea of what you want to achieve. In the course, your aim is always to improve your students' language proficiency. The course may also help them pass an exam or prepare them for a particular event, such as a job in an international company. At a lesson plan level, your skills-based aim might be to increase reading comprehension or to balance a student's spoken accuracy with fluency.

✔ An **objective** is to do with how you'll get students to achieve the aim. Objectives are more specific and require various procedures. So if the aim is for students to raise their score in the writing part of an exam, a lesson objective may be to analyse the differences between formal and informal language in letters. Or if the aim is to increase spoken fluency, an objective is to learn more conversation fillers, such as it's 'on the tip of my tongue'.

Most of the time, aims and objectives are bundled together. For your lesson plans you simply need to think about what the students need to be able to do better by the end of your lesson, with the syllabus in mind. Thinking about the aim and objective prevents you from simply teaching the students about your favourite topics or just having a laugh with them. (It's not that you can't have fun – after all, students learn better when relaxed – but that's the primary aim of an amusement park not a language school.)

Write your aim(s) and objective(s) at the top of the lesson plan so that you know why you're doing what you're doing. As well as writing the overall lesson aims and objectives, you may write them for each main activity also.

Listing the procedures

When you've worked out what your students need to learn, you need a variety of activities to help them grasp and practise the points you make. You plan each procedure in advance, paying attention to content, timing and who's involved in the activity.

No doubt it looks like the best lesson ever in your head, and perhaps it is, but when you write down your procedures you notice more of the important little details. A full essay for each activity isn't necessary, but some good notes make the difference between a good idea and a good lesson.

And even if you decide to use a ready-made lesson plan from this book, a course book, or a teaching website, you need to put your personal stamp on it, otherwise you come across as rather dry and stilted.

Here are some pointers to keep in mind when setting the procedures:

✔ **Analyse the new language point.** As I show in the section 'Looking at Different Ways to Plan Your Lessons', later in the chapter, you can call it the presentation, study, clarification, or teach stage, but you must have a part of the lesson that gets technical about the new language point that you're teaching. You need to go to the board and explain all the rules involved so that students know how to use the new point with minimal errors.

✔ **Don't overload students!** Work out what the students need to know to achieve the objective(s). How much will they be able to absorb mentally rather than just write down? Your answer determines the right amount to teach. Generally speaking, seven new words or one new grammar point per lesson is enough.

Find a link between the new information and what students already know so that learning is progressive. For example, you only teach your class how to describe patterns (stripes, checks, spots) after they know colours and clothing vocabulary well. Don't jump from the easy to the difficult in one huge leap. Your learners won't jump with you!

✔ **Establish a context.** Embed the language point into a natural setting. The students need to know why this information is useful. For example, if you're teaching the past continuous, the context could be explaining why you couldn't answer the phone ('Sorry! I was washing my dog when you called.').

✔ **Check understanding.** Think of concept check questions at every stage to make sure that the students understand what you're telling them. So if you're teaching items of clothing you could ask 'Do you wear socks on your head?' 'When do you wear gloves?' or, while holding up an item, 'Are these trousers?' Do the same for instruction check questions. Check that students know what to do before they begin a task. (For the low-down on concept check questions and instruction check questions, see the nearby sidebar on them).

✔ **Practise to make perfect.** Think of ways to give your students practice so that they can get used to the new language point in a controlled environment. They'll make some mistakes at first, but then you correct them and give them another try with a different but related communicative activity.

I discuss materials in the later section 'Preparing additional materials'. At this stage of planning, make a list of all the things you'll need.

Using concept check questions and instruction check questions

Concept check questions are questions you ask students to check that they understand what you have just taught them. For instance, when you teach vocabulary for fruit and vegetables, you hold up a picture of a carrot and ask 'Is this a lettuce?' or you say ' Which picture is a carrot?'

You use instruction check questions to make sure students understand a task you have just set. For example, ask the students 'Do you write the answers or just speak about it?' or you say 'Tell me what to do with this picture?' and see whether students can repeat or paraphrase your instructions.

Balancing the interaction patterns

As you know, a good TEFL lesson isn't a lecture. You can't just stand in front of your students and talk at them. Rather, you have to mix it up. So sometimes you talk to students, sometimes they talk to each other and at other times they talk to you, not to mention a bit of silent contemplation in between. These are called *interaction patterns*. Consider how often the dynamic changes during the lesson according to your plan, and make sure that the students get enough practice doing activities and that there is sufficient variety to keep it interesting.

It's easier to analyse the balance of interaction patterns in your lesson plan, by putting abbreviated terms next to each activity you plan. Most teachers write something like this:

T = teacher	St = student
Gr = groups	Sts = Whole class

So St–St means that one student speaks to another in a pair. T–Sts means that you talk to the class, and so on.

Use the terms that you prefer but make sure that you clearly indicate them on your plan and that they're easy to understand if somebody else is observing your lesson and following along.

Although it's valuable for students to listen to your voice/a CD and get a lot of input (see the information I provide on the Natural Approach in Chapter 2), they only make headway in their speaking by *practising* speaking. Pair and group work is the best method available to help the class achieve this. As a rule of thumb, limit your own speaking time to less than 30 per cent of the lesson.

Timing the activities

One of the most challenging aspects of lesson planning is predicting how long an activity will take. It's never an exact science. Do make a guess, though, and write the estimated number of minutes for each activity on your plan.

Preparing to finish too soon

Just in case a ten-minute discussion turns into a three-minute chat, I suggest you over-plan. By that I mean having extra optional activities at the ready.

If the students have been working in pairs, correct them, form new pairs and let them do the activity again (see the Test Teach Test model in the later section 'Looking at Different Ways to Plan Your Lessons').

Be aware that the reason students cannot sustain a speaking activity is usually because they don't know what to say or what you expect from them. Plan for this too by having a preliminary exercise that provides sample answers they can draw on in a discussion.

For example, if you want the class to talk about and compare national dishes, start off by setting an individual activity during which the students can get their dictionaries out and prepare information. By the time they have to speak they will feel more secure.

Planning for an activity to overrun

Decide how important each activity in your plan is. Be aware of the activities which you can remove without leaving students confused. For example, cooler activities at the end of the lesson can be dropped if necessary.

When you're delivering the lesson, be flexible with your plan if the students are accomplishing something important, leave them to it regardless. However, if they are just nattering and there other important points to cover, let them know that they only have two minutes left before you move on. If they are taking ages because they are struggling you can either stop the activity, go over it again and restart it, or float around the room offering assistance to the weaker ones.

Factoring in student information and possible pitfalls

All teachers want their students to succeed. Students feel more confident and accomplished if they do well in the lesson, and you as teacher enjoy a sense of satisfaction and can move on to the next teaching point knowing that you've built a good foundation. However, in order to enjoy success you need to think about possible hindrances that the students might face. Note possible problems at the top of your plan and write in strategies for dealing with them.

So what kinds of problems do you need to foresee and prepare for?

- **Age and background:** Your learners will most probably get bored if the material they're supposed to cover has absolutely nothing to do with their own lives. You might have to adapt or substitute it.

- **Equipment:** If you're depending on the Internet or a DVD player to pull off your lesson, you need to test the equipment out before you begin and have a back-up plan just in case it fails.

- **Environment:** Do you have the space and appropriate layout to do the activities you have planned? And think about the noise levels. Is it okay to make noise in your classroom, or on the other hand, will your silent reading/writing activity be disturbed by any exterior noise?

✔ **Knowledge gaps:** Are you sure that the students have enough information to complete the tasks? If some have been absent, you may need to do some revision first.

✔ **First Language interference:** You know where your students are from and the language(s) they speak. Make notes about the errors they are likely to make and how you will help them overcome these in your plan. For example, what do people from their culture(s) usually do when they speak English that marks them out as being a non-native speaker? Perhaps they mispronounce a particular sound, put words in the wrong order or use false friends. (*False friends* are words that students think they know because they look like something in their own language, whereas the meaning in English is very different. So '*actuellement*' in French means currently not actually. Students who speak Latin languages especially get very blasé about translating into English, and so you need to watch them!)

✔ **Motivation:** The students need the information but they'll do better if they want it too. What can you do to boost their enthusiasm and engage their minds?

✔ **Personalities:** Often more dominant speakers take over the lesson, whereas shy students struggle to handle the speaking activities without extra support. Some students clash or dislike each other and others have special needs. Do some students work faster than others? Think about the pairs and groups you'll form and prepare ideas for keeping everyone occupied.

Nothing on this list is insurmountable. As long as you think ahead and have a little something in reserve (an extra worksheet, game, or task), your lesson can be successful. And if you're over-prepared, you'll probably have more material for the next lesson.

Student information and possible pitfalls are individual to your particular teaching situation. I don't include them in the lesson plans in this book because you're in the best position to know what suits your group, and where their strengths and weaknesses lie.

Doing warmer and cooler Activities

Short activities that whet students' appetites for learning at the beginning of a lesson and round off a session with a bit of fun (students really should leave your classroom with a smile on their faces) are called warmers and coolers. They don't need to be tied into the lesson topic and can be as simple as a game of 'I spy' or a general knowledge quiz.

Write a warmer into all your lesson plans. Doing so helps you avoid the frustration of students straggling into the lesson and delaying the start of the main teaching. Have the cooler ready just in case the lesson finishes earlier than you expected.

Reviewing the Hardware

The preceding sections focus on the notes you (and an observer) will see. Now I consider what the students will see and what to bear in mind when planning this aspect of the lesson.

Practising board work

Practically all classrooms have a board, be it white, black, or interactive. Although I only refer to boards here, the principles apply to PowerPoint presentations or other media for displaying information to students.

What you put on the board goes down in your students' notebooks and is preserved forever (or for a very long time at any rate)! In fact, these days some students don't even write notes; they just take photos of the board.

Copying from the board is a memory aid in itself, whereas the 'phone camera generation' don't automatically review all the images they snap. You need to give students a reason to go back into their stored images; for example, a quick test. The teaching establishment you work for may have a rule about the use of photography in the classroom or you may agree the terms of camera use with your students.

When it comes to boards, you have two key considerations: visibility and accuracy.

Visibility

Consider the following:

- Rather than thinking of how much you information can cram onto the board, think about what your students can actually see from all angles of the classroom. You probably need to avoid using the bottom quarter of the board just in case someone's head obscures the information.

- Coloured pens are really helpful for highlighting smaller points, but for general writing only black or blue will do. Other colours don't stand out enough.

- Think about what needs to stay up on the board throughout the lesson and when to remove other items.

- If lots of information stays on the board, make sure it's organised and labelled. You may need to box off some points so that they don't merge with unrelated matters.

Accuracy

Every teacher I know has made an awful gaffe on the board at some point, either by leaving something out, putting things the wrong way round, or misspelling. Minimise errors by planning your board work beforehand.

Here are some tips for improving accuracy in your board writing:

- ✔ Write up a board menu (a list of things you'll do in the lesson written in the corner of the board) at the start of the lesson so that you and the students can see where the lesson is going.

- ✔ Use a simple equation to convey a grammatical point on the board. For example:

  Present Continuous = subject + verb to be + gerund

                 We   are   listening.

- ✔ Check which part of speech you are using and write it in brackets next to key vocabulary. For example, here I show the verb, noun and adjective forms of a word.

  restrict (v)   restriction (n)   restrictive (adj)

- ✔ Mark pronunciation features such as the stressed syllable or a phonemic transcription for trickier words.

  re<u>stric</u>tion/rɪstrɪkʃən/

- ✔ Make sure you designate errors. Strikethrough works well; for example: restrik̶t̶i̶o̶n̶.

- ✔ Have magnets or sticky tack at the ready for sticking up images or other information.

- ✔ Prepare complicated board work before the lesson and then cover it with paper. You can use a tantalising slow reveal tactic as you go along.

Interactive whiteboards

If you use an interactive whiteboard, you can save board work like brainstorms and email lesson notes directly to students. Use this stored work for use during revision sessions and future planning.

With an interactive whiteboard you can also play language games on the Internet; for example, at www.eslgamesworld.com.

Try not to be over-dependent on your interactive whiteboard, though. If your classroom is always darkened to benefit screen use, and the computer drones constantly, you may find that there is a tendency for everyone to become lethargic and suffer headaches or eye strain. Remember to vary your approach.

Writing and copying worksheets

Although you can present information on a computer screen or even dictate some questions to the students, which saves paper, using worksheets is beneficial too. Here's why:

✔ Sharing one worksheet encourages co-operation among students, which facilitates communication.

✔ You get to differentiate between groups/students by preparing different versions of a task.

✔ Students can make notes on them. Those who prefer computerised note-taking can still take a picture of the page.

If you produce a worksheet, it must look professional, even if you've drawn it by hand.

Photocopying from a book

You probably have a main course whose materials the students have bought too. However, inevitably you'll need extra information from other publications. As a professional, you're expected to provide the source for anything you photocopy. So before you print off a dozen sheets, write the name of the book and author at the bottom of the page on your master copy.

You're not allowed to photocopy a whole book in the UK. Schools need a licence to photocopy, and even so, you're limited to copying a very small percentage of the work. Some publications, such as workbooks, can't be copied at all. Fortunately, some resource books are designed to be copied. They're usually spiral bound and A4 size, which is highly convenient. You generally find copyright information at the front of the publication.

Designing your own worksheet

From the outset, let me say that time is of the essence when you're teaching many classes. I've seen a great number of novice teachers spend hours designing new worksheets in their enthusiasm for the job, only for their colleagues to say something like 'That's just that like an exercise in the English File resource book!' Do your research first! There's no need to reinvent the wheel, so only design what you can't find on the Internet or in a book.

Remember to:

- ✔ Take inspiration from the materials already available to you and then adapt what you find to suit your students.

- ✔ Save anything you design for future use.

- ✔ Set up a bank of shared resources with your colleagues.

Some of the best worksheets I've seen I found in the recycling bin next to the photocopier at my school. Most teachers are flattered when you ask them if you can use some of their work.

The English Raven website (www.englishraven.com) has instructional materials and design videos that help you create worksheets.

Preparing additional materials Apart from your plans and worksheets, it's a good idea to have other materials on hand, so that you can vary your lessons and keep students interested. Most schools aim to make the following available to teachers (even if you're teaching freelance, you can have a work area like this at home):

- ✔ Access to computers for students

- ✔ A selection of course books

- ✔ A selection of magazines or catalogues (either in English or just for cutting images out of)

- ✔ Board games such as Taboo and Scrabble

- ✔ Dice, counters, and a timer for homemade and improvised games

- ✔ DVDs suitable for student viewing and preferably with the option of English subtitles

- ✔ Graded readers, which are small books that are specially designed for students of English and each one states the level of proficiency it is designed to suit, for example intermediate or advanced.

- ✔ Posters about EFL

- ✔ Realia (some everyday objects for illustrative purposes; see Chapter 5)

- ✔ Reference books (dictionaries, grammar books, and so on)

- ✔ Various kinds of stationery (card, paperclips, scissors, glue, and so on)

Contact the publishers of EFL course books for help accessing books and posters. You can join their mailing lists, which opens you up to a world of freebies, samples and updates on EFL resources.

Looking at Different Ways to Plan Your Lessons

Almost every TEFL certificate course makes use of the Presentation, Practice and Production (PPP) method of lesson planning. In recent years, though, other types of lesson planning have become popular, despite the fact that the basic elements are often similar.

I don't believe that PPP has had its day, but in this section I want to introduce you to four more ways of approaching lesson planning that are a little more flexible.

In this book I draw on all of the approaches below without labelling them. As you become more comfortable with lesson planning you find that you are able able to balance the interaction and activities in the lesson without being tied to one particular model. However, using a planning model is a very good starting point.

You can also refer back to Chapter 2 in this book for information on approaches and methods to try. The Task-based Approach, for example, has a straightforward system you can follow.

The Presentation-Practice-Production Model

PPP is a three-step process:

1. **Presentation.** First you explain the new language items thoroughly using words, pictures, flashcards, or whatever is available to you.

2. **Practice.** You give the students an exercise to do that tests that they have understood but doesn't require free expression. The focus is on accuracy. These exercises might include gap-fills, multiple choice, or simple sentence construction.

3. **Production.** When the students have demonstrated that they get the idea by their success in the practice exercise, they can engage in a freer writing or discussion activity in which they incorporate what they already knew with the new language items. The focus is fluency and communication.

PPP has good points and bad points. The reason why PPP is taught on so many TEFL training courses is that PPP is an excellent starting point for new teachers. It is a tried-and-tested method that takes the teacher and the students through logical and progressive steps. PPP is based on communicative language teaching and so promotes pair and group work. By the end of the lesson students feel that they can, to some degree, do what the teacher taught them at the beginning of the session.

However, there are a few problems with this method of lesson planning. Unfortunately, although it can be reassuring for the students when the lessons follow a particular routine, eventually the routine becomes far too predictable and consequently boring. In addition, the human brain doesn't always need to be taught; it can discover information by itself and is excited by doing so. Therefore, PPP lessons inevitably end up teaching students what they already know. Students also have to wait until the production stage of the lesson to express themselves freely and this can be frustrating. That's why you ought to add a few other planning models to your armoury. In this way, you can adapt your lesson planning to suit your particular teaching situation.

The Engage-Study-Activate model

The Engage, Study, Activate (ESA) model became popular following the publication of *How to Teach English* by Jeremy Harmer (Longman, 1998). It appeals to teachers because, unlike PPP, you can move around the stages of the lesson. It is also used frequently by teacher trainers:

1. **Engage.** It is important that students are motivated to learn and use the new language items. So the teacher must find a way to lead them into their learning by arousing interest, emotion or curiosity. A fascinating story, unusual photograph, or song can facilitate this.

2. **Study.** During this stage you analyse structure and rules in the language, and give an opportunity for students to make sure that they understand the new items. However, unlike the first stage of PPP, the teacher doesn't necessarily have to do a presentation. Instead, you can give the students a guided activity to help them learn.

3. **Activate.** Now the learners can put the new language into practice using freer communicative activities such as role plays, games, and debates.

You can also use an EASA model (engage, activate, study, activate) so that students activate the language, then study it closely and try activating it again. This allows them to reflect on their development during the lesson.

The ARC model

ARC stands for Authentic use, Restricted use, and Clarification and focus, but not necessarily in that order. It was introduced in the book *Learning Teaching: A Guidebook for English Language Teachers* by Jim Scrivener (Heinemann, 1994). ARC is similar to PPP but often favoured because it's inductive and allows the students to discover language.

Here's how it works:

1. **Authentic use:** You expose students to the new language items in a context that shows how people use them naturally; for example, a dialogue. The students practise new language items while focusing on fluency, communication and meaning, like the PPP production stage.

2. **Restricted use:** Students follow the pattern of the sentences you've already shown them and make new sentences. This kind of practice concentrates on form, testing and accuracy and is similar to the practice stage in PPP.

3. **Clarification and focus:** During the clarification stage you either demonstrate to the students how to use the new language items, explain to them, or help them to find out for themselves. This is somewhat similar to the presentation stage of PPP and can include explanatory diagrams, some translation, and sentence analysis, among other things.

The Observe-Hypothesise-Experiment model

Here's a planning model that pretty much does what it says on the tin. It's a scientific approach, and encourages students to notice things for themselves. It's related to Michael Lewis's Lexical Approach (see Chapter 2 for more).

1. **Observe.** You present students with material that contains the information you want them to learn about; for example, a reading text featuring a particular kind of grammar. Apart from the new language point, the rest of the text should be quite familiar to the students so that they don't get bogged down. When they understand the information, you prompt them to notice the new language point and how it is used in the construction of the text.

2. **Hypothesise.** Next the students come up with a theory based on the language point they have now noticed in the text. With your help, they try to establish some rules which they can apply to their own language use.

3. **Experiment.** The class now undertake a task you set which allows them to try out the new language items for themselves.

The Test-Teach-Test model

The Test-Teach-Test approach to lesson planning requires you to think on your feet because you're not entirely sure which direction the lesson will proceed in. This method is ideal for advanced level classes. Here's the process:

1. **Test.** You give the students a speaking activity to do that allows for a lot of free expression; for example, a role play. You don't explain how to do the activity linguistically; you just let the students get on with it. Meanwhile you note down the errors they make and/or record the entire dialogue.

2. **Teach.** Based on the errors the students have made, you now teach them about the *important* points that need correcting. You can also prompt peer correction, in which the classmates help to correct each other, or self-correction by playing back the recording of the dialogue. Get the students to practise these points.

3. **Test.** You let the students repeat the same activity they started with or another similar one, so that they can use what you've just taught them.

Part II
Beginner and Elementary Classes

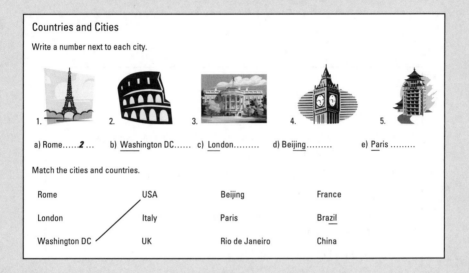

Countries and Cities

Write a number next to each city.

1.　2.　3.　4.　5.

a) Rome......*2*...　b) Washington DC......　c) London.........　d) Beijing.........　e) Paris ....

Match the cities and countries.

Rome	USA	Beijing	France
London	Italy	Paris	Brazil
Washington DC	UK	Rio de Janeiro	China

Visit www.dummies.com/extras/tefllessonplans for free online lesson plan ideas and outlines.

In this part . . .

✔ Get to know you beginner and elementary classes with ice-breaker activities.

✔ Use props and realia to teach the elements of English.

✔ Develop and deploy your own flashcards.

✔ Turn the functionality of mobile phones to your advantage with beginners in English.

✔ Use role-play with elementary students.

Chapter 4

Getting to Know Each Other on the First Day

*T*he way a course begins naturally sets the tone for how it continues. Taking the time to get to know your students, and for them to get to know each other, facilitates a friendly learning environment, co-operation, and an excellent team spirit.

Students are often apprehensive because they don't know what to expect from the teacher or indeed what you expect of *them*. In many cultures attending a course at any age means sitting at a desk, listening to a teacher or lecturer, and taking notes. To the dismay of many learners, in the modern TEFL classroom this is unlikely to happen. After all, the grammar translation method (which I cover in Chapter 1) went out of fashion some time ago!

In addition, learners of English have diverse needs, and because of this people from many different backgrounds may attend your course. They may have different positions in society or a certain status due to age and experience. As a result, new students wonder whether they'll be shown up or embarrassed in front of their classmates.

'Getting to know you' activities allow the students to get used to the classroom environment before they get into the process of learning in a deeper way. Hopefully, you allay some of their fears at this stage. For the teacher, finding out who your learners are before you put all your course materials together really helps. Abilities and disabilities, personalities, levels, ages, and interests are all relevant to your lesson planning.

In this chapter, I give you ideas for getting familiar with your students on the first day of a brand new course. I offer suggestions that you can use in various levels of classes, and then I set out a complete lesson plan for beginners.

As you go through the chapter note down a few ice-breakers you can use to begin your courses in a relaxed way. Then you'll be ready to have fun and observe your new students at the same time.

Looking at Activities for All Levels

Try these activities with your classes. I have arranged them by level.

Elementary

Activity 1: Get the students to rearrange themselves a few times throughout the lesson, sitting according to month of birth, the time they get up, or their names in alphabetical order. Make sure they actually have to ask each other questions to complete the task. Each time they have new partners sitting next to them, you can give the students questions to ask each other.

Activity 2: Here's another idea that is especially useful for children. Teach fidgety students the commands 'Stand up!' and 'Sit down!' by demonstrating yourself. Give a range of commands such as:

> 'Stand up if you like Manga! Sit down if you don't like football!'

Use gestures to help clarify 'like' and 'don't like' and use international or familiar vocabulary. After students get the hang of the activity they can work in groups, giving their own commands. Apart from getting familiar with these two commands as lexical chunks, the students get to know who has similar tastes to their own. The bonus is that the timid students don't have to speak if they don't feel ready to.

Pre-intermediate

Prepare a 'Find someone who . . .' activity. This is a kind of questionnaire that gets students mingling and writing down the names of students who fit each category. For example:

> **Find someone who** loves eating sushi . . . / plays the piano . . . /
> is hungry now . . .

Practise phrasing the questions before students start mingling; for example, 'Do you love eating sushi?'

Intermediate

Activity 1: Make 'Talk for a minute about . . .' board games, enough copies for students to work in small groups. Simply lay out a grid of squares on a large sheet of paper, number each square in sequence, and write a topic in each. See the example in Figure 4-1.

Figure 4-1: Example 'Talk for a minute about . . .' board game.

1. Your favorite meal	2. A funny movie	3. What you did yesterday	4. Your family	5. A good place for a holiday	6. Your city

Students use a dice or coin (heads for three spaces and tails for one space) to work through the board, talking for a minute about the topics in the squares they land on. Don't forget that one student in the group needs a timer. The winner is the person who gets to the final square first having successfully spoken about her topics.

Leave a few wild card squares. Perhaps have one that allows the speaker to choose her own topic. Have one that is the group's choice too.

Activity 2: Here's another idea, for teenagers. Sit in a circle. Each person has to think of an extra word or phrase to add to their name and an appropriate action to demonstrate it too. For example, my name is Michelle, so I introduce myself as 'Memory Michelle' while tapping my head. I tell students that I have to remember lots of things such as students' names. Another student may call himself 'Fashionable Fred' and straighten his collar in an exaggerated way explaining that he loves designer clothes, and so on. After all the introductions, the challenge is for each member of the class to remember the other students' names and actions one by one.

Upper intermediate

'Never have I ever' is an activity from www.icebreakers.ws/get-to-know-you. Everyone starts by standing in a circle and holding up their fingers and thumbs. Each person has to tell the group about something she has never done. Whoever has done that thing in the group themselves must put a finger down. The winner is the last person who still has a finger or thumb or two up.

Advanced

Set up a speed-dating type activity. Students quiz each other for three minutes, and then half the students remain in their place while the other half move along to someone else. The stationary students have an interview sheet listing some challenging questions that they can complete as they like; for example:

If you were a . . . which one would you be? Why?

What's your idea of the perfect . . . ?

You can have a second set of questions so that the students can switch places after the first round, allowing the other half to be in the driving seat as interviewers.

Beginner Lesson Plan

From the outset of a beginner lesson, you're likely to discover that you have a range of true and false beginners in your class. *True* beginners don't know any English whatsoever, whereas *false* beginners know a little.

Preparing for a class at this level is trickier than you might think. Explaining vocabulary without using other more difficult words involves a lot of thought.

In the first lesson your objective is to boost your students' confidence as well as teaching basic expressions. Use easy, snappy activities to ensure that your first lesson is fun.

Find out before meeting the students whether they're likely to know the English alphabet.

Lesson overview

Time: Approximately one hour

Materials: A soft ball or toy to throw; Images showing typical things from your home city; Map to show where you're from (perhaps a map of the world); map to show the country or city you teach in; sictures of celebrities from English-speaking countries; slips of paper on which you write the names of celebrities from the students' country or countries

Aim: To have fun, introduce everyone to each other in English and express opinions.

Vocabulary: To include: *Hello!; I'm . . . (name); What's your name?; I'm from . . . (place); Where are you from?; good/bad/so-so*

Emphasise clear, natural-sounding pronunciation skills so that even false beginners benefit from the lesson.

Doing a warmer activity

St >> T   2 minutes

Procedure: Arrange the seating in a horseshoe shape. Show the celebrity pictures and get the students to name the people.

Learning to introduce yourself

T >> St   6 minutes

Step 1: Sit in front of the class and say 'hello' repeatedly as you smile and wave. Drill 'hello' chorally and individually. Say 'repeat', but don't worry about actually teaching it; students will get the point as long as you gesture.

Cup your ear with one hand, showing you want to listen, and beckon with the other hand inviting the class to speak. Keep smiling!

If the students sound timid, be louder and more energetic with your prompts. Refuse to accept their version of the new vocabulary until they say it in a full-on, cheerful way. Most classes will laugh with you and join in when they see you have a sense of humour!

Step 2: Now point to yourself as you say 'I'm . . . . . . (name)'. Repeat this several times. Get up and shake a few people's hands and say 'Hello! I'm . . . . . .' Give the class plenty of opportunity to pronounce your name if it's unfamiliar to them. Now drill 'I'm' both chorally and individually. Write your name only on the board.

You can teach 'My name is . . .' if you prefer, but I find that in informal settings people more often introduce themselves by saying 'I'm . . .'. Also, by teaching 'I'm' you don't overload the students with vocabulary straight away.

Do open pairs activities (asking a student a question or eliciting a dialogue from student in front of the whole class) in a random order to keep students on their toes. If they know when you are going to ask them, they may switch off until it's their turn. Go back to students who are doing well again because they can be the role-models for weaker students.

Step 3: Introduce yourself personally to each student in random order. Go over to the student and say, 'Hello! I'm . . . What's your name?' The student will understand the meaning of the question because of the context, but you need to gesture towards the student to show it's the student's turn to speak.

When you want an individual learner to answer a question, point towards them with your whole hand instead of a finger (to avoid looking aggressive), palm facing upwards and with your eyebrows raised.

Make sure you get 'I'm', not just the name, from the students. If they do not do it, say the word yourself with great emphasis, *'I'm . . .'*, repeat the question and gesture once more.

Go around the class until everyone has had a chance to speak.

Asking others to introduce themselves

St >> St   3 minutes

Procedure: Students have already heard you say 'What's your name?' many times. Now it's their turn.

1. Drill the question chorally and individually.

2. Nominate two students and beckon for them to stand in front of the class. Say the introduction yourself: '*Hello! I'm . . . What's your name?*'

3. When the student answers, say, 'Hello . . . (student's name)!' and then shake hands or give a little wave.

4. Now point at each of the two students and step back, leaving them to demonstrate. Prompt with 'Hello!' or other individual words here and there if they seem stuck.

5. Give them a clap and let them return to their seats.

6. Get two more students on their feet to repeat the demonstration.

Whole Class Mingle   3 minutes

Procedure: Get all the students on their feet in a cluster. They must introduce themselves to each other. Demonstrate by rushing around and repeating the introduction to several students, shaking hands and moving on. Bring pairs of students closer together if they are slow on the uptake.

If the students understand and get involved, just step back and listen to how well they remember and pronounce the words. If they're struggling, get involved by mingling and introducing yourself again. By now you should have noted quite a number of names too!

When the class have repeated the introduction many times, draw the activity to a close by shouting 'Thank you!' and by gesturing for everyone to sit down.

If you heard a lot of mistakes, repeat and drill the phrases again.

Good pronunciation is vital. By that I mean that it should be clear what your students are saying regardless of accent. So it's worth doing extra repetition drills if necessary. Be careful to speak at a fairly natural pace, though. If you slow down or enunciate too much, your students will end up sounding very stilted.

Saying where you're from

T >> St　3 minutes

Procedure: Put images of your home city in front of the class (on the computer screen or stuck to the board).

1. Elicit the name of the city by saying the names of other locations in a quizzical way. For example, I use images that represent London, such as red double-decker buses, Queen Elizabeth, and Tower Bridge.

2. Encourage students if they offer the names of the things in the images, but don't waste time trying to teach this vocabulary in detail. If students are struggling to name the city, say 'New York? Sydney? Tokyo?' or similar cities until someone shouts out the right one.

3. Show the map as confirmation and point to the city and country.

4. Now drill 'I'm from . . .' thoroughly. Insert the name of their country, or city as you drill if all your students are from the same place. Remember that you may have to teach the English-language version of a place name too.

'I'm from' is a versatile expression to use for introducing personal information. The sentence may relate to schools, local areas, cities and countries. So there should always be enough variety in the class to use it an interesting way. For example, the answer to 'Where are you from?' could be 'I'm from School X/Westminster/London/England/Britain/Europe and so on.

Ask/gesture for one student to come up to the front. Give a full introduction and elicit a response from the student. Point to the map to give the student a prompt.

> T: Hello! I'm Michelle. What's your name?
>
> St: Hello, Michelle! I'm Ana.
>
> T: I'm from London. Where are you from, Ana?
>
> St: I'm from Moscow.

St >> St　2 minutes

Encourage the student from the preceding activity to introduce herself to another member of the class in the same way. Continue the same dialogue with a few more open pairs until students seem comfortable remembering it.

If you need to indicate to students that they should work in pairs, point at one with one hand (in the way I suggest in the earlier section 'Learning to introduce yourself') and say the name if you know it. Then do likewise with your other hand, saying the name. Bring your hands together and say, 'Two!'

T >> St / **St >> T**   **5 minutes**

Show the students how to write down the sentences you have just taught. A simple diagram on the board like the one in Figure 4-2 helps you elicit the words and write them down for the students to copy.

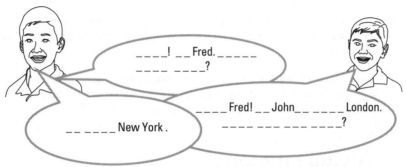

Figure 4-2:
Building
a simple
dialogue on
the board.

_ _ _ _! _ _ Fred. _ _ _ _ _
_ _ _ _ _ _ _ _?

_ _ _ _ Fred! _ _ John_ _ _ _ _ _ London.
_ _ _ _ _ _ _ _ _ _ _ _ _ _ _?

_ _ _ _ _ _New York .

Ask the students to shout out the words tocomplete the dialogue on the board. False beginners could have a go at shouting out the spelling of the words too. Give students plenty of time to copy the dialogue into their notebooks.

If you write everything on the board too soon, students won't pay attention to your pronunciation. Drill pronunciation first as much as possible.

Playing the celebrity naming game

St >> Sts   **8 minutes**

Hand out the slips of paper on which you've written names of celebrities the students will know (ask someone local for help with celebrity names if necessary and in multinational classes be careful to use celebrities from all around the globe). Indicate by the way you shield your piece of paper and hold your finger to your lips that the information you're handing out is top secret.

Keep one piece of paper for yourself and begin acting like the person whose name is on it. Walk like the celebrity, hold a microphone, dance, make karate movements, put your nose in the air, or whatever is necessary. Point to the dialogue on the board and beckon for students to ask you your new name. Wait and allow the students to shout out answers. After a few tries, put them out of their misery and say the answer.

St: .. What's your name? Jean Claude Van Damme? Chuck Norris?

T: No, I'm Jackie . . . Chan.

St: Where are you from Jackie Chan? (You can point to the question on the board.)

T: I'm from . . . (elicit a place name) Yes, I'm Jackie Chan from Hong Kong.

Now ask the students to act out their new identities in front of the class one by one, or in front of each other in small groups. If the class is very small, give them two or three identities each.

Get feedback by asking the students to say who they are. Point to the piece of paper so that they know you're not asking for their real identities but the fake ones. Remember to keep tweaking students' pronunciation whenever necessary.

Giving opinions

T >> St   3 minutes

Put all the pieces of paper from the previous activity face on a table So you can now teach the students to give opinions about each celebrity. Smile and put your thumbs up. Say, *'Good!'* Do the opposite and teach, *'Bad!'* Make an apathetic face for *'So-so!'* Drill each word/expression thoroughly. Prompt students to say the word that matches the gesture you make.

Now put the words on the board for the students to note down.

Whole Class   8 minutes

CElicit good/bad/so-so for a few of the celebrity names from the preceding activity (no doubt the class will argue a little, which is fine if they stick to the English vocabulary). When you point to one piece of paper with a celebrity name, write the word most of the students shout below the name on the paper as I show in Figure 4-3.

Figure 4-3:
Use cards to
assign new
identities
and prompt
opinions.

Take a vote if necessary. Give out a couple of pens. Ask the students to each write their (or their group's) opinion of the particular star under that individual's name – a kind of class poll. When they have finished, call out the more interesting results of the poll.

St >> St   6 minutes

Expand the students' usage of this vocabulary for giving opinions with a few international words. For example, pretend to eat or drink. Then select a student by throwing her your ball/toy.

T: Sara! Coca-cola – good, bad or so-so?

The students can express their opinions simply with the appropriate word. Now put your hands in the catch position. When you have the ball/toy back, go again.

T: Ayako! Pizza – good, bad, so-so?

St: Pizza? Mmmm, good!

Gesture for one student to throw to another. Prompt the thrower to say the name of the catcher too. Next the thrower needs to ask an opinion question such as '*Rap music – good, bad, so-so?*' Any international word suffices, and no doubt the students know a few. If they get stuck, throw in some names of tourist sites or famous companies to spur them on. Encourage the students to keep throwing, remembering each other's names and giving opinions.

Extension activity

Elicit the names of various countries or cities and teach the names of these places in English. Design a matching task worksheet with activities like those in Figure 4-4.

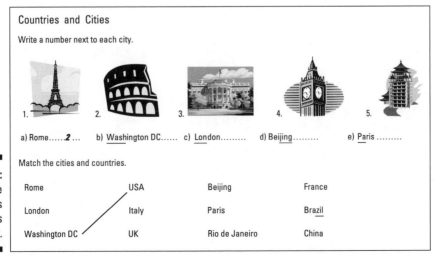

Figure 4-4:
Example
countries
and cities
worksheet.

Chapter 5

Back to Basics: Using Your Own Realia

- -

In This Chapter

▶ Seeing how realia helps learning

▶ Bringing vocabulary learning to life using everyday objects

▶ Using realia in a lesson with students of different levels

- -

*O*ne of the best things about TEFL is that it's a job you can take anywhere in the world. This also means a class can take place in an endless variety of settings. So, although the internet offers a wealth of resources for teachers, and libraries crammed full of TEFL books are out there, you occasionally find yourself in a setting lacking the resources you would usually depend on and in which you have to rely on nothing but the contents of your own suitcase to engage your students.

Realia is basically ordinary stuff you use in the classroom. In this chapter, I show you how you can entertain and engage your learners with everyday objects such as food, timetables, clothes and general bric-a-brac.

Using Realia as Lesson Context

Before you balk at the idea of lugging loads of gear into the classroom, look at some of the benefits of using realia:

✔ Holding an object yourself is far more memorable than seeing a picture of one. So the realia-based lessons stay in students' minds.

✔ You can appeal to the various intelligences and learning styles more easily (see Chapter 2 on NLP and Multiple Intelligences) when you have real props because some students learning better by moving an object around or by using visual input.

✔ Learners see language used in an authentic and contemporary way because realia tends to consist of things in current use.

✔ Realia teaches students about cultural differences because your realia may show something different from the typical objects in the students' culture.

✔ Personal realia helps your class get to know you, and by sharing it you come across as being open and interesting.

✔ It's quicker to hold up an object than to explain what its name means.

Of course you don't want your classroom to resemble a car boot sale and it doesn't have to. Realia might involve the creative use of things you bring in anyway. For example, dress in the clothing that features in your vocabulary lesson, and use class mobile phones for role play dialogues and a real email for writing practice.

Looking at Realia Language with All Levels

Teachers often use realia with lower level students but you can benefit all classes by incorporating it. Here I offer suggestions for using realia in a range of classes at different levels.

Divide vocabulary into categories and bring in realia to show the meaning of items in each vocabulary group.

✔ Fruit and veg

✔ Items of clothing: scarf, gloves, tie

✔ Hair and beauty: brush, lipstick, mirror

✔ Literature words: leaflet, book, poster.

✔ Numbers: dice, playing cards, price lists

Organise the vocabulary by level:

✔ **Pre-intermediate:**

• Times and schedules from timetables

• Personal data from application forms

• Sentence structure using objects to represent different parts of speech

✔ **Intermediate**

- Vocabulary for animals and vehicles using toys

- Computing verbs using a keyboard

- Holidays and festivals from a calendar

- Comparison of future simple and 'going to' using the weather forecast

- Describing buildings and homes from estate agent advertising

✔ **Upper-intermediate**

- Film and TV genres from reviews

- Museum leaflets and websites for culture

- Describing physical characteristics from fashion magazines

- Position idioms using an item of clothing (upside-down, back-to-front, wrong way round, inside out etc.)

✔ **Advanced**

- Pronunciation of place names from maps

- People watching for synonyms of 'walk' (stride, stroll, limp and so on)

- Supermarket items for tasting words (sour, land, crisp, aromatic and so on)

Elementary Lesson Plan

This lesson assumes students have basic knowledge of some language related to daily routine. It teaches learners how to describe some of the typical things people do on a daily basis.

You need to have taught morning/afternoon/evening and telling the time before you try this lesson.

Lesson overview

Time: Approximately one hour

Materials: toothbrush; shower gel; comb; a cup/plate; an item of clothing; the door

Aim: To teach lexical chunks (vocabulary which students learn as a set expression rather than one word at a time)for explaining a morning routine.

Vocabulary:

Get up	*brush my teeth*	*have a shower*	*do my hair*
get dressed	*have breakfast*	*go out*	

Doing a warmer activity

T >> Sts   5 minutes

Procedure: Put two anagrams on the board for students to decipher. Do the first one with them as an example. Then give them this one to lead into the topic:

dogo ringnom (good morning)

Alternatively, see how many smaller words students can make from this phrase.

Good morning (I, in, on, go, or, dog, door, god)

Presenting your morning routine

T >> Sts   **6 minutes**

Procedure: Tell students the story of your morning routine twice, by describing what you do after using actions. Use the realia to add meaning. For example:

> Every day, I <u>get up</u> at 7 o'clock. First I <u>have breakfast</u>. I have coffee and bread and butter. Next, I <u>have a shower</u> and <u>brush my teeth</u>. After that, I <u>get dressed</u> and <u>do my hair</u>. Then at 8 o'clock I <u>go out</u>.

Sts >> T   **3 minutes**

Now mime the morning routine story. Let the students provide the commentary.

St >> Sts   **5 minutes**

Pick up each item of realia in a random order, do the appropriate action connected with each item and elicit the vocabulary. Then step back and let a student do the actions and say the words for the class. The other students can help narrate the story.

Highlighting lexical chunks

St >> T   **6 minutes**

Procedure: You need to help your students to recognise the lexical chunks (See the section on the Lexical Approach in Chapter 2) in the morning routine story. See Figure 5-1: Unlike the typical board work you do in class, I can't use colour to group words here so I use shapes instead. The large shapes show the verbs used in more than one chunk. So where I put several words inside one shape, you may write those words together in the same colour to differentiate them from another group of words. In any case, set out these five verbs in separate parts of the board.

Figure 5-1:
Example of board work for teaching lexical chunks according to their verbs.

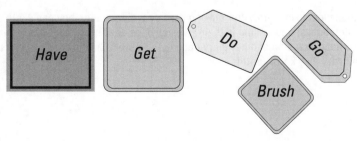

Verbs like 'get' are extremely common in expressions and tricky for students to understand because of the range of meaning. Use the same colour or shape every time 'get' comes up to make it easier for students to recognise and remember the lexical chunks that include this verb.

Call out these words, or pairs of words, one by one:

Up / breakfast / a shower / my teeth / out / my hair / dressed

Elicit the right verb from the board which combines to make a lexical chunk in each case. So when you say *up,* the students should say *get* because *get up* is a chunk. Then write the words below the appropriate verb. So write *up* under the main heading *get* on the board. When the students have helped to place all the words in the correct place on the board, instruct them to record the information for future reference.

Creating routine diaries

T >> St   **5 minutes**

Procedure: Ask students, one at a time, 'What time do you get up?' or 'What time do you go out in the morning?' Point to the clock as a clue.

Teach students the most typical pronunciation, fusing 'do' and 'you' together. Demonstrate which words carry the most stress in the sentence too and underline them. Drill until they sound natural and fluent.

What time /dʒə/ get up?   What <u>time</u> do you get <u>up</u>?

Now create two diary pages on the board and demonstrate how to fill them by eliciting the morning routine you taught earlier from one of the students and writing in the activities. Then ask another student about his routine and write in one or two of his activities as examples.

St >> St   **5 minutes**

Put the students in pairs. After making their own diary page (they can sketch it out in their notebooks) and writing in their own activities, they must interview a partner and note what he says on another diary page (see Figure 5-2). The students can use any vocabulary they know for this.

My Diary

Time	Activity
7.00	......................*Get up and have breakfast ......*
7.30	......................*Have a shower and brush my teeth*
7.45	.... *Get dressed and do my hair* ....
8.15	.... *Go out* ....

Mamita's Diary

Time	Activity
6.15	.... *Get up and have breakfast* .....
6.00	....
6.30	....

Figure 5-2:
Example
diary pages.

 Don't feel under pressure to create worksheets every time. Save time and paper by explaining the idea and guiding the students to draft something themselves. You could turn it into a dictation exercise so that the students practise listening and writing.

Transforming grammar

T >> Sts / **Sts >> T**   **10 minutes**

Procedure: Show students on the board that first and second person pronouns take the same verb structure in present simple sentences, as does the third person plural. Simply put it on the board like this (you don't need to use strict grammaticaljargon):

I/you/we/they   get up

Ask a student what time he gets up and elicit a response. Now see whether the class can complete the sentence correctly

Renny . . . up at 8 o'clock.

Ask another student of the opposite sex, if possible, and elicit a similar sentence.

Now it's time to put the third person singular pronouns on the board. Start with 'get up' because it changes in the simplest and most typical way. Then elicit the third person forms of the other verbs on the board by holding up the items of realia you used earlier one by one and beginning a sentence with he/she; for example, hold the brush to elicit: *She does her hair.*

Figure 5-3 shows three things you can highlight on the board:

 ✔ The error students are likely to make unless you warn them

 ✔ The correct form of the verb

 ✔ How to pronounce the third person form of the verb

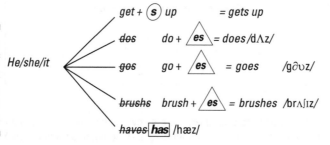

Figure 5-3:
Example of
board work
showing
verbs in the
third person

Notice how the verbs change in different ways. Again, I use shapes here to group verbs which change in a similar way in the third person, whereas you could also use colour to highlight this on the board.

TIP

The pronunciation of the five main verbs in this lesson is pretty unpredictable when you use them in the third person, so it is vital to drill them thoroughly.

Practising using the third person for daily routines

St >> St   5 minutes

Ask the students to find new partners. This time they need to use the third person in their discussion as they say what their previous partner's routine is like and compare it to their own.

> *St A: I get up at 7.00, but Renny gets up at 6.30. What time does Mamita get up?*
>
> *St B: Mamita gets up at 7.30 . . .*

Whole Class   5 minutes

Have a feedback session to round off the activity. Pick one student to ask another what they know about a classmate.Toss a soft toy or ball around to indicate whose turn it is talk about a classmate.

> T: Mamita, tell me about Renny. What time does Renny go out?
>
> St C: Renny goes out at 8.30. Vanessa, what time does Andre eat breakfast?
>
> St D: He eats breakfast at 7.00 . . . .

If the students make any mistakes, get their peers to correct them.

And finally . . .

Have a rapid-fire round of holding up the realia and eliciting the corresponding phrase. Put one of the students in the driving seat if you prefer and finish off with a big round of applause.

Extension activities

Give the class some writing homework. Teach more lexical chunks that use the same five verbs from this lesson, like the ones in Figure 5-4, and get them to continue the diary entry for a whole day in time for the next session. This activity prompts students to search for new and relevant vocabulary to describe their activities.

Figure 5-4: Show students other expressions for daily routine using the same verbs.

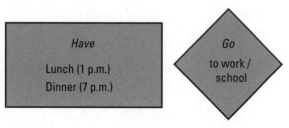

In the next lesson the students can talk about their typical day and share new words with the class. After that, you can show them how to turn the diary into sentences and paragraphs by teaching connecting words (next, then and so on).

Chapter 6

Getting Flash with Flashcards

· ·

· ·

Flashcards are a very traditional teaching resource. Many people envisage a teacher to be a person who sits in front of groups of children showing flashcards for vocabulary and spelling. In reality, flashcards are effective for this purpose, but they're also ideal for introducing ideas and fixing them in the memories of children and adults alike.

In this chapter, I talk about the advantages of using flashcards in TEFL and the different ways to use them. Then I give you an example of a lesson plan in which you use flashcards as the core resource with elementary-level students.

Using Flashcards as Lesson Context

Flashcards have become a popular resource among educators for many reasons:

✔ Learning by *doing* is effective, and flashcards prompt action on the part of the student.

✔ You can use them in various parts of the lesson to engage students' minds, introduce key points or to practise language.

✔ Preparing flashcards is cheap, quick, and easy.

✔ Flashcards with pictures provide context for vocabulary.

✔ Students can manipulate the cards (cut them out, turn them over, hold them up), which is interesting and motivating.

- ✔ You can easily shuffle and re-order them to provide a greater challenge to the memory.

- ✔ You retain the flashcards and can use them to review and repeat language points at regular intervals.

- ✔ Students can prepare flashcards themselves and carry them around as learning tools.

You should use any resource that you take time to prepare to full advantage. Here are some ways to use flashcards well:

- ✔ Put the picture on the front and vocabulary on the back.

- ✔ Have separate cards for a pair (picture on one, word on the other) to be matched together.

- ✔ Put English vocabulary on one side (*one* for example) and the students' first languages on the other (일, which is one in Korean, for example).

- ✔ Put the word in English on one side and its definition in English on the other.

- ✔ Put antonyms on either side of the card; for example, *hard* on one side and *soft* on the other.

- ✔ Get groups of students to prepare cards based on what they've learnt that week. Use them to revise at the beginning of the next lesson.

- ✔ On one card put many words related to the same topic.

- ✔ Put the individual words of a sentence on separate cards for students to put in order.

Incorporating Flashcards at All Levels

Here are some suggestions for using flashcards across the spectrum of levels.

Beginner and elementary

Make double-sided cards showing the letters of the alphabet in upper and lower case on one side (*A, a*) and a word or picture that starts with the same letter on the other (*apple*). Students practise calling the letters out, remembering the accompanying picture/word or putting the cards in alphabetical order.

Even students who speak European languages struggle with pronunciation of the alphabet and may forget certain letters that they don't use in their own language. Flashcards help students highlight the additional letters and practise using them.

Use a traditional pack of playing cards to teach the numbers to students who are a little 'too cool for school'. Play a simple game such as 'Snap', but don't allow students to take the cards they win unless they say the number shown on the front.

Start teaching colour vocabulary with coloured cards and the names of the colours written on them. In other words, write *blue* on a blue card. After the students have had sufficient practice drilling the colours, just put the colour words on white cards. When you hold up the card, students can rush to touch something in the room of that colour.

Pre-intermediate

Teach parts of the body with double-sided word and picture cards.

Drill pronunciation before you show the spelling of a word. This improves pronunciation, because students don't then try to pronounce every letter of the word unnecessarily. For example, *knee* must be heard as /ni:/ and not guessed as /kni:/.

Collect pictures of people working and create a set of jobs and occupations themed flashcards. Hand a student a flashcard and get her to act out or describe the job shown on it for the class to guess.

Find pictures of people expressing a range of emotions, such as surprise and fear. Make flashcards from them and use these to elicit ideas from the students about what the person is feeling. After teaching the emotion words, ask the students to create back-stories for the characters shown and write them down, as shown in Figure 6-1.

Figure 6-1:
Flashcard showing an emotion and used to elicit a story.

Angry

This is Michael. He is very angry today because he forgot to pay his tax bill and he got a big fine. He thinks the fine is too much.

Intermediate

For prepositions of movement (for example *off, onto, over, away, from, past*) show the same character in different positions on separate flashcards. Children enjoy pictures of a cute character, a teddy bear perhaps, so show it jumping over a chair, onto the chair, running past the chair, and so on.

Students who are interested in homes and architecture benefit from flashcards illustrating the vocabulary for buildings that are detached, semi-detached, and terraced, as well as sky-scrapers and bungalows, modern, or period. After using the flashcards to teach descriptions of various kinds of buildings, students can role-play the parts of estate-agent and home buyer.

Rows of terraced houses seem to be a particular feature of the UK landscape, and people from other countries can find the similarity among properties rather curious. Vocabulary about styles of homes allows students to compare and contrast the UK with their own land, and this makes for interesting discussions and essays.

Upper-intermediate

For exam students, use conversation cards showing the most frequently used speaking topics. For instance, IELTS candidates need to familiarise themselves with vocabulary for discussing family, work, study, and their hometown because these topics frequently crop up.

On each flashcard put a topic as the heading and some discussion questions beneath. Arrange students into small groups with a set of flashcards turned face down. One student in the group picks up and reads a card. All the students in the group make notes about the topic, but only one student is picked to speak about it for two minutes. The others listen and give feedback about grammar and vocabulary. Then the next student picks up a card and the challenge continues.

Put long, tricky words to pronounce on flashcards. Get the students to tap the desk to correspond with the number of syllables in the word your flashcard shows. For example, if your card says *literature*, the students need to tap the desk three times: /lɪtrətʃə /.

Advanced

Throughout the week, get the students who finish their activities first to prepare flashcards of the new vocabulary learnt that day. Get them to put a single item of vocabulary, a definition, and synonyms on each card. Then, at the end of the week, you have a ready-made revision game. The students can test each other using the cards to elicit either the vocabulary, synonyms or the definition.

On the front of a flashcard put a word that introduces a vocabulary group; for example, *thief*. Then on the back put a list of the more specific terms, such as *mugger, pickpocket, burglar, shoplifter*, and so on. Set a time limit of a minute and challenge groups of students to guess all the words on the list.

Elementary Lesson Plan

This lesson is designed to follow other sessions you run about rooms and items in the house. It introduces new vocabulary but draws on previously held knowledge, with speaking as the main skill.

Lesson overview

Time: Approximately one hour.

Materials: Flashcards for the household items and furniture students already know. Flashcards to introduce new words for bedroom items. Old catalogues or Internet access to online catalogues.

Aim: By the end of lesson the class will have learnt new vocabulary for bedroom items including <u>wardrobe</u>, chest of drawers, rug <u>cur</u>tains, <u>du</u>vet, bed and <u>pill</u>ow and they will have practised vocabulary for things in the house as well as prices.

Doing a warmer activity

Whole Class   **5 minutes**

Play a game of 'I Spy'. Someone says 'I spy with my little eye, something beginning with . . .' followed by the first letter of something in the room, like 'b' for board. The students have to guess what the challenger is thinking of, and the winner then starts a new round. This activity helps students practise the names of items in the room in addition to the alphabet. You should begin the game as the challenger but once the students have correctly guessed the first word, they can play it without you as a whole class.

Introducing the topic

T >> Sts   **10 minutes**

Students have already learnt words for basic furniture items such as *table* and *chair*. Now cut pictures out of a magazine and stick them to cards to show these nouns:

    <u>wardrobe</u>   *chest of drawers*   *rug*   <u>*cur*</u>*tains*   <u>*du*</u>*vet*   *bed*   <u>*pill*</u>*ow*

Draw the basic outline of a bedroom on the board but omit the items that comprise the target vocabulary on the flashcards. As you gradually teach the vocabulary, show each flashcard, drill the word and stick the card to the board. So step by step, you complete your bedroom picture.

Keep pointing to the flashcards to test that students know the word for each item. When they can remember the vocabulary, write the words on the board below each flashcard.

Playing silent bingo

T >> St   10 minutes

Prepare bingo cards for the students, but instead of numbers, show six words for household items on each card, including some bedroom vocabulary. Use all the vocabulary for house and home that your class know. Also prepare flashcards of pictures for all the household items on the cards. These you'll use instead of the traditional numbers called out in a bingo game. I show examples of some bingo cards and flashcards in Figure 6-2.

Figure 6-2:
Some bingo
cards and
flashcards.

Hand out the bingo cards. No more than two students should have the same card. Then silently hold up a flashcard. The students must recall the word for the picture and cross it off in its written form on their bingo card if it's there. The winner is the student who's first to cross out all six words on her card. Play four or five rounds of the game.

Doing a bedroom makeover

St >> St   10 minutes

Tell the class you don't like your bedroom because everything in it is old, and you want the students to help you change your room. Introduce old catalogues or online ones (such as Argos and IKEA websites) to the class. Point to each bedroom flashcard and ask students how much they think the item shown costs.

Next, prompt a student to look up a price and help her to do so. For example:

> *Teacher: How much is a nice, new wardrobe, Miyuki? Find the wardrobes in this book.*
>
> *Student: A nice, new wardrobe costs £300.*

Divide the students into small groups and allocate each one a catalogue or website to check. Give each group a few flashcards for bedroom furniture and set the task of checking the price of an item like the one shown on the card. They must write the price on the back of the flashcard.

This activity helps students become accustomed to authentic material from the real world outside the classroom, which increases their confidence.

St >> St   5-10 minutes

The groups quiz each other by holding up their flashcard and saying, 'How much is this? What do you think?' (You may need to review these questions first.) The other groups then guess. Finally, the group holding the flashcard turns it over to reveal the price. Each group has a turn at quizzing the others.

Let each group have a turn at guessing the price of an item before the true price is revealed. The holder of the flashcard can gesture to make the guesses higher or lower, and build up some anticipation like the old game show *Play Your Cards Right* (which is a nice game for students to play along with on YouTube, by the way).

Discussing design

St   3 minutes

Ask students to prepare a drawing of their ideal bedroom in their notebooks. They may also check in the dictionary for particular vocabulary they need to describe their picture which is required in the next exercise.

St >> St   8 minutes

Put the students in pairs. They must describe their picture to their partner. Put these conversation questions on the board to help the students fuel their discussions:

- ✔ Which colours do you like?
- ✔ Do you prefer this item of furniture to be big or small?
- ✔ How much does this cost?
- ✔ Would you like a TV/fire/desk/big window in your bedroom?

St >> T   4 minutes

Get feedback from the students by holding up a flashcard, eliciting the name of the item shown and asking a student whether this item appears in their partner's ideal room. Elicit sentences about the partners of a few of the students like this:

> *Teacher: Is there a rug in Charlotte's room? Tell me about it.*
>
> *Student: Yes, there's a big white rug near the bed and the fire.*

Extension activities

Lay out all the flashcards for things in the house. Put the students in pairs. Take the first pair, and arrange one student standing in front of the flashcards and the other with her back to them. State the name of a room in the house. The student near the flashcards must listen to her partner call out the names of things that may be in that particular room. The other student responds by finding the flashcards to match her partner's words. When the first pair have had a two-minute turn, start again with another pair and a new room.

Chapter 7

Making Use of Mobile Phones

. . . .

In This Chapter

▶ Identifying the mobile phone features that are useful for language classes

▶ Using mobile phones with students from beginner to advanced

▶ Employing phone features to teach pronunciation

. . . .

*L*et's face it, mobile phones are so commonplace in many parts of the world that if you don't work with them, you'll only be fighting against them. Rather than viewing phones as a constant distraction, in this chapter I present many suggestions on how to incorporate the technology into your lesson and I give you tips on how to do so. I also present a pronunciation lesson for elementary classes that encourages students to use their phones as a learning tool.

Using Mobile Phones as a Lesson Resource

Never before have students had so much technology available to them in such a portable format. Most the students already have a mobile phone. Just consider the range of features available that you can use for an educational purpose: calculator, calendar, camcorder, camera, clock, games, Internet access, learning applications, maps and/or a GPS system, phone calls, radio, SMS, voice recorder and media player.

Incorporating Mobile Phones at All Levels

Whatever class you teach, your lesson will seem more fun and engaging if you make use of the things students already enjoy. Here are some ways to use mobile phone activities with students at all levels.

Make sure you tell students ahead of time that they'll be using phones in class so that they charge them up.

Beginner and Elementary

Try the following exercises:

- ✔ Dictate sums to students, which they then tap into their phone calculators. Their answer to the sum shows whether the students understand the numbers in English well and also facilitates teaching the useful words *plus, minus, times, divide, point,* and *equals.*

- ✔ After students have learnt the cardinal numbers (*one, two* and so on), calendars are useful for prompting students to say the days of the week, months, and ordinal numbers (*first, second* and so on). For instance:

    Teacher: What's this date, Charlotte? (Points to 10/10/13).

    Student: It's Thursday the tenth of October, twenty thirteen.

    Just offering the date allows students use their technology to find the day of the week.

- ✔ The clock feature is, of course, great for telling the time in both digital and analogue formats (for example, *twelve thirty* and *half past twelve*). Challenge the students by giving them a time, preferably one within the next five minutes or so, and asking them to set their alarm to ring at that moment. It will soon be evident who understands the time in English.

Pre-intermediate

Try out these ideas:

- ✔ Instead of copying, inventing or bringing in maps, teach directions using your actual location on a phone's map or GPS system. Ask the students to write directions for getting to another address from the present location.

- ✔ The video recorder function enables students to make short movies out of role play tasks. Recorded role plays enable students to assess their own errors, instead of relying on your feedback, and also allows them to measure their progress over time by comparing the footage of different role play performances over a period of time. For more on role plays, head to Chapter 9.

Intermediate

Try these exercises:

- ✔ Using the voice recorder, you and the students can record announcements heard outside the classroom and bring them to the lesson for the class to comment on. For example, students may complain that they can't understand what announcements on trains mean (*'All aboard!'*, *'Stand clear of the doors!'* and so on). Get students to collect announcements using their phones. Then students 'show and tell', and other classmates try to explain the meanings. (You can also ask students to take pictures of signs on the street.)

- ✔ Students can download learning apps for use in dead time (when they've finished an activity before everyone else), such as the free Android 250 Grammar Quizzes app.

- ✔ Get students to practise using the imperative form by writing instructions to a mobile phone game. Another student can then try playing the game according to the instructions. If the player can't follow them, the writer needs to improve the instructions.

Upper-intermediate

Give these ideas a go:

- ✔ The camera feature is often reversible, so students can take normal photos and also pictures of themselves. This latter function is great for getting a snapshot of the correct mouth position for pronunciation of tricky phonemes.

- ✔ Students who find it difficult to write notes, or do so rather slowly, can record information in photos instead. It's less embarrassing for the slower student than lagging behind.

- ✔ Make calls on speaker phone in class to gather and practise vocabulary. Of course, teachers shouldn't allow students to make a nuisance of themselves for the sake of an English lesson. However, if you're planning a class outing, for example, the students can compile a list of valid questions (such as *'Are tourist information leaflets available in Chinese?'* and *'Can we come without booking first?'*). One student then makes the call to the information office of the intended venue while everyone listens and records the answers. Some offices also have recorded information for callers, which means you can prepare for exactly what the students will hear (for example, *'Your call is very important to us. Press one to hear our opening times and press two to speak to one of our customer service advisers'*). If the student is struggling during the call, step in with assistance.

Advanced

Try these exercises out:

- ✔ Give students a list of radio stations available in the area that have an hourly news bulletin. With their headphones, students listen to the radio news individually and then discuss the news headlines and big stories of the day.

✔ Use the Internet for research tasks. Students research and summarise points on a particular story or one aspect of it. They can then feed back information to their class-mates. For example, a course book may have a reading about a particular person and his noteworthy activities. Ask students to find a video clip of the person, an interview, comments of fans, or background information about the person's home town.

✔ Set up an email forum to discuss a class novel or review class trips. Pick out inter-esting posts and good use of English to highlight in class.

✔ Teach text messaging in English as a skill for higher -level students. You can teach which words students can omit in a sentence while retaining meaning clearly. (*'Would you like to come for dinner tomorrow night?'* can become *'Come for dinner tomorrow night?'*). You can also look at 'textspeak' in English (For example, *'Come 4 dinner 2morrow night?'*).

✔ Compare emoticons too. For example western and east Asian styles differ and may confuse the reader at first.

Happy, :), becomes ^_^. And sad, :'(, becomes ;_;.

Put different nationalities together in class to compare the meanings of emoticons and symbols. They can prepare an explanatory chart.

Elementary Lesson Plan

Lesson overview

Time: Approximately one hour.

Materials: Simple flashcards showing sets of minimal pairs. Students' phones with cameras, camcorders and voice recorders. Worksheets showing minimal pairs.

Aim: By the end of this lesson, students will have used their phones to record information about voiced and unvoiced phonemes and they will have practised using them by means of minimal pairs (pairs of similar words which differ in pronunciation because of one phoneme only, such as pull and pool) and tongue twisters.

Doing a warmer activity

T >> Sts   **6 minutes**

Do a minimal pairs exercise with flashcards. Show words that have the same pronunciation with the exception of one phoneme and ask them to repeat the pair after you. Make sure that students can pronounce each word distinctly. Figure 7-1 shows an example using /k-t/ words, but you can also use words such as *full, fall, fell, feel, fill, fool, foal* and similar word groups or pairs. Make sure that students pay attention to and copy the mouth shape you make for each word, as well as the sound. In addition, give plenty of opportunity to repeat after you.

Figure 7-1: Minimal pairs flashcards exercise using /k-t/ pronunciation.

Introducing the voiced and unvoiced consonants

T >> St   10 minutes

Show students a copy of the phonemic chart and drill these phonemes.

| /p/ | /b/ | /f/ | /v/ | /s/ | /z/ |
| /t/ | /d/ | /θ/ | /ð/ | /k/ | /g/ |

Look up Underhill's version of the phonemic chart – its layout is especially good for this activity See `www.onestopenglish.com/skills/pronunciation/phonemic-chart-and-app/interactive-phonemic-chart/`.

Write the phonemes on the board. Ask the class why /p/ and /b/ are together and why /f/ and /v/ are together, and so on. The answer is that you produce these pairs with the same mouth shape.

Students may not know the terminology (the phonemes on the left are unvoiced and the ones on the right voiced), but they may be able to point to the mouth and throat areas respectively. You can explain the distinction between the two groups by drawing a head and neck sideways on, and drawing arrows to the mouth and Adam's apple. Repeat the pairs of phonemes again, pointing to the appropriate area on your own body as you say each one. Show that /p/ is from the mouth but /b/ is from the throat.

Ask students to repeat the phonemes again, this time holding their Adam's apple area so they can feel the difference between voiced and unvoiced production of sound.

Students who are unable to distinguish between /p/ and /b/ can practise using the appropriate amount of force by holding a sheet of paper in front of their faces at forehead height. If they can say /p/ with enough force, the paper will move away from the face, but /b/ cannot produce the air needed to move the paper, no matter how hard they try.

Photographing phonemes

St >> St   10 minutes

Ask students to use their phone cameras and camcorders. They're going to record themselves demonstrating the mouth positions for the pairs of voiced and unvoiced phonemes. They should look at you pronouncing the phoneme, try to do it the same way, and then record themselves, as I show in Figure 7-2.

Figure 7-2:
Images
based on
phone
camera
pictures
showing
phonemes.

/s/ or /z/   **/f/ or /v/**   **/b/ or /p/**

The camcorder is more effective than the camera when the movement of the tongue is more important to the students' pronunciation than the lips and teeth (as with /t/ and /d/).

Over a number of lessons you can get the students to record all the phonemes on their phones, or at least all the ones they have trouble with.

Teaching Tongue Twisters

T >> St   **5 minutes**

Give the students some practice pronouncing the phonemes they find tricky to pronounce. Start with minimal pairs.

This website helps you find minimal pairs for practically any two phonemes in English: myweb.tiscali.co.uk/wordscape/wordlist/minimal.html. The classic books Tree or Three? and Ship or Sheep? by Ann Baker (Cambridge University Press) do the same job and are usually lurking somewhere in your school resources cupboard (if you have one).

Isolate the minimal pairs that best suit your students' pronunciation problems. For example, a number of my students from Colombia struggle with /v/ and pronounce /b/ instead. On the other hand, Korean students tend to confuse /p/ and /f/.

From a list of minimal pairs, create a tongue twister to help students see that in English you confuse words if you don't make the distinction between two different sounds. Help them feel the physical difference between the pronunciation of each one.

Here's an example tongue twister for /b/ and /v/:

> *Brenda the vendor went biking with a Viking.*
>
> *But her ballet-loving valet said, 'I vote for a boat'.*
>
> *When Brenda the vendor and the young biking Viking*
>
> *Saw cupboards quite covered with marbles, they marvelled.*

And here's an example for /p/ and /f/:

The chief has a passion for cheap-looking fashion

There's far too much pressure to make him look fresher.

So from packs of cool facts he just picks a quick fix.

It isn't necessary to teach students the meanings of the words in a pronunciation exercise. They'll look them up in a dictionary if they choose to.

Put the tongue twisters on the board for the students to note down. Read the tongue twisters to the class slowly and ask the students to repeat them line by line until they begin to distinguish the tricky phonemes more clearly.

St >> St   **12 minutes**

Next the students practise reading the tongue twisters aloud in pairs. When they feel confident, they record their own voices reading the tongue twisters on their phone voice recorders. They may also record a good example of pronunciation such as a classmate's voice or yours. The students should play back the recording and re-record if they're not content with the quality of their pronunciation.

I usually allow students to go out of the classroom to make their recordings, so that they can hear themselves clearly and feel less self- conscious speaking into the microphone.

Dictating to peers

T >> St   **5 minutes**

Prepare minimal pairs worksheets like the ones shown in Figure 7-3, but use phonemes suitable for your students' needs. Each numbered section is a minimal pair, for example 1) *Brenda* and *vendor* and 2) *biking* and *Viking*. Swiftly drill all the words on the worksheet chorally and individually.

1.Brenda	vendor		6. ban	van
2. biking	Viking		7. best	vest
3. ballet	valet		8. marble	marvel
4. boat	vote		9. banish	vanish
5. cupboard	covered		10. berry	very

1. copy	coffee		6. clip	cliff
2. picks	fix		7. past	fast
3. pattern	fatten		8. passion	fashion
4. paint	faint		9. cheap	chief
5. pair	fair		10. pressure	fresher

Figure 7-3:
Minimal
pairs
worksheet.

St >> St   8 minutes

Put students in pairs, perhaps of different nationalities, so that they can help each other with different problems. Give the pairs two identical worksheets. Get the pairs to sit back to back or with a book between them so they can't see each other's mouths. Each student must say one word in the minimal pair while his partner listens and circles the word he heard. Finally, the students compare their answers. This activity facilitates greater awareness of clear pronunciation on the part of the speaker and improved distinction of the sounds on the part of the listener.

Doing a cooler activity

T >> St   5 minutes

Show the students how to work on their pronunciation skills using their phones. Introduce them to free pronunciation applications such as Sounds - the pronunciation app by MacMillan (www.soundspronapp.com) or Pronunciation Power by ECLI (itunes. apple.com/us/app/pronunciation-power/id368753108).

Extension activities

Give each student a copy of the phonemic chart. Mouth a phoneme silently. Students watch and point to the phoneme(s) on the chart they think you said. Different answers are possible for the voiced and unvoiced pairs. After students get the hang of the game, they can play by themselves in small groups.

Ask the students to find four new words that begin with the phoneme they struggle to pronounce. They can do it as homework and explain the words to groups of classmates in the next lesson.

Challenge the students to learn and recite a short poem to practise clear pronunciation. Children's poems like 'Do Not Feed the Animals' by Robert Hull and 'Time' by Valerie Bloom are manageable for low-level students.

Chapter 8

Covering Clothes and Fashion

. . . .

In This Chapter

▶ Using clothes and fashion as a context for practising grammar and feeding discussions

▶ Practising the present continuous tense

▶ Teaching a fun, practical lesson for elementary students of any age

. . . .

*L*ower level students need lesson content that they can use practically in their everyday lives. If they can't put into practice the language items they acquire, they soon forget them. Fortunately, everyone uses clothes and many people have at least a passing interest in fashion. This topic always encourages students to offer an opinion.

In this chapter, I show you how to apply the topic of clothes and fashion to many different lessons and I present a lesson plan that combines this topic with the present continuous tense in a practical way.

Using Clothing and Fashion as Lesson Content

The great thing about discussing clothes is that you cover and expand into a broad range of topics. For example:

✔ Budgeting

✔ Comparing countries and cultures

✔ Conforming in society

✔ Describing colours and patterns such as stripes and zigzags

✔ Describing cut and texture such as wide and narrow, rough and smooth

✔ Discussing retail and consumerism

✔ Conducting ethical studies of large clothing companies

✔ Expressing personal taste

✔ Talking about formal and informal situations

✔ Knowing the difference between the generations; each has its own style

Incorporating Clothing and Fashion at All Levels

Here are some suggestions you can use for classes incorporating clothes and fashion.

Beginner and elementary

Practise words for clothes and colours regularly. For instance, ask someone who is a wearing red t-shirt to answer a question or someone who is wearing blue shoes to write on the board.

Use realia (real everyday objects) that help kinaesthetic learners. For example, students can race in teams to find and put on certain items of clothing to practise remembering the lexis for the different items.

Pre-intermediate

Students can show photographs of themselves in different outfits and then describe the clothes and occasions. They can write about what they wear for various events in life.

In English-speaking countries, send the class to the shopping centre to find out which shops sell, for example, sportswear, party clothes, or formal suits. Give them a whole list to check out, which has the dual purpose of helping them get to know the town they're staying in and get used to the vocabulary at the same time.

Intermediate

Ask students to brainstorm as many jobs as they can. Following this, give each group of students a certain number of jobs to work on, and ask them to find the vocabulary to describe what people wear while working. For example, useful words such as apron, helmet and uniform arise. Then the groups can teach each other the new vocabulary.

Upper-intermediate

Teach some useful phrases for debating, such as those you use to agree, disagree, and interrupt. Then set up some topics based on the fashion world to debate. You might ask:

- Does fashion encourage extreme behaviour, such as eating disorders and bullying?
- Is it shallow to believe that you must always dress in the latest fashion trends?

Advanced

Show photographs of various aspects of British fashion culture; for example, teddy boys, mods, skinheads, punks, new romantics, and goths. Ask the students to compare and contrast the various images, saying what messages the people shown want to convey through their clothes.

Now ask students to give a short presentation about fashion styles through history in their countries.

Elementary Lesson Plan

This lesson teaches students how to name items of clothing and also give an opinion about them. They need a basic knowledge of the present simple and present continuous tenses to do so make sure you teach these tenses before you use this plan.

Lesson overview

Time: Approximately 1 hour.

Materials: Flashcards of clothes (details in 'Introducing the topic'). Coloured pens, pencils, and markers. A drawing of a person wearing clothes based on the new vocabulary. Photographs from fashion magazines showing various interesting outfits. Some items of clothing of your own or borrowed from the students.

Aim: By the end of this lesson the students will have learned vocabulary for seven items of clothing (skirt, trousers, shirt, jacket, tie, dress and shoes) and practised the present continuous.

Doing a warmer activity

Whole Class   3 minutes

Whizz through the alphabet from A to Z. Get each student in turn to say the next letter.. Then try it again from Z to A.

Introducing the topic

T >> St   7 minutes

Procedure: Make seven simple flashcards using pictures of items of clothing.

Write the word and phonemes on the back of each flashcard.

a skirt	/skɜːt/
<u>trousers</u> (pl)	/traʊzəz/
a shirt	/ʃɜːt/
a <u>jacket</u>	/dʒækɪt/
a dress	/dres/
a tie	/taɪ /
shoes (pl)	/ʃuːz/

If possible, give each item of clothing a different colour so that your students can practise colours and so that visual learners remember the pictures better.

Start the lesson by writing 'clothes' on the board as a heading. Drill the word. Quickly show all the flashcard images and say, 'These are clothes!'

Clothes is a tricky word. I must admit I teach 'close' instead for students who just can't manage the pronunciation.

Now deal with the flashcards one by one. As you show each picture, say the word and get the students to repeat. Don't show the spelling until you've drilled the pronunciation of each word several times.

You need to point out that trousers are always plural, and highlight the single and plural form for 'shoe'.

Students usually struggle to absorb any more than seven new language items per lesson. That's why I don't include the word 'pair' in this lesson plan. Have a lesson on pairs another day (glasses, gloves, socks, and so on).

Using the present continuous with 'wear'

T >> St   **10 minutes**

Procedure: Draw the outline of a person on the board; a simple figure will do. Point to the figure and elicit the clothing to put on it. For example, you point to the torso and say, '*Trousers?*' or '*Shoes?*' Pick a student, who should say '*Shirt!*' or '*Jacket!*'. Elicit the colour also.

Make sure students understand that the adjective comes before the noun. So they need to say 'a blue shirt' not 'a shirt blue'.

Continue the activity by pointing to the legs and the feet and draw on the clothes that the students call out as you go. Ideally, use coloured markers – or just write a label for the colour.

Now show the students how to construct a full sentence about clothing in the present continuous. Write a sentence like this on the board, based on your drawing:

> *He/she . . . . . . a blue shirt, black trousers and brown shoes.*

Elicit from students suggestions for the first missing word by pointing to the gap. If the students need extra help then narrow down the choices by saying:

> *'He am? No! He are? No!'*

Try to elicit *'He is'*. Write *'is'* in the gap and then move on to the verb. Write *'to wear'* on the board somewhere underneath the sentence. Hopefully, students remember how to construct a sentence in the present continuous and can say *'he is wearing'*. (You could use the contraction ('s) if students know it.) In any case, write *wearing* in the gap.

> *He/she is wearing a blue shirt, black trousers and brown shoes.*

Drill the sentence chorally and individually around the class.

St >> St   **3 minutes**

Next, point out what people are wearing in the class. Get students to make sentences about their friends to check they can use sentence present continuous sentence structure.

> *T: Today Pedro is wearing a white shirt. Pedro tell me about Rashida.*
>
> *St: Rashida is wearing . . .*

St >> St   **10 minutes**

Explain and gesture for students to draw a person in their notebooks. Show the students how to hold the book so that nobody else can see their pictures. Tell them to draw clothes on the figure. Use gestures and simple language, so pretend to be drawing and give a commentary.

> *'Red jacket, yellow shirt, blue trousers, green shoes . . . '*

Students now design their own outfits for the figures they've drawn.

Have a pre-prepared drawing of your own. When everyone has finished drawing, hand the picture to a student and ask whether the picture is of a man or a woman. Ask what he/she is wearing. Draw a figure on the board dressed in an outfit like the one the student's describing.

Now put the students into pairs. In each pair, one student is A and the other is B. Student A needs to put down her pen and Student B needs to be ready to draw on a new page. Student A must dictate her picture to Student B. For example:

> *It's a man. He is wearing a grey shirt and a grey tie. His jacket is black . . .*

Then it is Student B's turn to dictate. Finally, both students compare their pictures.

Giving student feedback

T >> St   5 minutes

Correct any errors you spotted during the picture dictation activity. Students often have some trouble with the present continuous, and they may mispronounce some of the vocabulary. Or else ask a few individuals to tell you about their drawings.

Working on positives and negatives

T >> St   10 minutes

Use one of the students as an example and write an erroneous sentence on the board; for instance:

> *Lucas is wearing a blue **skirt**.*

Ask the students whether it's a good or bad sentence and thereby elicit a correction. So, in this example the student crosses out *skirt* and writes *shirt* instead.

Now write the name of another student on the board and get someone else up to complete the sentence. Whisper to the student what to write and make it something untrue so that the other students will correct the sentence.

> *Lucas is wearing a blue skirt shirt.*

Tell the students to write sentences in their books about what each person in the class is wearing. Half the sentences should be right and the other half wrong.

After the students have finished, remind them how to make a present continuous sentence negative. Use your sentences on the board to demonstrate.

> *Lucas isn't wearing a blue skirt. He is wearing a blue shirt.*
>
> *Audrey isn't wearing black trousers. She is wearing black shoes.*

Students now correct their untrue sentences in their books.

Go around the room and monitor. Make sure the students write the new sentences correctly. As feedback, ask students to read out what they wrote and discuss any problems.

Exploring fashion styles

`St >> St`   8 minutes

In a very obvious way, put on some items of clothing you've brought along or secretly taken from the students, where appropriate (there is a usually a scarf on the back of someone's chair). For example, throw a jacket over your shoulder, roll up your trousers, and take off one shoe. Pose like a fashion model and ask the students whether they like your clothes. Elicit opinions around the class.

> *T: Do you like my new clothes Mikako?*
>
> *St: No, I don't like your shoes.*

Put students in groups of three or four and give each a set of photos from fashion magazines. Make sure they can say:

> *I (don't) like his/her/the . . .*

They now discuss their opinions, saying what they do and don't like. Afterwards, ask one or two students about specific pictures.

Doing a cooler activity

`St >> T`   4 minutes

Hold up the flashcards again and elicit both the vocabulary and spelling for each item.

Extension activities

This lesson covers only seven items of vocabulary, but students need to learn words for many more items of clothing. Build up the entire wardrobe by teaching words like hat, scarf, socks, gloves, belt, jumper, trainers and so on.

A fun activity is to send one or two students out of the room and get the others to change their clothing somehow. They might put on a hat, or take off a jumper. When they return, the students who went out have two minutes to say what has changed. They can use the present continuous for this.

> *You're wearing that hat now. He's wearing Pedro's jacket . . .*

If you have an old clothing catalogue or two, bring them in and set a timed task in which students have to list the page numbers for various items of clothing. For example:

> *Which page has a long, blue skirt for £17.99? Page . . .*

Chapter 9

Acting It Out: Using Role-Plays

. . . .

In This Chapter

▶ Getting students to interact and use their imaginations

▶ Making role plays as effective as possible

▶ Using a transport role play

. . . .

Given the chance, most teachers would love to introduce their students to all kinds of situations in the real world that require the use of English. However, because time and opportunity rarely allow for this, practising differing contexts through role-play is the next best thing.

In this chapter, I talk about the advantages of role-playing and how to get your students involved in this very effective form of interaction. I also provide a level lesson plan for a taxi journey role play.

Using Role-Playing as a Lesson Resource

People use the term *role-play* to cover more than one thing these days. The basic meaning of the term refers to taking on another character and acting out a situation as that person. However, in class you often allow students to play themselves within a foreign situation too. This second type of enactment is really called a *simulation*, but most teachers tend to put it under the umbrella of role-play as well, and so I stick to that definition in this book too.

Here are some of the advantages of using role-plays:

✔ Acting out situations is good practice for using English in the outside world, but no harmful consequences result from errors.

✔ Students can practise an endless number of situations, including those they'd love to encounter but have little opportunity to do so. Putting yourself in someone else's shoes leads to wider perspectives and sensitivities, which is very valuable when students are dealing with a variety of languages and cultures through language learning.

✔ Students use their imaginations and creativity, which is fun and motivating for them. Pretending to be someone else means students can throw off their usual inhibitions and be rude, devious or bossy – lots of scope for fun!

✔ You can be in character too, so the students don't look to you for information. Instead, they exercise learner independence by keeping the scenario going using their own skills, and through collaborating with peers.

✔ Role-playing improves overall communication skills. Collaborating on role-play tasks allow students to put forward their own opinions, and overall speaking fluency improves.

✔ Giving students input in the form of watching, instead of just reading or listening, is good for retention. So when students watch others role play, they remember the content well. And acting things out is more memorable still.

Follow these basic steps to make sure that role-plays run smoothly.

1. **Decide on the objectives of the role play.**

   For example, establish a language point, situation or aspect of cultural awareness for your class to practise. Put this information on the board or on a worksheet for students to review and focus on.

2. **Demonstrate the role play yourself.**

   Then students have a good idea of what to do. Choose a confident student to role play with you. The other students can coach you by shouting instructions to you (that means you need to be hesitant in your performance here and there, until the class give you some input).

3. **Put students into groups of mixed abilities and personalities.**

   Either set up the role play yourself by providing students with the plot (not script) of the play and assigning each student a role within it. (When assigning roles, get students to try new things rather than always playing themselves.) Alternatively, allow students to organise the plot and script themselves, based on a few instructions from you.

4. **Get timing.**

   Make students aware of the timeframe: how much preparation time they have and how long the role play itself should last. As the activity unfolds, let students know how the timing is going, so the students can embellish or summarise according to how much time is left.

5. **Discuss.**

   Follow up with a discussion of how the role plays went, what could be improved and what the class have learnt.

You may get the class to perform a short, spontaneous role play from time to time if you're sure that the students have the skills and confidence to pull it off. After all, many situations arise in real life that the students are not well-prepared for. So this kind of spontaneity is good practice for the world outside the classroom,

Above all, keep the atmosphere fun and light so students feel they can try dialogue out comfortably . . . and make the odd mistake!

Incorporating Role Plays at All Levels

You can use role plays very effectively with students at all levels. In this section, I show some role play ideas with language points or useful scenarios they practise.

Beginner and elementary

Use roleplays to help low-level students to see the practical value of the their English lessons and to help them cope in situations they may encounter.

- ✔ Collect some takeaway menus and bring them in for waiter and diner role plays. Practise ordering food items as well as introducing countable and uncountable nouns: *I'd like **some rice** and **a steak**, please.*

- ✔ Practise describing parts of the body by role playing a doctor and patient scenario. Teach the verb 'to hurt' for this. For example: *It's my arm, Doctor! It hurts.* If your students are living in an English-speaking country for an extended period, you may role play the whole procedure from making the appointment to attending the surgery and dispensing the prescription.

- ✔ Practise attending a cocktail party. Then students get used to introducing themselves and stating basic personal information such as nationality and length of stay in the country: *Hi, I'm Alishka, and I'm from India, but I'm only here for a month.*

Pre-intermediate to intermediate

Try out these role plays:

- ✔ Use a travel agency scenario to practise talking about modes of transport, dates, times and personal data. Students can role play choosing a holiday and booking it.

- ✔ Role plays based on romantic relationships always raise a smile. Compare using polite and impolite register by role playing break-up scenarios or asking someone out on a date.

✔ Assign students to play interviewers and job candidates. This role play is very practical because many students look for part-time work and the vocabulary in employers' questions is often tricky. For example:

What's your best achievement?

What are your strengths and weaknesses?

What is your availability?

✔ Practise telephone conversations through role play. Many telephone expressions need to be committed to memory such as:

Speaking!

Hold the line!

Sorry, it's engaged!

I'll call you back.

It's regarding . . .

Upper-intermediate to advanced

Give these exercises a go.

✔ Assign students the role of taking a particular stand in a debate. Teach expressions such as *devil's advocate* and *NIMBY* (not in my backyard).

✔ Practise the tasks involved in finding accommodation, such as calling to make enquiries, being interviewed by potential flatmates, and getting landlords to fix things.

✔ Role play making a sales pitch and negotiating a deal (which may involve a particular business etiquette, not just vocabulary).

✔ Get students to role play complaining to a shop assistant about a purchase. Teach them to be courteous yet firm with language such as:

I'm afraid that's unacceptable.

I insist on speaking to the manager!

It's written in the terms and conditions.

Elementary to Pre-intermediate Lesson Plan

This lower- level lesson teaches students very useful everyday expressions and allows them to work as a team to create and act out a taxi journey role play.

Lesson overview

Time: 60 to 70 minutes.

Materials: As many role cards as there are students (some roles can be duplicated in a large class). A vocabulary sheet is optional (you could put vocabulary on the board).

Aim: By the end of the lesson, the students will have role played a typical taxi journey and practised useful expressions for this situation.

Doing a warmer activity

T >> Sts   5 minutes

Put the students into small groups and give them two minutes to brainstorm and list as many different kinds of transport as they can. The lists may include:

car	bus	taxi	(underground) train
bicycle	motorbike	skateboard	boat (various kinds)
helicopter	aeroplane	hot-air balloon	

After two minutes, a representative from each group gives you his group's list. Count who has the most correct answers and declare that group the winner. Point out any particularly dodgy spelling by putting the correct form on the board (without identifying the culprit).

Introducing the scenario

T >> St   10 minutes

Draw or show a picture of a taxi with a driver and passenger. Elicit or teach the words *taxi*, *driver* and *passenger*, along with the words *fare* and *cab*.

Position five chairs as though they were the seats in a car and get a student to sit in a front seat (left or right to represent the driver, depending on the country you're in). Shout 'Taxi!' and then pretend to get in the back seat.

Say hello to the driver, who will certainly reply. Then, look quizzically at the students and 'driver'. Wait for someone to suggest the driver's question (such as *Where are you going, please?*) and then take out a small piece of paper on which you've written the address. Again, pause for the students to suggest the next line of the conversation (such as *I want to go to . . .*). Pretend to put your seat belt on and, after a little pretend driving, point frantically as though you've seen your destination. Again, let students suggest the words. Mime getting out and prompt the students to stop you and make the driver ask for the fare.

Teaching taxi journey expressions

T >> Sts   10 minutes

Hand out a vocabulary sheet like the one shown in Figure 9-1, or put the vocabulary on the board. Explain and drill all the vocabulary thoroughly.

Taking a Taxi

Figure 9-1:
Vocabulary
sheet for a
taxi journey
role play.

In the taxi: driver   passenger   fare   cab

Questions and answers: Where to? / Where are you going?   I want to go

to....... / Take me to......What's the address and postcode?

It's **on**..........street / road.

It's **in**..........(area)   How long does it take to get there?   It takes...... Are we

there yet?   We are ....minutes away

What's the fare? / How much is that?   That's.........

To help explain the questions and answers you could write a full dialogue on the board using the taxi driver and passenger as characters, like this:

> Taxi driver: *Good morning! Where to, please?*
>
> Passenger: *I want to go to the sports centre. It's in Holborn, on Chancery Lane.*
>
> Taxi driver: *What's the address and postcode?*
>
> Passenger: *It's 1543 Chancery Lane, London WC1Z 9DF.*

Now put two more students in the 'taxi' (without vocabulary sheets). Give the passenger student an address and get the passenger and driver to act out a role play. Other students can assist by jogging their memories with vocabulary.

Organising the students

St >> St   10 minutes

Explain that in groups students are going to act out one longer taxi journey or a couple of short ones, totalling approximately three minutes. Put the students in groups of three or four. In each group someone must play the role of the driver and the others are passengers. The passengers can travel together or one after the other.

Prepare secret role cards to add more drama to the role play. For example, passenger cards may read like the ones in Figure 9-2. You could give the taxi drivers similar cards to add colour to their performances too. Put your finger to your lips as you surreptitiously hand the cards out so students know the information is top secret. It's more fun for other students to guess what's going on with the various characters than to know for sure.

Figure 9-2:
Examples of role cards for a taxi journey role play.

Passenger: You drank six beers this evening!	Passenger: You are very late for your new job.	Passenger: You think the other passengers are stupid.	Passenger: You think all taxis are very dirty.

Students now work together note down and learn their role plays. They must choose a destination, and use expressions from the vocabulary sheet and their own general knowledge of English. Incorporating the information on their role cards affects what students say or simply how they say it.

Get the groups to move the furniture to make 'taxis' and act out their scenes privately before they show them to the class.

If one group finishes more quickly than the others, get them to switch the cast around. So let someone else try being the driver instead of being a passenger.

Acting out the role play to the class

St >> St   10-15 minutes

Tell the groups to put their furniture back in the normal position except for one 'taxi' at the front of the classroom. Each group acts out their role play. The students watch each group respectively, and after the performance they try to guess what was on each person's role card.

Discussing the role play

`T >> St`   **10 minutes**

Discuss questions like these with the students:

- ✔ Which sentences from the vocabulary sheet can you remember easily? Why?
- ✔ Could you make your role play better? How?
- ✔ What did you like about each group?
- ✔ Which drivers and passengers were very polite?
- ✔ Which students are very good actors?
- ✔ What else do you sometimes talk about with a taxi driver?

Extension activities

In subsequent lessons use similar role plays to practise expressions for booking train and aeroplane tickets. You can then teach students how to handle single and return tickets, seat reservations and luggage restrictions.

A community language learning approach is effective here. Refer to Chapter 2 of this book for more information.

Part III
Pre-Intermediate and Intermediate Classes

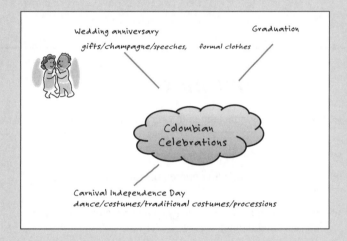

Visit www.dummies.com/extras/tefllessonplans for free online lesson plan ideas and outlines.

In this part . . .

- ✔ Cultivate classroom language with you intermediate students.

- ✔ Learn how to develop discussions.

- ✔ Adapt readers and other printed resources to meet your needs.

- ✔ Ride the technological wave by using i-players to stimulate interest and learning.

- ✔ Draw language from art and photographs.

- ✔ Show your students the value of story-telling.

Chapter 10

Cultivating Classroom Language from Day One

In This Chapter

▶ Helping students clarify, check and respond to information

▶ Teaching idioms to make students more fluent

▶ Following a lesson plan to improve students' classroom language

*P*ractically all TEFL teachers agree that one of the main objectives in a lesson is for students to maximise the amount of time they spend speaking English. Yet an obstacle to doing that is when students tend to fall back on their native language with the teacher or other classmates when they need help. So, as a teacher, you need to teach all levels of students' *classroom language:* the words and phrases to say when they've got lost.

The first day of a course is very important for setting the tone. You can very quickly set the standard for what you expect from students. Whether you intend to operate a full immersion programme (entirely in English) or accept translation, you must give students the tools they need in the real world. Out there learners need a strategy for when things go wrong and they don't understand.

So in this chapter, I show how you can establish a routine right from the first lesson of a course by giving students the language they need to clarify, check and respond to information in English.

Looking at Classroom Language at All Levels

Here are some ideas for phrases you can teach your various classes. Why not put the phrases on classroom posters. Perhaps the students could create them, according to their level.

Beginner and Elementary

Start by teaching a few imperatives, or commands, that you are likely to use often. Use actions to demonstrate the meaning.

- ✔ Open/close your book
- ✔ Listen!
- ✔ Repeat!

Play Simon says with some of the basic teachers' commands to practise with beginner students.

Next teach the students expressions that they need to speak to you:

> Excuse me!
>
> Please /thank you
>
> (Can you) repeat please?
>
> I (don't) understand.
>
> Right/ wrong
>
> What is . . . . .in English/ my language?
>
> What does . . . . mean?
>
> How do you spell/ say that?

Polite phrases such as 'please' and 'thank you' are absolutely critical when speaking English, whereas in other languages politeness is built into the grammar. For this reason students often fail to see the importance of those little words. Emphasise and insist on them from the outset.

Use words in current usage but avoid slang for the lower levels. For example, teach 'Sorry?' rather than 'I beg your pardon' but don't teach 'Cheers!' instead of 'Thanks'.

Pre-intermediate/Intermediate

As students become more aware of the subtleties of English grammar and vocabulary, teach them how to express questions that require detailed answers and also how to respond to information in a natural way:

Is it irregular ?

What is the past participle?

Does this make sense?

Can I say. . . . .?

I see!

I have no idea!

What's the opposite/ synonym of that?

What's the difference between . . . . . and . . . . . .?

Students tend to confuse 'How do you say . . . . . . ?' and 'What do you call . . . . . . ?' all the time! Spend some time explaining the two expressions. The difference between right/wrong and true/false often presents problems too.

Upper intermediate- Advanced

At this level, students cope with idiomatic language more easily and can incorporate into their vocabulary. So, teach classroom language that reflects this:

I (can't) get the gist of it!

Could you go over that again please?

Just a minute please!

What is that in simple terms?

Can I put it like this?

In other words . . . . . .

Intermediate Lesson Plan

It's relatively easy for students to find polite phrases for classroom language. However, in reality we use idioms that are much trickier to understand. In this lesson, I introduce students to common idioms they can use as responses when they aren't sure of the correct response or need the speaker to repeat.

Lesson overview

Time: 60+ minutes. Remember, you need to do a 'get to know you' exercise first so that you can introduce yourself (see Chapter 4 for details on exercises).

Materials: A complete story text and the same text cut into segments. Discussion questions and a questionnaire (you could make a worksheet containing the discussion questions and questionnaire but students don't need one each as they can easily share).

Aims: By the end of the lesson, students will be able to use classroom language in a more idiomatic way.

Vocabulary: Students know the meaning of these phrases and when to use them:

I don't get it!

Sorry, I didn't catch that!

Could you give me a hand?

I haven't got a clue!

That rings a bell.

Hold on, please!

Doing a warmer activity

T >> Sts then **Sts >> T**   5 minutes

Procedure: Prepare a short reading passage. It can be the one you'll distribute later in the jigsaw task. After general introductions, tell students to get ready for a short dictation by getting their pens and paper out. They have to write down whatever you say. Then, deliberately frustrate them by reading the text first ridiculously quickly then by muttering it so that the words are unintelligible.

When they're unable to write, ask students what the problem is in an exaggeratedly innocent fashion, so they understand you're playing with them, and see whether they can express the problem in English. Note what they say on one side of the board; for example, 'Too fast!' or 'Not clear!' Explain that today the lesson is about idioms they can use when they have problems in your classroom or in the outside world.

Vocabulary discussion 1

St >> St   6 minutes

Procedure: Write these expressions on the rest of the board.

I don't understand	*Repeat, please!*	*Help me!*
I don't know	*I remember that*	*Wait, please!*

In small groups, students must brainstorm other ways of saying these six things. For example, they may suggest 'I have no idea' for 'I don't know'.

Don't allow dictionaries for this stage of the lesson. This exercise is a good revision tool.

Whole Class   10 minutes

Procedure: Ask representatives from each group to write their suggestions on the board under each expression from Vocabulary discussion 1. As a peer correction exercise, let the rest of the class say whether they agree with each group's suggestions. Make sure the final version on the board is correct and give students time to write all the expressions down.

Jigsaw task

St >> St   10 minutes

Procedure: The story below contains all the key vocabulary in context. You can use my story or one that you create to suit your students, but you need two versions. Have the complete text ready to read, and then another copy of the same text that you've cut up into little sections. Each section should contain one or two sentences and they areand distributed equally amongst the class.

If you create your own story, make sure that the text contains structural clues. That means that there are connecting words that refer to previously mentioned information (such as *after that happened*) or ones that continue the story (such as *next*). In this way you subtly train students to notice connecting words.

Students cheat! They'll try to match the pieces by shape, like a literal jigsaw puzzle, instead of going by the story content. So use straight lines to divide the segments; a guillotine will help.

The students must now co-operate to put all the pieces of the story together and make one complete tale. To do this they all show their segments of the story and together work out which is first, second and so on. Eventually, they should all stand up in a line holding the story segments in order from start to finish. Read the students' version of the story aloud and help them correct any parts that are in the wrong order.

You could give each pair of students a full set of segments to organise. However, for a first-day lesson, it's good to get all the students interacting.

Full text

Richard was planning a family holiday. The only problem was that he **didn't have a clue where to go.** *One day he saw an advertisement for a hotel in Cornwall.* **That rings a bell,'** he thought. 'I'm sure my wife went there with her grandfather when she was a child.'

He decided to call the hotel. When the receptionist answered, he began to organise the room, but the telephone line was very bad.

'Sorry, sir, I **didn't catch that**! Did you say Mr Richards for one night?' asked the receptionist at the hotel.

'No, I said Mr Richard Smith! It's a family room for May 1st. We want to stay four nights, leaving May 5th.'

Richard repeated the details many times because the receptionist just **didn't get it**. In fact, he thought that the receptionist might be very old and a little deaf.

After a few minutes the receptionist began to explain some necessary information. Richard asked the receptionist to **hold on** while he got himself a pen. He asked his young son, who was playing in the room, to help. 'David, **could you give me a hand**, please? Pass that pencil and notebook over there.'

As soon as David stood up, the living room door opened and Richard's wife walked in. Richard quickly put the phone down.

'We did your secret surprise, Mummy! We're all going on holiday to Cornwall!' said little David.

The text in segments

Richard was planning a family holiday. The only problem was that he **didn't have a clue where to go**.

_____

One day he saw an advertisement for a hotel in Cornwall.

'**That rings a bell**,' he thought. 'I'm sure my wife went there with her grandfather when she was a child.'

_____

He decided to call the hotel. When the receptionist answered, he began to organise the room, but the telephone line was very bad.

_____

'Sorry, sir, I **didn't catch that**! Did you say Mr Richards for one night?' asked the receptionist at the hotel.

_____

'No, I said Mr Richard Smith! It's a family room for May 1st. We want to stay four nights, leaving May 5th.'

_____

Richard repeated the details many times because the receptionist just **didn't get it.**

_____

In fact, he thought that the receptionist might be very old and a little deaf.

_____

After a few minutes the receptionist began to explain some necessary information.

_____

Richard asked the man to **hold on** while he got himself a pen.

_____

He asked his young son, who was playing in the room, to help. 'David, **could you give me a hand**, please? Pass that pencil and notebook over there.'

_____

As soon as David stood up, the living room door opened and Richard's wife walked in. Richard quickly put the phone down.

_____

'We did your secret surprise, Mummy! We're all going on holiday to Cornwall!' said little David.

_____

Text comprehension

`T >> St`   6 minutes

Procedure: Students can put their story segments from the jigsaw task on the floor and then read the story again for themselves. Allow a couple of minutes for this. Then make sure that the students have understood the gist of the text by asking some basic questions. Here are some simple yes/no questions (more confident students can provide an explanation for their answers):

1. When Richard wanted to organise a holiday, was he worried about the cost of the hotel?

2. Did Richard want to go on holiday with his wife's grandfather?

3. Did Richard want to take his child on holiday?

4. Why did Richard repeat what he was saying on the phone a few times?

5. Was little David helpful?

Vocabulary discussion 2

`St >> St`   5 minutes

Procedure: Focus on the phrases in bold in the story in the jigsaw task. Explain that each of the six highlighted phrases is a synonym for one of the six phrases you wrote on the board during Vocabulary discussion 1. By reading the story again in context, students should be able to guess the meanings of the phrases. For example, '*Hold on*' matches '*Wait, please*'. Depending on how many students you have, they can do this as a whole class or in smaller groups.

Elicit the correct answers and write them on the board under the six phrases. Make sure students take notes.

Idioms in context

`St >> St`   10 minutes

Procedure: In pairs or small groups get students to discuss the following, or similar, questions. Monitor their language use and have a brief feedback session.

Give an example of British culture you just don't get. For example, why do Brits always talk about the weather?

When American people speak, are you able to catch what they say most of the time? How can you improve your listening skills?

In what situations do you prefer to ask the teacher for a hand and in what situations do you prefer to do things yourself?

Do the names of any of these movie stars ring a bell with you? Which films are they famous for? Angela Bassett; Anthony Hopkins; Lucy Liu; Hugh Grant

Which of these English-speaking countries can you say you haven't got a clue about? Say what you know about the others in this list.

Republic of Ireland	*Canada*	*Bahamas*
Sierra Leone	*Guyana*	*New Zealand*

Getting student feedback

St individually or **St >> St**   **10 minutes**

Procedure: Give your students a say: use the questionnaire in Table 10-1 with your class so that they can tell you what they'd like to include in the course. Collate the results and tell the students which topics proved to be most popular.

Table 10-1	First day class questionnaire
I was taught this but I just don't get it!	**I haven't got a clue about this but I'd like to learn about it!**
2nd conditional	UK culture

If you want the students to spend more time thinking about this, you can give out personal copies and ask them to hand back the questionnaire next lesson.

Doing a cooler activity

Repeat the warmer activity with another text. Students don't have to write, but they need to respond to you with the new vocabulary. Slow down your reading when the students say *'Hold on!'* or *'I didn't catch that!'* but not for long – keep giving them a reason to stop you.

Extension activities

Have a revision session in which you cover issues raised by 'I was taught this but I just don't get it!' in the questionnaires from 'Getting student feedback'. Pair students who get it with those who don't get it to do an activity based on the topic. One will help the other.

Cover the 'I haven't got a clue about this but I'd like to learn more!' topics highlighted in the questionnaires as warmers and coolers, or the basis for whole lessons if the subject matter warrants it.

Chapter 11

Back to Basics: Developing Discussions

In This Chapter

▶ Reviewing the skills students need to make conversation

▶ Incorporating discussion activities in all your classes

▶ Using a questionnaire to teach follow-up questions

. . . .

*H*earing your students chatting away in English and incorporating what they've learnt in their discussions is very satisfying. Speaking fluently is perhaps the most important skill to develop in a foreign language and one which involves many sub-skills. However, the question is: how do you get students talking?

This chapter shows you that student conversations seldom happen by chance, but with your support students can develop excellent fluency and speaking skills. I show you how to help students build and sustain conversations. I also present a lesson plan that combines discussion activities and active listening.

Using Discussions in Lessons

The vast majority of learners want to *speak* English, not just read, write or listen to it. After all, our most important human relationships are conducted face to face by means of spoken language. However, although students may well have conversing in their second language as a main objective in learning English, relatively few students realise that the ability to hold a good conversation, in any language, is a skill.

So many considerations are at play in holding a good discussion that students need to practise this as a life skill, not just a linguistic one. And because discussions with foreigners involves the added pressure of cross-cultural communication, you need to give students plenty of opportunity to get the basics sorted in the safety of the classroom before they venture into the wider world.

So what does the art of conversation involve? Students may think that if they learn vocabulary and grammar they can then hold discussions. However, they soon discover that this knowledge alone is frequently inadequate. This list of discussion skills could provide the basis for a whole discussion course or perhaps a regular weekly slot in your syllabus. Raising awareness of these points and practising them facilitates better student discussions:

- ✔ Demonstrating that you're listening with interest (not thinking about what you want to say next)
- ✔ Disagreeing with respect
- ✔ Displaying tact/sensitivity to social and cultural factors
- ✔ Fuelling the discussion with open questions
- ✔ Having an interesting topic to talk about
- ✔ Having the confidence to speak
- ✔ Knowing when to conclude the conversation and how to do so
- ✔ Responding appropriately, including paraphrasing
- ✔ Telling stories and anecdotes
- ✔ Using open body language
- ✔ Using well-phrased questions to invite others to respond

Although some learners develop an alter ego when they speak English, most people don't do better at speaking in a foreign language than in their own. Quiet or standoffish people are going to be a little limited in discussion lessons no matter what you do. So be realistic about what you expect your students to achieve and commend them for their own individual progress.

Incorporating Discussion Skills at All Levels

Teach discussion skills at every level progressively. By doing so students gradually increase in confidence.

Elementary

Teach *'How about you?'* or *'And you?'* to get students extending any dialogue by asking for opinions after giving one themselves.

Even at this level you can introduce students to conversational responses such as:

Wow!

Fantastic!

Interesting!

Okay!

Oh/Oh no!

When you're introducing the phonology of English, take the opportunity to teach single phoneme expressions (which differ from language to language) like these:

Oh!/əʊ/ = surprise

Aah! /ɑ:/ = how sweet

Pre-intermediate

Go through all the WH questions (the question words beginning with W or H) one by one (Table 11-1 offers guidance). This helps students develop open, instead of closed, conversation starters. In other words, their questions elicit more than a 'yes' or 'no' answer.

Table 11-1	WH Questions for Low-level Students
W Questions	*H Questions*
What (action/object/idea)	How (manner)
Which (choice)	How much (uncountable)
Why (reason)	How many (countable)
Who (person)	How long (time or measurement)
When (date/time)	How far (distance)
Whose (possession)	How old (age; teach students to use this with caution when speaking to adults!)
Where (place)	How come (reason; informal)
What kind (description)	
What time	

You don't need to teach the use of *whom* until upper-intermediate level at least. Even then students need to recognise it more than say it these days.

Learners always have a tendency to omit auxiliary verbs and say sentences like *Where you go?* instead of *Where do you go?* So question structure needs constant practice.

Intermediate

Get the class using direct speech to generate opinions. So give each student a topic to discuss with a partner. After a few minutes reconfigure the pairs This time the students can say something like:

> *I asked Alex what he thought about X and he said . . .*
>
> *I agree/disagree with him because . . .*
>
> *What do you think about that?*

You can allow an extra minute or two of discussion time each time the pairs change. In this way the students should become more fluent due to the repetition of the topic and extended conversations as they gradually have more opinions to comment on.

Upper-intermediate

Question tags are like mini questions, usually made up of an auxiliary verb and a subject pronoun, that you add to the end of a sentence. They help the speaker to involve the listener in the topic and the listener to demonstrate interest, but they're tricky for students to master. Here are the rules in brief:

Always use an auxiliary verb and then a subject pronoun to make a question tag. They are different depending on whether you are asking for information or just expressing interest in what you hear.

Main speaker question tags: In a question tag use the first auxiliary verb in the main part of the sentence. Use the verb 'to be' if it is the only verb in the main part of sentence or else a form of the verb 'to do' when there is no auxiliary verb. A positive sentence takes a negative tag and a negative sentence takes a positive tag.

> *You have been there*   *You've been there, **haven't you**?*
>
> *It's great*   *It's great, **isn't it**?*
>
> *You eat meat*   *You eat meat, **don't you**?*

Listener question tags: The rules are similar to the main speaker tags but if you are just showing interest you don't have to mix positives and negatives. Rather, stick to positive verb forms in the question tag.

Person A: I went to Wimbledon and it was hot.

*Person B: Oh! You went to Wimbledon, **did you**? And it was hot, **was it**?*

Advanced

At this level students are able to speak quite fluently, but some may hesitate to express their opinions in class. At times it's good to give students an opinion by assigning them to play the devil's advocate or take up a particular position in a debate.

One idea for generating class debates is to put a broad selection of random topics in a hat. They can include anything the students are familiar with. Divide the students into two teams. One person from each team picks a topic from the hat and, after consulting with team mates, they both debate why their topic is better than their opponent's. For example, the debate may be why *interior design* is more important than *sound effects*, or why *investment properties* are better than *the popular press*.

Class debates in general provide great speaking practice, but if the quieter students are hiding behind the extroverts, let the students prepare as a team but debate in pairs (one from each side).

Scaffolding a discussion

Always use a scaffolding approach if you want students to enjoy a final, extended conversation without your help. As with a scaffold surrounding a building, you remove the support only when the main structure is ready. Follow these steps:

1. Start by brainstorming and pre-teaching vocabulary or by finding out what students know about the topic.

2. Give students input – something to watch, look at, or read on the matter.

3. Set the question for discussion. Allow the students time to make notes and consult reference material, or ask you, if necessary.

4. Give an example of an opinion – your own or just a typical one.

5. Invite a response from one student as an example of agreement or disagreement. Respond again. This stage demonstrates that a discussion is by no means a monologue and reminds students of the type of language they ought to use.

6. Give the students adequate time to discuss.

7. Get feedback.

Intermediate Lesson Plan

In this lesson I use a traditional questionnaire as a tool for teaching students to extend conversations and be active listeners. You don't need any sophisticated resources and you can adapt the questionnaire to suit your students' interests.

Lesson overview

Time: Approximately one hour.

Aim: By the end of this lesson students will develop follow-up questions and show they're listening by offering appropriate short responses. They will use these questions and responses in short discussions.

Materials: A questionnaire on the board, or typed and copied as a worksheet.

Doing a warmer activity

Whole class mingle   **8 minutes**

Hand out a 'Find Someone Who' questionnaire such as the one in Figure 11-1, that covers about ten activities of general appeal to the class. If you're not able to type or photocopy a questionnaire, write the questions on the board before the class begins. It won't take long for students to copy them down in their notebooks.

Sneak in revision of tenses the class should know by using them in the questionnaire.

Check that the students understand the questions before they begin. Also, check that they can structure the questions correctly; so, not 'You use an iPod often?' but 'Do you use an iPod often?'

Find Someone Who...	Name of Student
. . . uses an ipod often	Danilo
. . . can cook quite well	Risa
. . . is feeling hungry	Ryoko
. . . watched TV last night	
. . . has read a book in English	

Figure 11-1: Example of a 'Find Someone Who' questionnaire.

Get students up on their feet and begin a class mingle exercise. They need to go quickly from one student to another, asking the questions and noting the names of students who say yes.

By way of feedback, briefly ask some of the students which names they've written down and for which activities.

Preparing open questions

T >> St   **5 minutes**

Tell the class that they now have some useful information for building conversations because they know about the activities of their classmates. Then choose one question topic from 'Find Someone Who' and elicit follow-up questions on the board so that the students can continue discussing each questionnaire topic. A layout like the one in Figure 11-2 helps you to do this and serves as a written example. (Use Table 11-1 of WH questions to prompt the students, if necessary.)

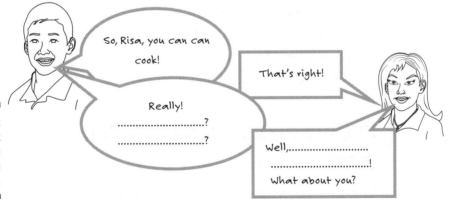

Figure 11-2: Board work for eliciting discussion questions.

Elicit several follow-ups for one topic (such as 'How often do you cook?' or 'What do you like cooking?'), and then role-play the dialogue by acting as the responder while a student asks you the questions. Make sure that you ask the student a question or two in return.

St >> St   **10 minutes**

Put the students in pairs to write some interesting follow-up questions for at least five 'Find Someone Who' question topics to which someone said yes. (I say at least five because this allows for differentiation of speed and ability within the class. (Some pairs will manage all ten.) Monitor and check grammar.

Ask a selection of students for at least one follow-up for each topic as class feedback.

Using active listening skills

`T >> St`   10 minutes

Explain to students that you need to to show you're interested when you are listening to someone speak and we often do this by saying something. Elicit and teach the students some responses used in casual conversation. Drill them thoroughly and be as animated as you can. Intonation conveys much of the meaning here.

Here are some examples of listeners' responses:

- **Negative:** How awful! That's terrible!
- **Neutral:** Really! Interesting! I see!
- **Positive:** Great! Amazing!

Practise using the responses by asking one student at a time to respond to something you say. Here are some statements you can use here:

I lost my favourite book.

I forgot to buy lunch today.

You're going to have a new English teacher.

I am very famous in my country.

I love rock music.

Putting all the skills together

`St >> St`   15 minutes

Get students back on their feet for a new mingle activity. They have to find a person who previously said 'yes' to a question on the 'Find Someone Who' questionnaire. As the two students speak about that topic, they have to

- Ask follow-up questions: *When did you do that?*
- Show interest by responding while listening: *I see!*
- Ask a question about the same topic in return: *And you?*

Shout 'Change!' every three or four minutes so the students are forced to speak to a number of different students. If you have an odd number of students, get involved in the mingle yourself.

T >> St	**3 minutes**

Find out who got some interesting information from a classmate. Ask for a few examples.

Finishing with a cooler activity

St >> St	**10 minutes**

Play the 'Yes/No' game. Put two people together to begin a conversation. You aren't allowed to say yes or no. and you can't nod or shake your head or make noises like *mmm* or *err*. When one person breaks the rules, he's out of the game and the winner gets a new partner to talk to.

Extension activities

Here's a game that you can use for general speaking practice. Give each student a folded slip of paper with an unusual sentence on it, such as 'I don't eat green apples when I'm at the beach.' The students keep the sentence secret. Then, in small groups, the students must begin conversations and somehow use their secret sentences while speaking. The other students try and guess the secret sentence. The others in the group shouldn't be able to guess their classmate's secret sentence because of the skilful way the student brings it into the discussion. Allow five to ten minutes for the discussions.

Chapter 12

Thinking Outside the Book

In *Teaching English as a Foreign Language For Dummies* (Wiley) I wrote about using a course book and why it's often beneficial to do so instead of creating all your own materials. Basically, using a course book is less time-consuming for the teacher because it reduces planning time, it usually contains a logical course syllabus and the book enables you to draw on the experience and research of well-informed teacher-authors.

In this chapter, however, I show you what to do if the course book isn't meeting your students' needs. I give you suggestions for eliminating, expanding on, and substituting the material in the book.

Building on Course Books as a Lesson Resource

What do course books usually contain? This list covers the typical features:

- A syllabus
- Practice exercises
- Discussion/writing questions
- Photographs and images
- Grammar boxes with rules
- Extended grammar reference sections

- ✔ Verb tables
- ✔ Glossaries for particular exercises
- ✔ Extended word lists
- ✔ Material for communicative activities
- ✔ Scripts of listening texts
- ✔ Answer keys (in the students' book or teachers' book)
- ✔ Short reading texts
- ✔ A CD/ DVD with listening texts

When you take the course book apart, figuratively speaking, and think about ways of manipulating its features, you tend be more creative.

Just because your students have a course book, it doesn't mean you have to use it all the time or follow exactly what it says. In fact, here are some reasons why you may deliberately choose to 'go rogue' with the book:

- ✔ You realise that your students already know the topic so there will be no challenge or new input for them.
- ✔ The students aren't ready for the lesson because they haven't mastered some of the basic principles embodied in it.
- ✔ The course book is out-of-date so the information it presents is no longer accurate.
- ✔ The course book presentation is rather boring.
- ✔ Students have a negative attitude to learning from the book.
- ✔ Students have no need to learn a particular language point.
- ✔ The book doesn't have a broad enough range of activities.
- ✔ You can cover more information in the time permitted without the book.
- ✔ The book presents only one point of view when the students would enjoy exploring other angles.
- ✔ Students seem to be too book oriented and unable to see speaking as the language as a real life skill.
- ✔ You need to help students develop a particular skill, such as speaking or reading, in a more in-depth way.

Having said all that, you need to be ready with strategies for overcoming these problems. Finding supporting materials and resources is the first step. So be aware that you need all kinds of reading books, magazines, examples from the Internet, CDs and DVDs to enhance lessons. Of course, if these things aren't available, you can still use realia, drawings, personal anecdotes, and students' own experiences to create interest. Flick to the table of contents of this book to find chapters dedicated to all kinds of different ways to approach learning beyond the course book.

Find ways to use a scaffolding technique with the course book material too and that means you need to provide support for the students before they can approach a task. For example, before jumping into the book, survey the students on what they know about the topic or set them a research task on it to prepare them.

Adapting Course Books at All Levels

There are many ways to use a course book, both traditional and more creative. Here I give you suggestions for using course books in interesting ways with a variety of classes.

Elementary

Try these ideas out with your elementary students:

- ✔ Transform reading texts into pronunciation exercises. Read the whole text aloud first while students listen. Drill the trickier words. Afterwards the students read the text aloud around the class or in small groups, one section each.

- ✔ With books closed, give the students the key words for an upcoming activity. Allow them some dictionary time to create their own glossaries by translating into their mother tongue, using English definitions, or using pictures.

- ✔ Most general English course books set the students short discussion topics. When students are discussing a topic in the course book, get them to make an audio recording of the discussion, identify their errors, and then switch partners and discuss the topic again. Transforming the exercise in this way gives the students the opportunity to self-correct and consolidate the corrections through use.

Pre-intermediate

Check out these exercises for pre-intermediate classes:

- ✔ Use a photograph in isolation from the unit in the book and get the students to create a story based on it. They can decide on the names of the characters, how they arrived at the situation shown in the photograph, or what happened next.

- ✔ Turn grammar tables into quizzes. Give the students four minutes to scan about fifteen verbs and remember the past simple form of each one. Then have a rapid-fire quiz to see how many they can remember.

- ✔ Give students the homework of researching in advance and making notes about a particular person who's featured in a reading text you're going to cover later that week.

Intermediate

Try these intermediate activities:

- ✔ Play the course book DVD without the sound on and get the students to predict information about the speaker(s) such as nationality, interests and personality type.

- ✔ Flip a comprehension exercise on its head: take a set of answers from the answer key and have students predict the questions instead.

- ✔ Rather than giving students a written test based on the book, assign small groups of students a particular unit of the book each to review. The groups then prepare mini-tests based on their unit, which they hand to another group.

Upper-intermediate

Try using these exercises with your upper-intermediate students.

- ✔ Get teams of students to prepare questions for each other based on the tape scripts of listening texts. In this way, they begin by practising their question construction skills, and a sense of competition builds interest in the activities.

- ✔ Students prepare their own versions of grammar rules as posters to put on the classroom walls. The grammar boxes in the book are usually dull, but personalised examples of the grammar provided by students are far more memorable, as is the process of creating the poster.

Advanced

Try these ideas out with your elementary students:

- ✔ Begin with a discussion of the syllabus. Groups of students can discuss the areas they think they already know about and the ones they'd like to learn about most. A class representative then reports back their findings, and together you and the class agree which topics will be presented as revision (or omitted) and which get priority status. Ask students to suggest other areas they want to cover too.

- ✔ Provide definitions of words shown in a word list. Students race to find the word you're referring to first by scanning the list.

Pre-intermediate Lesson Plan

For this lesson plan I use as an example the class I'm working with at the time of writing and their course book. It's a class of pre-intermediate general English students aged 20 to 60 (some of the students would qualify for an intermediate class if their speaking ability were stronger). The majority are artists and designers of some kind and they're from four countries. The book for this class has a wide range of activities and topics. However, my students don't feel that their lessons are fun when they're tied to the book. So during a three-hour lesson I often delay using the book for the first hour at least, but subtly prepare students for the topic or grammar the book contains. In this case the students will be studying a unit on special days.

Lesson overview

Time: Approximately one hour.

Materials: A recording of 'I Just Called to Say I Love You' by Stevie Wonder and the lyrics. Basic materials for creating posters (A3 paper and marker pens). Pictures of unusual festivals.

Aim: By the end of the lesson, students will have engaged with the course book topic of special days through brainstorming, vocabulary building, and discussion.

Doing a warmer activity

T >> Sts   10 minutes

Find out what students know about the musician Stevie Wonder and his many hit songs. Ask students to listen carefully to a song and write down any special days people celebrate that are mentioned. Then play 'I Just Called to Say I Love' on CD or on YouTube. Students compare their answers and then listen again while reading the lyrics (play the video with lyrics or print them). The singer specifically mentions a wedding, New Year's Day, and Halloween, but there are other enjoyable ideas for a good day too. Make sure students understand the meaning of the three main celebrations days.

Comparing cultures

St >> St   15 minutes

Give students some A3 paper and pens and put them in groups of those from similar cultures. The students create a poster showing the special days most people celebrate in their cultures, as I show in Figure 12-1.

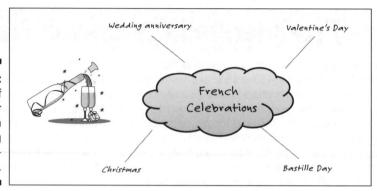

Next the students share their posters by laying them out on a table or along the floor. In this way, the entire class can look and compare the celebration events on each poster. The students then browse and ask other classmates about any celebrations they don't recognise.

If all the students are from the same culture, they can check they've included all the possible celebrations by comparing their poster with those of their classmates. Variations may occur according to the region students are from.

Describing ways of celebrating

Whole Class   **10 minutes**

While the students are preparing and comparing posters, put all these celebration words on the board, leaving a little space in between them. I underline the stressed syllables here.

champ*agne*	cakes	ball*oons*	gifts
conf*etti*	flags	b*a*nners	c*a*ndles
face paint	f*a*ncy dress	f*o*rmal dress	trad*i*tional costume
songs	f*i*reworks	b*o*nfires	proc*e*ssions

After discussing the posters, the students focus on these words. Ask students to come to the board and draw explanatory pictures next to any words they understand. Have a picture ready for the more difficult words such as *processions*, just in case. Make sure the meanings of the words are clear and that you drill the pronunciation.

Allow the students to add words that describe other forms of celebration in general (such as *party* and *feast*) or something important to their own cultural celebrations, such as *piñata*, *garland* or *lantern.* They can use a dictionary to find out whether an English translation exists or not, but they ought to explain the meaning of the additions they make.

St >> T   **10 minutes**

Students now go back to their poster teams and on the poster write under each celebration the appropriate words for celebrating it. Figure 12-2 shows an example of a completed poster.

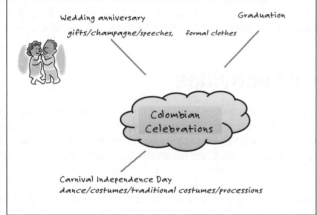

Figure 12-2:
Example
of poster
preparation
showing
ways of
celebrating.

Get feedback by asking individual students' questions, such as, *When do people wear special costumes in your culture?*

Put the posters on display in the classroom for future reference

St >> St   **10 minutes**

Take a question from the course book without referring to the book itself: *What's the most special day of the year for you? Why?* Then add your own question: *How do you celebrate it?* In pairs students discuss this for five minutes with the help of the vocabulary on the board and the posters.

Stop the students after five minutes and create new pairs. They must now relate to the new partner what their previous partner had said.

Thinking about photos

T >> St   10 minutes

Show students a photo of a particularly unusual festival, such as the Gloucestershire Cheese Rolling Festival. Ask the class some 'wh' questions (*What is it? Where is it? Why did it begin?*).

Don't be too quick to agree or disagree. Let students explore their ideas.

After finally explaining the photograph (the cheese rollers follow the tradition of chasing a cheese round down a steep hill, which involves an awful of lot tumbling!), instruct students to turn to the correct page in the course book but to fold the following page over so that the corresponding reading is concealed. In pairs the students discuss the photographs on the page and ask each other, *Which celebrations do you think the pictures represent and why?*

Extension activities

The course book contains a reading text about three special days. You may do the exercises in the book during class time, but for homework, students can write some questions about the reading that the book doesn't answer. For example, after reading about World Teachers' Day, a student may note the questions: *Do people celebrate World Teachers' Day in Europe? What do they do?*

The students can then swap questions and research the answers on the Internet at the beginning of the next lesson.

Chapter 13

Watching TV Online

. . . .

In This Chapter

▶ Using TV programmes from the Internet with a variety of students

▶ A lesson plan to stimulate vocabulary learning and practical role plays

. . . .

*I*n recent times there has been a substantial rise in the number of people watching TV online via their phones and computers. In the UK many channels offer catch-up services and online programme archives enabling viewers to watch programmes they missed on TV and even download programmes to their own devices. At present in the UK you can access scores of popular shows on services such as BBC iPlayer, ITV Player, 4oD and Demand 5. There are also many shows to watch on YouTube. The availability of television programmes online is excellent for students to increase their knowledge of the English language and the cultures of English speaking countries.

Watching TV offers heaps of benefits:

✔ Whenever you watch a little bit of online TV in class you will pique your students' interest. Here are some reasons why:

✔ When students watch what the general population do, they feel more integrated and have a better handle on popular culture.

✔ Internet TV services often have good subtitling options and a wide variety of programmes so there are many ways to use them.

✔ You can employ all the language skills (listening, speaking, reading, writing, plus pronunciation analysis) by discussing shows and getting the learners to write about what they've seen.

✔ Because the programmes are stored online and not live you can divide one programme into short segments, or mini-episodes, very easily.

✔ You don't have all the bother recording programmes yourself or getting hold of DVDs.

✔ Most students are TV and film fans, so it's entirely natural for them to use modern media rather than just course books.

✔ Enjoying media in English is a final outcome that many students consider a mark of success. They want to be able to do what they like in their first and second language.

In this chapter I show you ways to use online TV shows with a range of classes. I demonstrate how to base a lesson plan on a popular TV show.

Using Online TV Content at All Levels

Here are some pointers for incorporating online TV content into classes:

Beginner to elementary

Ask questions about the size and colour of objects in a particular clip. For example:

> *Is there a red car?*
>
> *Is there a blue house?*
>
> *Is there a big shop?*

You could also give students a list of words to listen out for and tick off as they appear. In both cases, students don't feel overwhelmed by the dialogue taking place because they have something achievable to focus on.

Some shows might be based on slapstick or other visual performance so scenes have hardly any dialogue. Try, for example, *Mr Bean* or an act from *Britain's Got Talent*. The task you set for the students can then be about words they know rather than the performers' speech.

Pre-intermediate

At this stage students have a few more tenses under their belts so you can try a 'What Happens Next?' guessing game. Teach students how to create sentences predicting the future but based on what they see now using 'going to' (this should help them to avoid being overly dependent on 'will').

Equally, you can use a clip to practise past simple sentences. Just pre-teach some useful and relevant verbs that feature in the clip and then get students to describe what took place.

Intermediate

Use a short documentary or factual programme as a source of debate. You might raise a question before watching a clip and then separate the students into two groups to list points for or against, based on the points presented. They collate their answers as a group and then break into pairs, one from each side to debate the matter. Figure 13-1 offers an example worksheet students can fill in.

> *Question: Should rich property developers be allowed to buy many houses in an area where people are quite poor?*

> *Complete one side of the table after watching a clip from the BBC's Homes Under the Hammer show.*

Upper-intermediate

Watch a dramatic scene from a soap opera without the words (maybe the last part of an episode of *Neighbours* before the music kicks in) and get the students to split into pairs and write a script. Just give them a character guide and leave them to it. After every pair has come up with a dialogue and shared it with the class, watch the real thing again complete with sound.

Prepare a straightforward comprehension exercise, but use formal synonyms for all the informal and common slang words the speakers use in a clip. You can match the clip to the variety of English the students need (*EastEnders* for London, *Corrie* for Manchester, *River City* for Scotland and so on). So if a character needs £5,000, but says '5 grand', make a multiple choice question out of it to focus attention on this useful expression:

> *Does Connor say he needs a) £5; b) 5 grams; c) £5,000?*

Advanced

Get students to invent and pitch a new product to a panel of their fellow students after watching *Dragons' Den* or *The Apprentice*.

You could also have a regular news slot. Compare and contrast the reporting of major news events in different parts of the world by watching clips on Aljazeera.com, Foxnews.com and BBC.co.uk.

Do keep cultural sensitivities in mind when choosing a clip to use. Make sure everything said and shown is suitable for your students and won't cause offense.

Argument	Developers should buy lots of houses in a poor area	Developers shouldn't buy lots of houses in a poor area
Reasons	The houses are empty and nobody uses them. It's okay for clever people to make money. It's just a job.	They make rents very expensive. They don't need so many – they're being greedy!

Figure 13-1:
Worksheet for documentary debate.

Pre-intermediate Lesson Plan

No TV show stays online forever. For that reason, I give you ideas here that you can transfer easily to other programmes. In this case I use an episode from a long running cooking series which reveals a great deal about how people in the UK live. In particular I show my class an episode from *Come Dine With Me UK* about a man called John who cooks a Filipino meal for guests but you could use a similar plan with any episode of the show.

Lesson overview

Time: Approximately one hour.

Materials: Copies of a wordsearch. Access to *Come Dine With Me* See 4oD for this programme (www.channel4.com/programmes/4od).

Aim: By the end of this lesson the students will have watched segments from a popular show and practised the language of dinner parties, including food words, invitations, and responses including:

courses   starter   main course   dessert

I'd like to invite you round/to my place for dinner on . . . . . . at . . . . . .

Can you make it?   I'd love to!   What should I bring?

Sorry but I'm busy on that day!   Another time maybe!

We're having . . . . . . (food items).

Doing a warmer activity

T >> St   6 minutes

Procedure: Make a wordsearch using Figure 13-2 as a model. How many words connected with food can the class find in three minutes? Give students an extra minute if they haven't found all seven, and then compare answers.

H	D	A	B	C	F	A	O	S	C
U	I	A	P	D	U	S	E	A	H
N	N	B	P	P	E	R	P	U	I
G	N	D	F	G	L	J	K	L	C
R	E	Z	X	C	Y	E	Y	O	K
Y	R	G	J	I	F	O	R	K	E
V	E	G	E	T	A	B	L	E	N
S	P	O	O	N	E	A	D	A	W

H	D	A	B	C	F	A	O	S	C
U	I	A	P	D	U	S	E	A	H
N	N	B	P	P	E	R	P	U	I
G	N	D	F	G	L	J	K	L	C
R	E	Z	X	C	Y	E	Y	O	K
Y	R	G	J	I	F	O	R	K	E
V	E	G	E	T	A	B	L	E	N
S	P	O	O	N	E	A	D	A	W

Figure 13-2:
Quick pre-intermediate wordsearch using food vocabulary.

Brainstorming

Whole Class   8 minutes

Ask students whether they like going to a friend's house for dinner. Explain that when you invite friends over, cook for them, and sit at the table together eating and drinking in the evening, this is called a dinner party. What do the students think makes a good dinner party? Brainstorm answers on the board. You might set the brainstorm out like in Figure 13-3 to elicit as much vocabulary as possible.

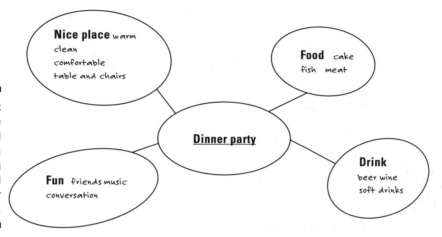

Figure 13-3: Example of board work for a brainstorm on good dinner parties.

Come Dine with Me

T >> St   3 minutes

Explain the premise of the programme. Five people go to each other's homes for five dinner parties (one each). After each dinner party they give marks out of 10. The best host (make sure you teach this word along with *guest*) wins £1,000.

Find out who knows this programme. Who likes this idea?

St >> St   4 minutes

In preparation for the chosen episode

Courses: starter/main course/dessert

Ask students to discuss what kind of food they think British people eat for each course. Give them a couple of minutes to note down ideas, allowing the use of dictionaries. Then listen to their ideas.

The menu

T >> St and **Sts >> T**   4 minutes

Write the four main headings and the vocabulary that features in the menu on the TV episode on the board. Here I show an example using John's menu. Elicit the meaning of each item. Use pictures (or allow students to investigate using the Internet) and ask them to predict under which headings the items go.

Starter	**Main course**	**Dessert Drinks**
flan salad	pork	chicken sausage
rice a hibiscus flower	vegetables	fruit cocktail
mushroom	coconut cream	onions garlic

Watching   8 minutes

Students watch the video and check which items go under each Heading in John's menu. After watching, they compare their answers.

Note down time markers for each stage of the episode so that you can go directly to the segment of the show you need.

The entertainment
St >> St   6 minutes

Ask students what kind of entertainment they think would be good at John's house. Put students in pairs to think of three things John might do. They have two minutes to share ideas. After their discussions, get some feedback.

Now ask the class to watch the two-minute video segment. Ask the students: What is the entertainment and do the guests like it? Check answers as a class after watching.

The score
T >> St   2 minutes

In this episode, all John's guests give him the same score. Write ?/10 on the board and elicit a score for John based on the clips the students have seen. Watch the video to reveal the answer.

Planning your perfect dinner party
St >> St   6 minutes

In pairs students plan a dinner party for four friends from class. They must decide on date, time, and location (whose house? indoors or outdoors?), the full menu and the entertainment.

`T >> St`   **6 minutes**

Elicit vocabulary for inviting friends to a dinner party and responding to an invitation:

>*I'd like to invite you round / to my place for dinner on . . . . . . at . . . . . .*
>
>*Can you make it?*
>
>*I'd love to!*
>
>*What should I bring?*
>
>*Sorry but I'm busy on that day. Another time maybe.*
>
>*We're having . . . (food items).*

Invitation mingle
`Whole Class`   **6 minutes**

Get students up on their feet. Have a full class mingle in which students invite others to their dinner parties and note those who can come.

`St >> T`   **2 minutes**

As feedback, find out who got the most acceptances.

Extension activities

Play more clips from *Come Dine With Me* and pick out key vocabulary. Then get students to do an extended role play of a dinner party, from greeting the guests at the door to seating them and serving the food. They can set up the classroom furniture to represent a dining table and spend twenty minutes or so in character as hosts and diners, discussing the meal and making polite conversation. Practise phrases such as:

>*Welcome!*
>
>*Come in.*
>
>*Take a seat.*
>
>*Would you like a drink?*
>
>*Make yourself at home.*
>
>*Can I introduce? . . .*
>
>*Help yourself.*

Chapter 14

Culture: Extracting Language from Art

In This Chapter

▶ Seeing why art is a great subject for TEFL

▶ Honing the vocabulary of art

▶ Running an art-based discussion lesson

Art is everywhere and in every culture. From cave drawings to graffiti, from mosaics to old masters, art provokes a reaction. So because it is vital to grab the attention of your learners, why not build a lesson around an arty theme? After all, visual images give your students something to discuss and at the same time teach them a variety of new expressions that are useful in other areas of life.

In this chapter, I get you up and running with an intermediate art-based lesson that will further your students' English skills. Students may disagree about what art actually is! For the purposes of the lesson, I talk mainly about drawings, paintings, photos and posters put together in a creative way that you can use as a basis for discussion.

Using Art as Lesson Context

Here are some of the best reasons to use art in the classroom:

✔ Everyone can find an image they like.

✔ You have a choice of an enormous range of material to use.

✔ Art is associated with leisure and relaxation, so students feel your lessons are more informal in style.

✔ Students can share their own creativity with others.

Selecting artworks

Art is so varied! Think about your students' tastes and backgrounds when you select images to use. Ask yourself (or the class):

✔ What will get students talking?

✔ Which language points will come out of the discussion?

For example, there is no need to intimidate teenagers by making them debate the meaning of a Picasso or something else considered high-brow; a quirky photograph you've taken is sufficient. Or perhaps a Banksy on a city wall or some other graffiti will do the trick.

It is great to have an image bank at your disposal, which means collecting postcards and magazine clippings ready to use. Language schools often prepare these resources, and you can easily find thousands of pictures online. Also keep a personal stash of hard copies of pictures. Students like to sort through them to choose one and touch something as they speak to calm their nerves.

Students can also use their own artwork or favourite images in class. They will likely have more to say about their choices than yours.

Students don't always have to focus on language itself. If they have a topic they like dealing with, they can learn about that in English and as a result, they generate English to support the topic. Read about Content and Language Integrated Learning, Task-based Approach and NLP in Chapter 2 of this book for more information on this.

Looking at Art Language at All Levels

Consider the grammar and/or vocabulary that come naturally to a discussion on art. Which tenses do people generally use to describe pictures? (It's present continuous and present simple by the way!) How do people describe the different areas of an image? Consider too the different expressions used to offer an opinion.

Below are some of the vocabulary and concepts that you can teach your learners by means of artwork. Pick one of these points as a language focus or think up one of your own.

Beginner – elementary

Language elements you should try to use include:

- ✔ **Grammar:** There is, there are; It is, it isn't.
- ✔ **Straightforward colours:** Blue, red, yellow.
- ✔ **Prepositions:** behind, next to, near, below, above,

Pre-intermediate – intermediate

Try to cover the following:

- ✔ **Positions and directions:** Horizontal/ vertical/ parallel/ diagonal, top right, bottom left
- ✔ **Expressing opinions:** it seems, in my opinion, it appears, I believe
- ✔ **Comparing and contrasting:** This picture is . . . . . . while the other is . . . . . . This is more/less . . . . . . than the other image. Whereas this one seems . . . . . ., the other looks . . . .

Upper-intermediate – advanced

Look to stretch more advanced students with the following language elements.

- ✔ **Colour vocabulary:** Subtle, shade, dull, vivid, pale, brilliant, deep, bright and so on.
- ✔ **Modal verbs:** It might/may/could/must /can't + infinitive verb

  For example, *That must be a bird* ('be' is the infinitive verb)

  It might/may/could/must/can't have + past participle

  For example, *It must have been difficult to take that picture* ('been' is the past participle)

- ✔ **Metaphors and idioms:** These can include
  - to foreground something
  - to be in the background
  - a bird's eye view
  - a different perspective
  - to picture something
  - to be in the frame

✔ **Arty vocabulary:** This includes

- still-life

- portrait

- landscape

- abstract

- sculpture

- installation

- collage

✔ **Useful art verbs:** These can include

- to symbolise

- to represent

- to resonate

- to depict

- to portray

Students need to compare and contrast photos for exams like the Cambridge First Certificate, so it's good to get them practising well in advance.

For additional variety, try to find artists who have a theme you can exploit. For example, students can work together to put Rembrandt's self-portraits in sequence or identify the process of change (first, later, eventually) in his paintings.

Intermediate Lesson Plan

In this section, I present an intermediate level art-based Lesson Plan. But the lesson packed with ideas for you to adapt, so you can use the framework to come up with a similar lesson for any group of learners. It is broadly PPP in structure (see Chapter 3). Think about your particular group of learners and any adjustments you can make to suit them.

Lesson overview

Time: One hour

Materials: A simple drawing for the warmer stage. Worksheets with typed questions for the practice exercise. Role play cards for the main activity.

Aim: To practise speaking by describing art.

Vocabulary: For describing pictures, including this list:

(in the) <u>foreground</u> (n)	(in the) <u>background</u> (n)	in the frame (n)
(at) the edge (n)	(in the) <u>cen</u>tre (n)	(on the) hor<u>i</u>zon (n)
on the right/left (of something)		

Students should already know *right* and *left* as adjectives but may not know how to use the words correctly within a sentence structure. Many tend to say : *There is a left tree and a right car and a house in the middle* instead of *The tree is on the left <u>of the</u> house but the car is on the right.*

Doing a warmer activity

If there is one thing we have learnt from Humanistic lessons (see Chapter 1), it's that relaxed students learn better. So this warmer activity helps students to prepare their minds for the harder stuff and enjoy themselves by working as a team (not to mention laugh at each other's drawing skills).

Multiple intelligences theory, which I touch on in Chapter 2, can help teachers match their students to activities that engage their interests. Many students need bodily-kinesthetic activities, so moving and drawing is great for them. Others are linguistic and do well at describing things.

Prepare a simple line drawing: a house in the mountains, a cat in a garden or something else which students can describe easily because they know the words for these things already. However, make sure the picture suits the target vocabulary in the lesson overview. For example, you need to position something you draw on the horizon, or on the left and so on.

St >> St   8 minutes

Put the students in pairs. Sit half your students with a pen and paper each facing away from the board. Sit the other half of the class facing the board, to which you attach the picture. The students facing the board must dictate instructions for drawing the same picture to their partners. Give an example like this: 'Start on the left. Draw the sun at the top in the corner.' Set a time limit of for the activity.

After the students have described the scene well, using whatever vocabulary and gestures they can, gather all the pictures together on the desk and see whose picture is most similar to the original.

Class Feedback   4 minutes

Get some feedback by asking various students to say where the objects in the pictures they have drawn are. Ask which things were most difficult to describe. By doing this you can find out which vocabulary the students already know and which additional words they might need. Make notes in case you need to add a word or two to the vocabulary list later.

Introducing the topic

T >> St   3 minutes

Procedure: Explain that today's lesson will be about art and elicit some responses from students about these and similar questions:

- ✔ Do you know about any famous works of art?
- ✔ Who are the best artists from your country, past and present?
- ✔ Do you paint?
- ✔ Do you like taking photographs?

Setting up the activity

`St >> St`   3 minutes

Procedure: Put today's vocabulary on the board (see the lesson overview). Divide the students into pairs or small groups and give them two minutes to discuss what they know about each word/phrase. Do they know the meaning and how to use it? In this way students pool their knowledge.

`Whole Class`   8 minutes

Procedure: Go through the meaning of each word and phrase, making sure to drill pronunciation and highlight which part of speech the word is (noun, verb, preposition and so on). Let the students tell you what they know about each word first before you provide additional details and information as necessary. Give plenty of examples using the images available in the classroom, even the view from the window.

Doing a practice exercise

This exercise shows whether students know how to use the vocabulary and provides examples of how to use it even for those who aren't art lovers.

Give each student a copy of the worksheet which I show in the numbered list below. Ask the students to put one of the new words or phrases from the lesson overview into the spaces. Do the first one with them as an example.

`St`   alone first, then   `St >> St`   8 minutes in total

Fill in the gaps using these words:

    (in the) <u>fore</u>ground (n)   (in the) <u>back</u>ground (n)   frame (n)
    (at) the edge (n)   (in the) <u>cen</u>tre (n)   (on the) ho<u>ri</u>zon (n)
    on the right/left (of something)

1. If you want to give someone a picture as a gift, it's best to put it in a . . . . . .
2. In the picture, the tall lady is standing in front of the camera, but lots of other people are in the . . . . . .
3. The bank's in the middle but the cinema is . . . . . . the left.
4. A long time ago, people thought that it was possible to fall off the . . . . . . of the world. Now we know the earth is round.

---

5. If you want to see the price of your newspaper, look on the ....

6. 'Don't stand so far away! I want you in the ...... of the picture!'

7. 'Can you see that ship? It's far away on the ......, but if you look carefully you can see it.'

There is an error in each of the following sentences. Correct the sentences:

1. On this picture there is man with a child.

2. There are two men there and the left man is fatter.

3. The tree is just at the frame of the photo.

Students should compare answers, and then you confirm the answers for the whole class.

Moving on to the production exercise

St >> St   **25 minutes (3 minutes to prepare each role play, 6 minutes to act it out in pairs and few minutes for feedback)**

Put the students in pairs. They are going to talk about Role Play 1. Give each pair of students the role play cards, with the text shown in the boxes below, one for each of them. Read both cards aloud and make sure they understand the role play instructions, for example, you need to explain commissions (when someone pays an artist to create work especially for them). One student is a millionaire who wants to commission a new portrait of himself, and the other student is the artist who will paint it. The students need three or four minutes to think, check the dictionary and make some notes before they begin acting it out. Set a time limit of five or six minutes for the students to act it out. Monitor the pairs, noting down any errors.

Student A: You are the millionaire

You are commissioning a portrait of yourself with your favourite people and objects in it. You must explain to the artist the painting you would like, saying what needs to be in each part of it. Describe colours, people, objects and positions. Find out how much the painting will cost, but tell the artist that you won't pay if it isn't correctly done.

> Student B: You are the artist
>
> A millionaire is commissioning a portrait from you. You should ask as many questions as possible and make a note of all the details. If you don't get the painting right the millionaire will not pay for it. On the other hand, this buyer will spend thousands on good art. You must agree a price.

Next get feedback from the pairs about the prices they agreed for the paintings. Also, correct some of the errors they made, especially the ones that are connected to the vocabulary you taught in this lesson.

Then, follow a similar procedure for Role Play 2. Explain the role play and vocabulary. Make sure the students swap roles (the artist from the first role play is the editor this time, and the millionaire is now the pap) so that they both have the opportunity to practice being the creative person and the demanding one. Allow some preparation time and monitor the students as they act out the scene.

Again get class feedback about what the pairs decided and correct errors.

> Student A: You are the editor
>
> You are a magazine editor. Before you'll buy the picture you want a detailed presentation of it from the pap and you also want the pap to make some changes, such as the background and the colours of certain objects. Obviously, magazines love a bit of photo manipulation! Explain what you want to the pap.

> Student B: You are the pap
>
> You need to explain everything about the image you want to sell (where and when it was taken and everything that you can see in the photo). Make a note of all the changes that the editor wants. Agree a price for the picture after you make changes to it.

Extension activities

Set up an art gallery by sticking copies of famous artworks and photographsto the walls around the room. Students might be willing to contribute their own pictures too. Ask them to wander around and discuss the images with each other as though they were art critics.

For higher-level students you could use a set of role plays similar to the earlier ones but include information about what the image should represent (honour, success, scandal and so on). For lower levels a role play could simply involve the things the millionaire wants in the picture and an idea of where to put each thing/person ('Paint Mum in a red dress next to Dad in a blue suit').

Chapter 15

Communicating through Story-telling

In This Chapter

▶ Sparking students' imaginations so that they create their own stories

▶ Using stories to practise grammar and pronunciation

▶ Teaching a lesson that gets students working together to produce a range of stories

*F*rom infancy people listen to stories. It's the way that people communicate tradition and culture, warnings, and insight. Actually, listening to a story is far more natural to human beings than sitting in a classroom. So teachers have good reasons to make use of stories, not only from fables, books and films but also those generated by the students themselves.

This chapter provides plenty of ideas for using stories with students of all ages, encouraging them to express their imaginations in the English language. I show you an intermediate lesson that helps students to plan and create stories well.

Using Stories as Lesson Content

You can hear, tell, write, or read a story. You can put it across using images, gestures or even sounds with no voices. Such is the power of the human imagination that with the most basic of stimuli people can fill in any gaps and understand a complete story. For these reasons, stories are perfect for generating language.

Stories are

✔ Closely related to real life

✔ Common to all cultures and generations

> ✔ Easy to remember
>
> ✔ Fodder for imagination and creativity
>
> ✔ Motivating because they make you want to tell stories you know

In the EFL classroom teachers can maximise the power of a story, and take advantage of various benefits such as:

> ✔ Giving more autonomy to the students; they can direct the stories themselves.
>
> ✔ Creating a change of pace and routine: story-telling classes are less formal than book exercises.
>
> ✔ Running lessons on stories and narratives with less preparation than other kinds of lessons, because the content comes from the students. Does this work? How about- Reducing preparation time because the lesson content comes largely from the students instead of you.
>
> ✔ Using the medium to introduce and review language in a clear context and stretching the students' language skills.

Incorporating Stories at All Levels

Don't think that story-telling is just for children. All your students can try it in one way or another. Here are some fun ways to get students telling a tale.

Elementary

Give your class a simple picture story, perhaps showing the daily routine of an imaginary character. You may draw the pictures or use photos. Students can assign the character a name, nationality, and personal details to add interest. Using the present simple, they can write a short story, individually or in pairs, describing the character's routine as shown in the pictures.

Figure 15-1 gives an example of a picture story to inspire elementary students.

Figure 15-1:
A picture story with a sample student response.

The book *Teaching Tenses* by Rosemary Aitken (ELB Publishing) features some great photocopiable picture stories. It's a classic TEFL resource.

Getting students to repeat a story is excellent for pronunciation and memorising chunks of language. Students can practise retelling each other's stories as a group. So each student in the class contributes a sentence in the story until it has been completely retold.

Pre-intermediate

After students have learnt how to use the past simple, repetition and memorisation of a story can help to familiarise them with the various pronunciations of '–ed' verb endings. For example, here I show you a story to demonstrate three ways of pronouncing past simple regular verbs. The phoneme at the beginning of the paragraph indicates the sound which appears at the end of each past simple verb within that paragraph.

/t/	*Fiona <u>walked</u> to work through the park and <u>picked</u> some flowers. She <u>talked</u> to a neighbour and <u>kissed</u> her baby.* /wɔ:**kt**/ /pɪ**kt**/ /tɔ:**kt**/ /kɪ**st**/
/d/	*At the office she <u>called</u> some customers and <u>interviewed</u> a new secretary. She <u>showed</u> her the office and then she <u>signed</u> some cheques.* /ɪntəvju:**d**/ /ʃəʊ**d**/ /saɪn**d**/
/ɪd/	*After work she <u>waited</u> for a taxi. She <u>wanted</u> to go to the theatre. The play <u>started</u> at 7.00 p.m. and <u>ended</u> at 10 p.m.* /weɪt**ɪd**/ /wɒnt**ɪd**/ /stɑ:t**ɪd**/ /end**ɪd**/

Challenge your students to add appropriate sentences to each paragraph. They must be careful that the main verb in each sentence fits the pronunciation of the paragraph it is in. So they can't put *looked* in the paragraph with /d/ verbs for example, because it's pronounced /lʊ**kt**/.

For an inductive approach, eliciting the story by using props and visual aids works well. Acting the story out incorporates some principles of Suggestopaedia, and if you get the students to do the actions too, you appeal to more of the multiple intelligences. See Chapter 2 of this book for more information about these methodologies. So for this story you pretend to be Fiona. You walk around the classroom, bend to pick a real flower you have conveniently put in the classroom, mime talking and so on.

Intermediate

In a class of mixed nationalities, ask the students to think of a folk tale from their cultures. Everyone in the class must tell a story and make it exciting. Give students time to research and prepare if necessary.

Divide the class into groups of four or five for the storytelling. Each group can vote on the best student to progress to the next round, in which the best storytellers from the groups tell their story in front of the whole class, who then vote for the best one overall.

Upper intermediate

Give the students an extract from a story text, but provide only the infinitive forms of the verbs. The students discuss and select the appropriate tense for each verb. Then they try to retell the story in pairs without looking.

Jake . . . was . . . (to be) terrified. It . . . was . . . (to be) the most frightening experience he . . . had ever had . . . (to have, ever). Suddenly, while he . . . was sitting . . . (to sit) at the bus stop, he . . . realised . . . (to realise) that the   man . . . was still watching . . . (to watch, still) him.

Advanced

Create a mock-up of a daily newspaper, but provide only the photos and headlines. Working in pairs, each group of students has to provide the articles for a page of the newspaper. Put the pages up on the wall for everyone to read. Figure 15-2 provides an example.

The English Language Gazette 18/07/2014

TRIUMPH FOR BRITISH TEAM

DANIELLA DEVASTATED

Figure 15-2: Photos and headlines to inspire articles.

Intermediate Lesson Plan

This mid-level lesson plan gets students analysing, the structure of stories, and creating stories together.

Lesson overview

Time: Approximately one hour

Materials: A worksheet that serves as a template for story writing, and a timer.

Aim: By the end of the lesson the students will have practised telling a story, reviewed the elements of good writing and created stories together as a class.

Doing a warmer activity

Whole Class   5 minutes

Show pictures of a popular story such as The Three Little Pigs and get the students to help you tell the story. As a class, see whether the story changes according to the students' nationality and compare different versions

Seeing how good stories work

This activity covers the basic elements of a good story, and introduces the idea of a story arc.

Basic elements

St >> St   10 minutes

In pairs, ask students to talk about what they think makes a good story and then make notes. Start them off with a suggestion, such as 'a hero'. Put students' ideas on the board.

Make sure that you put these points on the board even if students don't mention them and go over the vocabulary with the class:

> Setting: For example location and time period
>
> Characters: For example a hero and a villain
>
> Plot: for example, a problem, suspense and a resolution

Looking at the story arc

Whole Class 8 minutes

Clean the board and draw a story arc, a diagram to show how a story develops, but label only the start and end. Elicit from students what the missing parts might be. You can do this by asking what every plot needs to make it interesting. Variations on any of these elements are fine:

✔ Setting

✔ Description of characters and what they want

✔ Climax/problem (this must be at the top)

✔ Resolution

✔ Consequences/result

Figure 15-3 gives you an idea of how the board looks.

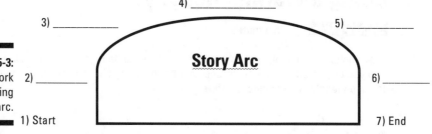

Figure 15-3:
Board work
for eliciting
a story arc.

3) _____

4) _____

5) _____

Story Arc

2) _____

6) _____

1) Start

7) End

The story arc is a useful guide that takes students through typical stages in creating stories. It also provides a great framework for discussing plays, novels and films.

Good grammar, interesting sentences

St >> T 6 minutes

Remind students about the narrative tenses they know. Elicit the usage and structure:

✔ **Past simple** for finished actions:

He **thought** for a few minutes then **decided** to go out.

✔ **Past continuous** to show that one action was longer than another, or an action happened at a particular moment in the past.

While he **was reading** he saw an advertisement.

At 7.30 she **was watching** TV.

Next, remind the students to use adjectives and adverbs to make sentences more inter-esting. For example, put a simple sentence on the board and elicit additional language from the students to enhance it.

/\ *Peter walked*/\ *to the*/\ *supermarket.*

```
Handsome, young Peter walked excitedly to the huge supermarket.
```

Narrative collaboration

St >> st   **25 minutes**

The advantage of using a worksheet is that students can see clearly how much they should write.

Create a worksheet like the one in Figure 15-4 and copy one per student. Distribute the worksheet to the class.

Each student must write in the space provided the start of a story using the instructions in point one of the worksheet . Tell the students they have two and a half minutes to complete this.

When they have all finished, each student must pass the worksheet to a classmate and receive one from another student. If the students are in a circle, for example, everyone can pass their worksheet to the student on the right.

Make it clear that each student must read the start of the story written on the worksheet in front of him and continue that story following the instructions in point two. They must forget about the story they had started in point 1.

Again, set a time limit of two and a half minutes minutes reading and writing before everyone passes the worksheets on again and addresses the next point.

Continue the process of reading, writing and passing it on until all eight points on every worksheet is filled in.

The advantage of a worksheet is that students can see clearly how much they should write.

If you have a large class, you need to put them into groups of eight. Without this kind of organisation, students may lose the feeling that they have a personal investment in the story. Groups of four are good too, because then the narrative can go around the group twice.

**Narrative Writing:
The Unforgettable Event**

1) **Start:** Name the hero/heroine of the story. Where and when is the story set?
   ....
   ....
   ....

2) Who are the other main characters? Describe them.
   ....
   ....
   ....

3) What did the hero/heroine want to do that day and why?
   ....
   ....
   ....

4) **Problem:** Describe the big problem the hero/heroine suddenly had. How did he/she feel about the situation?
   ....
   ....

5) What did he/she decide to do about the problem? Why?
   ....
   ....

6) Was he/she successful?
   ....
   ....
   ....

7) **Consequences:** What were the results of the hero's/heroine's actions?
   ....
   ....
   ....

8) **End:** What happened in the end?
   ....
   ....
   ....

Figure 15-4:
Worksheet
for col-
laborative
story-
writing.

Giving student feedback

St >> T   5 minutes

Ask students to read out examples of the stories that they think are particularly good. Put some of the stories on display in the classroom.

Extension activities

An in-class collaborative writing activity is a semi-controlled practice for students. However, if you set them a story writing task for homework, they are free to spend as much time as they want and research the language they need without constraints. Brainstorm a good story title in class. As well as writing, which only you and the student see, each learner can tell a partner about their story orally.

Another idea is to get students to write plot spoilers for their favourite movies. Do this activity in class, whether in pairs or small groups, because if students work at home, they're likely to cut and paste too liberally from the Internet. Recalling and reconstructing the story together is also a good speaking exercise for students.

Finally, assign each member of the class a short reading from a famous literary work. Have each student read aloud to the class, practising intonation and pronunciation. You might combine this activity with video by asking students to predict how a movie director might portray the scene. Then you can watch the scene to see whether the predictions were correct.

Part IV
Upper Intermediate and Advanced Classes

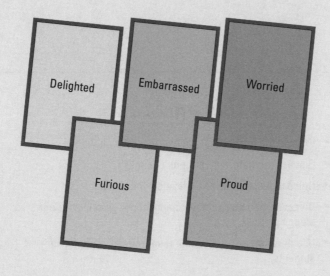

In this part . . .

✔ Work with your students to improve their intonation.

✔ Discuss the different varieties of English.

✔ Delve into dictionaries to develop vocabulary.

✔ Discover the value of developing language skills through blogging.

✔ Use news stories and media resources to engage your students.

Chapter 16

First Day: Improving Intonation

. . . .

In This Chapter

▶ Knowing why intonation is a good opening gambit for a new course

▶ Showing features of intonation visually on the board

▶ Teaching intonation to upper-intermediate students using rhymes and flashcards

. . . .

Good pronunciation is critical to effective communication. No matter how accurate a student's grammar or vocabulary is, she'll be met with quizzical looks if what she says doesn't sound English.

Pronunciation teaching in general is a great first day topic for students because it tends to be an overlooked area, grammar and vocabulary taking precedence. Non-native speaker teachers are sometimes less comfortable with this aspect of the language due to their own accents and a lack of access to authentic communication in English. But no teacher should overlook this area because students are hampered in their learning if they find that no one can understand them when they speak.

In this chapter, I look at one aspect of pronunciation: *intonation*. You can add meaning, emphasis and emotion, or differentiate a sentence from a question, simply by controlling the way your voice rises and falls. And on top of that, teaching intonation is great fun too!

I show you how to use intonation with all classes, but concentrate mainly on higher levels. Upper-intermediate to advanced students are often jaded and reach a plateau because they feel they've studied all the grammar and already comprehend well. Actually, intonation helps students to use what they already know far more effectively, giving them a new perspective on their learning. Hopefully, a look at intonation gives learners new energy as they begin your course.

Developing Intonation at All Levels

There are various aspects of intonation teaching. Just as you mark the stress on a particular syllable in a word, you can also highlight to students the words that carry the main function in a sentence and are therefore pronounced with more force. The other words may then have a weaker pronunciation.

Plenty of drilling is the ideal way to keep pronunciation features in sharp focus. Do this for all levels.

Here are specific ideas to improve intonation at different levels.

Beginner and elementary

Get students used to stressed syllables, by showing these syllables on the board when you teach new words.

In my examples I show how to indicate stressed syllables on the board using both the alphabet and phonology.

In the following example I mark stress by underlining and by an apostrophe before the stressed syllable:

> inton<u>a</u>tion /ɪntəˈneɪʃən/

In this full sentence I underline whole words that are stronger , rather than individual syllables, and circle the altered pronunciation of the weak words (where there is the schwa).

> <u>Intonation</u>'s for <u>students</u> of <u>all levels</u>
>
> /ɪntəneɪʃənz (fə) stɪuːdənts (əv)ɔːlleʋəlz/

Don't forget to write pronunciation between slashes to distinguish it from ordinary spelling!

Pre-intermediate and intermediate

Introduce students to *emphatic stress*, which means pronouncing some words with more stress because they emphasise the point you're making, by comparing the different meanings achievable by shifting stress.

In the example that follows, I compare to ways of saying the same sentence. A different word is stressed in each version and below I show what the stress in the sentence implies.

> Don't do **that** now! /Don't do that **now**!
>
> Do something else!/Why now?

Upper intermediate and advanced

Practise *contrastive stress*, which means using intonation to differentiate one thing from another. The contrast may be stated or implied.

In the examples that follow, I show one sentence that states a contrast (not Belgian but French) and one that, by stressing the verb (speak), implies a contrast with another verb.

Stated contrast:	*She isn't **Belgian**, she's **French**!*
Implied contrast:	*I **spoke** to him. (I didn't just email him)*

Upper-intermediate Lesson Plan

This first day lesson gets students exploring the way different attitudes and emotions alter the way you vocalise sentences. It increases awareness of how the *way* you say things influences the listener as much as *what* you say.

As with all first day lessons, introduce everybody to each other at the outset.

Lesson overview

Time: Approximately one hour.

Materials: Flashcards with emotion adjectives written on them and some nursery rhymes to display on screen or on worksheets.

Aim: By the end of this session, students will be more aware of the role of intonation when speaking English and will consider strategies for improving their own speech habits.

Doing a warmer activity

T >> Sts, then **Sts >> T**   5 minutes

Prepare some flashcards displaying a range of emotions. Choose emotions that you express with adjectives and that students can act out visually.

When you have everyone's attention, say 'Good morning!' (or the appropriate greeting for the time of day). Keep repeating the greeting slowly, but each time hold up a different flashcard and use the corresponding intonation.

Now switch and hold up the cards while you stay silent. Elicit the greeting chorally (whole class together) and see what kind of intonation they come up with. Then elicit greetings from individual students too. Figure 16-1 shows examples of some flashcards.

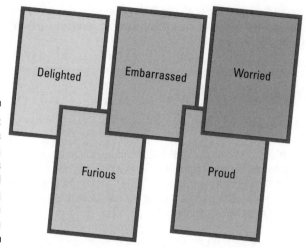

Figure 16-1:
Flashcards
showing
emotions
are useful
for eliciting
a change in
intonation

Using a sound to replace a real word

T >> St   **6 minutes**

The students are going to practise 'words' that have little or no meaning without intonation. Write 'uh huh' and 'uh-uh' on the board and elicit the pronunciation. Ask what
these very similar sounds mean; for example, 'yes', or 'I'm listening' for 'uh huh' and
'no' for 'uh-uh'. Put 'oh' on the board and say it with different kinds of intonation such
as surprise, disappointment, excitement and interest, Ask students what they think 'oh'
means each time.

Ask the students to compare a word/sound in their native language that requires a
particular kind of intonation to make the meaning clear.

Tell the students that you will now speak to them, but that the only response they're
allowed to make is 'oh', 'uh huh' or 'uh-uh' (using the appropriate intonation). Throw out
a range of sentences/questions that require agreement, disagreement, acknowledge-
ment, and anything else 'uh huh' might mean in natural speech. For example, say:

Can you lend me £200?

Would you mind passing this to him?

If you are 30 minutes late, you can't come into the classroom.

You're Mexican, aren't you?

You're Lorraine, right?

I'm only twenty years old.

The students may not think that they can speak to you in such an informal way. As a facilitator, you need to adopt a playful attitude and do some coaxing to help them understand that the teacher can change roles.

Listening with relish

St >> St   6 minutes

Practise 'oh', 'uh-uh' and 'uh huh'. Divide the class into pairs. Student A has to tell Student B all about an activity she particularly likes doing and one she hates. Student B must listen intently and demonstrate by saying 'oh' or 'uh huh' in appropriate places and with suitable intonation. The two then swap so that Student B talks and Student A responds. The listener must not remain silent.

Depending on culture, one person's respectful silence might come across to another as a lack of interest. Really encourage active, but non-intrusive, listening.

St >> st   2 minutes

Have a brief feedback session in which one or two students relate what their partners told them. You and the whole class respond with 'oh' and 'uh huh' in all the right places.

Dialogue building

St >> T   4 minutes

Tell the students that they're going to create a dialogue together and then use it to practise intonation. Put four headings that help to elicit a story on the board and elicit the content of each section from the students. Table 16-1 shows you how to begin eliciting a story with basic headings

Table 16-1	Eliciting a story with basic headings		
Setting	*Two Characters*	*Problem*	*Solution*
Shop	Customer, Bob Assistant, John	Trainers don't fit but Bob has no receipt.	John reluctantly exchanges them.

It's always good for students to invest in a story themselves. Don't just tell them, ask them for the details.

St >> st   **15 minutes**

Break the students into small groups and ask them to discuss and write down a dialogue of 8 to 12 lines using the notes you have elicited. Five to six minutes should be sufficient for this part of the task.

While the students are preparing the dialogues, put a scale of emotion on the board like that in Figure 16-2 (which is advanced level, but you could make it easier).

Figure 16-2:
An emotion   ☹ *depressed----------distraught----------apathetic----------enthusiastic----------ecstatic* ☺
scale.

After the dialogues are ready, each group must act theirs out but in the manner of one of the adjectives from the scale, which another group dictates. They can choose one emotion for each character. For example, Group A is ready to act and Group B asks for the group members to play Bob as a distraught character and to play John enthusiastically.

Giving student feedback

T >> St   **5 minutes**

After each group has had a turn or two, select a few lines from one dialogue for analysis. Put the lines on the board and elicit the normal and natural intonation. Make sure that key words stand out and that the students sound fluent and polite.

Demonstrate the intonation by humming the sentence and/or drilling.

Reading the rhyme

T >> St   **5 minutes**

Select a children's rhyme that has a sufficient number of lines to share, perhaps twenty or more, and preferably a narrative that the students can follow. I like to use these:

- ✔ Jack Spratt
- ✔ The Owl and the Pussy Cat
- ✔ There Was an Old Lady
- ✔ This Is the House That Jack Built

Read the poem aloud so that the class can hear the rhythm that is created by intonation.

Get students to clap the rhythm as you read. If they'd like to see a master class in rhythmic rhyme, show them a clip of the dub poet Benjamin Zephaniah. 'Dis Poetry' is a great example of his work (www.youtube.com/watch?v=Q2jSG2dmdfs).

Get the students to repeat each line after you. You can also help them to 'see' how the rhythm works. Write a line of the poem on the board and highlight the key words. that carry more stress. This helps the students to recognise that the less important words are pronounced in a quicker, more contracted way. In this way the students won't try to say every word and syllable with equal stress. Doing so just interrupts the rhythm.

You can also show on the board how to break up a line into chunks, each with a falling tone on the final word of each chunk.

>   The **owl** and the **pussy cat / went** to **sea** / in a **beautiful pea green boat**

Sts   10 minutes

The students read the rhyme one line at a time around the class. The aim is to keep the rhythm and intonation going from person to person.

If possible, record the students' reading and play it back to them so that they can compare it to your version. Discuss what they need to do to make their reading more similar to yours.

Doing a cooler activity

St >> T   4 minutes

Procedure: Put this sentence on the board (without punctuation):

>   I'm telling you right now I'm ill

Get students to read this sentence in as many ways as possible while attempting to change the meaning each time.

Extension activities

Try these activities:

- ✔ Give students a poem or nursery rhyme to practise at home. They must then recite it to the class (or to a group, if the students are many in number).

✔ Use an extract from a speech for intonation practice too (then you combine reading and discussion of the events that inspired it). Martin Luther King's 'I Have a Dream' speech is the obvious choice for most teachers, but how about some movie speeches? The website `www.filmsite.org/bestspeeches.html` lists a staggering number of speeches and monologues. Give students a homework challenge to select a monologue from one of their favourite films to recite. Perhaps the others could guess which film it is and then watch the real clip.

✔ Watch a clip from the iconic film 'My Fair Lady'. Professor Higgins' use of the xylophone to teach 'How kind of you to let me come!' always gets my students repeating and analysing their own speech.

✔ As a revision activity, use the word 'really' as you use 'uh huh' in the earlier activity 'Using a sound to replace a real word'. Get students to respond to conversation with surprise, boredom, disbelief, and so on using this one word.

Chapter 17

Back to Basics: Teaching Varieties of English

Sometimes my students say, 'I can understand you but I can't understand voices on TV or on the CD.' Well, I've been teaching for many years and so my voice has become very student friendly. However, in the real world outside the classroom, such a wide variety of people use the English language that it makes sense for students to become accustomed to different accents as well as slight grammar and vocabulary changes that occur from region to region.

Varieties of English around the world are, for the most part, mutually intelligible except for the odd phrase or two. However you may be a speaker of one variety who's teaching in an area where another is used. Or perhaps your students ask you which form is correct, and rather than continually saying 'It depends!' you need a lesson or two that deal with the differences.

In this chapter, I tackle the differences between English used in the UK and in the US. Many other varieties exist, of course, but this chapter gives you ideas about how to make a comparison between two varieties and in doing so assist your students.

Don't try to teach your students that one variety of English is superior. It won't wash! Rather, find listening texts that reflect a wide range of speakers, and use readings showcasing different Englishes too. At the same, focus your teaching mainly on the variety of English that's most relevant to your students.

Considering types of speaker

When teaching the subject of English varieties, keep in mind the different types of speaker:

✔ **Inner circle:** The core English-speaking (inner-circle) nations such as Ireland, Australia, New Zealand, Canada, the UK, and the US, have a rather small combined population compared to the number of people learning or using English in the rest of the world. Pronunciation differs quite distinctively among these lands and there are regional features of grammar and lexis too. A range of grammars and dictionaries support the 'correctness' of these Englishes, yet they are, in fact, very similar.

✔ **Outer circle:** From countries that recognise English as one of their official languages but use a variety of English that's noticeably influenced by local languages.

✔ **Expanding circle:** From countries that give English no official status but use ELF (English as lingua franca), which is often more simplified than the variety used in the inner circle but very effective for international communications.

Using Varieties of English at All Levels

Rather than divide the differences between the varieties into levels of ability, I suggest you cover the points on this issue as the need arises. Intermediate-level students and above are able to absorb the variations in spelling, pronunciation, vocabulary, and grammar, whereas lower level students ask about a few specific points when they encounter them.

American spelling and grammar tends to be easier to grasp than British English. However, students mustn't switch between the two varieties when writing or else the differences will be viewed as errors.

Looking at US and UK English Differences

The following sections outline key differences between the varieties of English to teach.

Verb forms

Past simple and past participle forms can differ between varieties and consequently cause confusion. Irregular forms become regular in some cases. For example:

UK	USA
smelt	smelled
spilt	spilled

Other noticeable differences include:

UK	USA
got (he's got fat)	gotten (he's gotten fat)
pleaded	pled
dived	dove

Spelling

Explain why different spellings and verb forms appear in literature from various parts of the world. These examples cover the main areas of difference:

UK	USA
col*our*	. . . *or*
thea*tre*	. . . *er*
leuk*ae*mia	. . . *e* . . .
organi*se*	. . . *ze*
fulfi*l*	. . . *ll*
progra*mme*	. . . *m*
preten*ce*	. . . *se*

Verb tenses

In the UK, the present perfect tense is used liberally to connect past time events with their consequences in the present. American speakers, on the other hand, make more use of the past simple for this function.

UK	USA
Have you seen Dave yet?	*Did you see Dave yet?*

Higher Level Lesson Plan

I have designed this lesson to be used with or without the aid of technology. The lesson raises students' awareness of language varieties by comparing UK and US English. These two main varieties provide a good sample of 'inner circle' usage (see the nearby sidebar 'Considering types of speaker'). However, you can treat ELF (English as a Lingua Franca) or outer circle varieties in a similar way.

Lesson overview

Time: Approximately one hour.

Materials: Either copies of the worksheet shown in this chapter or slips of paper to write pairs of words on.

Aims: By the end of the lesson students will be more aware of language varieties and the implications they have on their studies. They will have compared the UK and USA varieties with a focus on differences in everyday vocabulary.

Doing a warmer activity

T >> Sts then **Sts >> T**   6 minutes

Procedure: Put students into teams and run this quiz about countries that use English as an official language:

1. Name the country. It has four letters and begins with F, and English is its official language. *Fiji*

2. Which is the only English-speaking country on the continent of South America? *Guyana*

3. English and Arabic are the official languages of Pakistan. True or false? *False – English and Urdu*

4. Aagimb is an anagram for one of the smallest countries in Africa. It shares most of its border with French-speaking Senegal. However, it is an English-speaking country. Solve the anagram. *Gambia*

5. Which country in Asia has a capital city called Manila and English as an official language? *The Republic of the Philippines*

Comparing US and UK vocabulary

St >> St   **10 minutes**

Start students off with an example or two of the lexical differences between the two varieties of English. For example, elicit the UK words for an elevator (lift), a pair of pants (a pair of trousers) and a buddy (a mate).

Using the worksheet in Figure 17-1, do one of these exercises:

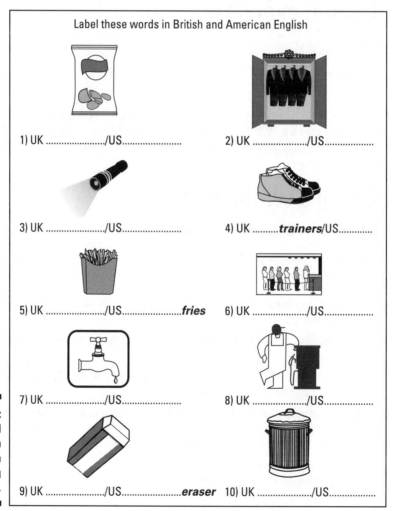

Label these words in British and American English

1) UK ..../US......................

2) UK ..../US..................

3) UK ..../US......................

4) UK ....***trainers***/US............

5) UK ..../US......................***fries***

6) UK ..../US..................

7) UK ..../US......................

8) UK ..../US..................

9) UK ..../US......................***eraser***

10) UK ..../US..................

Figure 17-1:
British and American English naming exercise.

✔ Give out the worksheet and explain to the students that they must label each item using the two varieties of English. Dictionaries are not allowed. After two minutes alone, put students in pairs or small groups to help each other.

✔ Write each word pair from the worksheet in the figure on a slip of paper. Put the students into two teams. Pick a student from each team to come to the front. Show the chosen students the word pair and get them to mime the item while their team-mates shout out the answers.. The teams get one point for shouting out the UK word and one for the US version. Mark on the board the scores for each team and move to the next word pair as soon as one team gets both versions right.

Answers:

1. crisps/chips

2. wardrobe/closet

3. torch/flashlight

4. trainers/sneakers

5. chips/fries

6. queue/(stand in) line

7. tap/faucet

8. petrol/gas

9. rubber/eraser

10. bin/trash can

Go over each word pair and drill the pronunciation.

Translation exercise

 5 minutes

Procedure: Tell students that you're going to read a text in US English and that they must listen to it carefully (the text follows in this section). They need to make notes of 12 examples of US English that they will later translate. For example, the first one is the name of the character in the text, Chuck. This is a typically American nickname or friendly form of Charles. What would it be in the UK? (Charlie)

You may choose to read out the UK version instead. Choose whichever one your students are less familiar with so that the key words stand out to them.

Read in the appropriate accents if you can.

Here's the US text:

> **1) Chuck** loved sport. He was a huge **2) soccer** fan and he couldn't wait for his school team to start playing again in the fall, after the long, dull summer **3) vacation**. Sometimes he practised with his brother Billy in the **4) yard**. They were the only family in their **5) apartment building** who had a yard because none of the others lived on the **6) first floor**. So Chuck made sure he was out there with his ball every day.

Determined to be a sporting success, he avoided **7) candy, 8) cookies** and other junk food. Every week he took one of the crisp ten-dollar **9) bills** he'd earned to the **10) drugstore** where he bought the protein drink all the professional players were photographed with in the magazines. 'I'm gonna do it! I'm gonna be the best soccer player this town **11) ever saw, period**!' he'd say.

And the UK version:

1) Charlie loved sport. He was a huge **2) football** fan and he couldn't wait for his school team to start playing again in the fall, after the long, dull summer **3) holiday**. Sometimes he practised with his brother Billy in the **4) garden**. They were the only family in their **5) block of flats** who had a garden because none of the others lived on the **6) ground floor**. So Charlie made sure he was out there with his ball every day.

Determined to be a sporting success, he avoided **7) sweets, 8) biscuits** and other junk food. Every week he took one of the crisp ten-dollar **9) notes** he'd earned to the **10) chemist's/pharmacy** where he bought the protein drink all the professional players were photographed with in the magazines. 'I'm gonna do it! I'm gonna be the best soccer player this town **11) has ever seen, 12) full-stop**!' he'd say.

> **St >> st**   5 minutes

After the first reading, students compare their ideas in groups. They discuss the UK version of the words noted and together come up with a list of 12 translated items.

> **T >> st**   5 minutes

Now read the UK version aloud and ask students to listen and check their notes. Again, the groups must compare before you finally confirm the answers.

> **St >> T**   3 minutes

Elicit any further examples students may know of lexical differences between these two varieties of English. Quickly revise the pairs of UK and US words covered in this lesson.

Discussing varieties

> **St >> St**   10 minutes

Work with these discussion questions:

- What kind of accent would you like to have when speaking English?

- Do you think some varieties of English are more respected than others?

- Is it good or bad to have teachers who speak different varieties of English? What might be the advantages and disadvantages of this?

✔ If you moved to live in an area where people spoke English in a regional dialect, would you try to learn that dialect or would you use standard English instead?

✔ Are there different varieties of your language? Do people view them as equal? Why (not)?

✔ English is used by millions of people all over the world. Should we spend less time learning English and more time on languages that are at risk of disappearing? Explain.

First ask a volunteer to read through each discussion question and give students the opportunity to clarify the meaning of each one before the discussion.

Give the students some time to think about their answers to the questions individually and then break them into small groups to discuss the questions.

You may need to teach the word *dialect*. It refers to a particular variety of a language that is identified as belonging to a geographical location and that includes somewhat different grammar or vocabulary than the standard form of the language.

Giving feedback

St >> T   **5 minutes**

Find out from the students which points they agreed on. Now that you have raised awareness of varieties of English, elicit and offer suggestions for incorporating this knowledge into the students' study routine; for example, by reading texts from a wider range of sources.

Doing a cooler activity

St >> T   **5 minutes**

Play a game of 'Where Are They From?'. Select a number of actors and celebrities who use English in their work. Show their names or photos. Students then shout out the nationality. For example, here are a few actors who might elicit more than one response:

✔ Arnold Schwarzenegger (Austrian/American)

✔ Daniel Craig (British/English)

✔ Charlize Theron (South African/American)

✔ Keanu Reeves (Canadian but born in Lebanon; holds US and UK citizenship through descent)

✔ Russell Crowe (New Zealand; born Australian)

✔ Nicole Kidman(Australia ; grew up in Hawaii)

Extension activities

Run pronunciation sessions featuring acceptable options for pronouncing the same word. For example:

class = /klɑːs/ or /klæs/   schedule = /skeʤuːl/ or /ʃeʤuːl/

Advocates of ELF highlight /θ/ and /ð/ as phonemes that aren't essential to intelligible communication. Students who haven't already mastered these sounds enjoy learning the common alternatives /f/ and /v/. Drill words with the 'th' spelling for example:

/θ/ Try /f/   **/ð/** Try /v/ or /d/ at the beginning of a word

thanks   /fæŋks/   *this* /dɪs/

thought   /fɔːt/   *mother* /mʌvə/   *depth*   /depf/   *with* /wɪv/

Chapter 18

Traditional Resources: Delving Into Dictionaries

· ·

In This Chapter

▶ Knowing what dictionaries can tell your students, apart from meaning

▶ Getting students to use dictionaries more fully

▶ Teaching advanced students how to better use dictionaries

· ·

*D*ictionaries are a basic resource in any study of language. These days they exist in many different forms; for example, most students use electronic ones and apps, for translation purposes. However, traditional single language references exist: thesauruses, encyclopaedic works, lexicons of particular fields of study, and so on. All these materials contain valuable information for you and your learners to dip into.

Although at first glance the density of language in printed dictionaries may seem intimidating to some, they're a treasure store of information for TEFL, provided you know how to use them. When teachers are aware of how to use dictionaries well this leads to improved learner *differentiation* (planning for/ accommodating different student needs in the lesson) and greater learner independence.

In this chapter, I talk about the valuable information in dictionaries you should highlight to students. I give you ideas for training students to get better use out of dictionaries and I present an advanced level lesson in which students find many dictionary definitions of the same word, which expands their vocabulary.

Using Dictionaries as Lesson Content

Dictionaries are a traditional resource, so you should find that your language school has many copies available. Even schools with a basic level of resources usually have a set of dictionaries available in each classroom.

Check when your class set of dictionaries was published in case it's a little archaic. If you need new ones, request them – the school should find your request entirely in keeping with good practice.

Dictionaries offer input in a range of areas, including

- ✔ Collocations (expressions that typically contain the word)
- ✔ Etymology (explains the background of the word)
- ✔ An example of how to use the word
- ✔ Spelling (and alternatives)
- ✔ Grammatical input (for example, separable and inseparable phrasal verbs, and irregular verbs forms or plurals)
- ✔ Meaning(s)
- ✔ Part of speech (verb, noun, article, and so on)
- ✔ Phonology to aid pronunciation
- ✔ Register (level of formality)
- ✔ Synonyms and antonyms (words of the same and opposite meanings)

When students are aware of the different ways in which dictionaries can help them they're more likely to use them in their own research rather than always asking you. This takes the pressure off you to provide all the answers (not that the teacher has all the answers anyway) and allows an individual student to look up a point of interest without involving the rest of the class. It's good self-management that will likely continue outside the lesson.

Although you should encourage dictionary use, students should have specific periods of the lesson during which they can research. Guessing meanings from context or other clues is a valid learning strategy, and the effort to work out the meaning results in better memorisation of the word. So constant dictionary use throughout the lesson may mean that students aren't listening to you or are focused on getting the answer right rather than learning.

You need to choose between two types of dictionary:

✔ **Translation (such as French–English):** This helps when you have a low-frequency word that's relevant to the understanding of one particular discussion or text. Take looking at a menu, for instance. It's far more efficient to translate the name of a particular herb, say parsley, than to describe the difference between one of those little leaves and another variety.

✔ **Monolingual (such as English–English):** This is ideal for students who already have a basic vocabulary in English, from intermediate level upwards. It allows for full immersion into the language and avoids the pitfalls of trying to translate word for word one language into another, which is rarely possible. For example, it's very tricky to traSome monolingual student dictionaries include:

- Highlighting of the most important words to learn

- Pictures of word groups such as vegetables or clothing

- Examples to help students improve writing skills

- Exercises on CD-ROM

Still ask concept-check questions after students use a dictionary to translate because otherwise you can't be sure that they have the right meaning (there may be several) or even the right word (a spelling mistake could lead them to a different word entirely).

Incorporating Dictionary Use at All Levels

Dictionaries contain such valuable information about language that you should train your students to use them from beginner level upwards. Here I give ideas for activities to facilitate this.

Beginner to elementary

At this level students tend to use translation dictionaries, which generally they buy themselves, liberally. However, use English–English dictionaries to familiarise students with the alphabet in English (even closely related European languages omit certain letters or pronounce the letters differently). Set a true or false quiz in which the students check simple definitions using a dictionary.

The lower frequency letters of the alphabet are K, V, X, Z, J and Q. The ones that students struggle to pronounce are A, C, E, G, H, I, J, K, Q, R, V, W and Y. Make sure that the tasks you set feature these letters.

Create a word wall in the classroom. When interesting new words arise, get the students to write them up on cards using the dictionary for spelling, part of speech and so on. Then make a display wall of these cards, which you can use in revision sessions and for reference.

Pre-intermediate to intermediate

Use dictionary work to highlight *false friends*, which are words that look the same as a word in the students' first language but have a different meaning in English. For example, speakers of Latin languages can compare *sensible* and *sensitive,* which tend to be switched in meaning, or find out why *sympathetic* does not translate into 'simpatico'.

Give students a list of phrasal verbs and get them to mark each one as separable or inseparable. Many dictionaries show this by using 'something' or 'someone' to illustrate. For example, *pick up* is entered as *pick **someone** up* (therefore separable), whereas *fed up with **someone*** has the object at the end to show that it's inseparable.

Teach new lexis and then use a dictionary training session to investigate whether you can add any prefixes or suffixes; for example, *mobile/**im**mobile/ mobil**ity***. This extends the students' vocabulary considerably.

Upper-intermediate to advanced

Have a writing session in which you plan an essay together. Use dictionaries or thesauruses to find synonyms so that students don't repeat themselves in their work.

Do you remember the old TV show *Call My Bluff?* Play this game with students to help them improve their ability to define and explain vocabulary. The idea is to have one word and three definitions. Teams have to research the correct meaning and then offer true and false definitions convincingly while the classmates on the other team guess which definition of the word is correct.

Advanced Lesson Plan

This dictionary skills lesson raises awareness of dictionaries as an excellent resource. It gets students searching through the book and the definitions for pronunciation, synonyms, and more.

Lesson overview

Time: Approximately one hour.

Materials: A good supply of English–English dictionaries. Students need access to a set of sentences and a set of questions, whether you use a worksheet or put them on the board/screen.

Aims and objectives: Students will have practised using an English–English dictionary for lexical input and a pronunciation aid by the end of this lesson. They'll be more aware of the value of monolingual dictionaries as a learning resource.

Doing a warmer activity

Sts >> Sts   8 minutes

This is an exercise about *homophones* (words that sound the same but are spelt differently and have different meanings; for example, court/caught).

Give students the word groups in Table 18-1, which may or may not be homophone groups. In pairs or threes they must decide whether all the words in each group are pronounced in *exactly* the same way. Some words will be familiar to them, but for unfamiliar words they should check in a monolingual dictionary using the phonemic transcriptions (the word written out in phonemes) to compare.

Do the first one as an example: look up each word with the class and write the phonemes on the board. The phonemic transcription is the same each time so this is a true homophone group.

Table 18-1	Table showing vocabulary and phonemes for homophone activity
Word Groups	**Phonemes**
peak/peek/pique	/piːk/
seas/sees/seize	/siːz/
coarse/course/cause	/kɔːs/ /kɔːz/ (not true homophones)
flew/flu/flue	/fluː/
gnu/knew/new	/n(j)uː/
ware/wear/where	/weə/

Drill the pronunciation of the groups to round off the warmer activity.

Examining 'issue' thoroughly using dictionaries

T >> St   3 minutes

Following the warmer exercise, write /ɪʃuː/ on the board. Elicit the pronunciation and spelling of the word. Explain that the word 'issue' has various meanings and is used as two parts of speech. Put the headings 'Noun' and 'Verb' on the right of the board and write up this sentence to the left: 'This is the January issue of *Vogue*.'

Elicit the meaning of issue in this context (a magazine that comes out at a particular time). Ask whether it's a noun or verb. Now connect this sentence to the 'Noun' heading and write the definition in the same section.

St >> St   10 minutes

In small groups, get students to brainstorm other meanings of 'issue' and write example sentences for the same word. Let them know that dictionaries aren't allowed just yet.

Next, make sure that each group has access to an English–English dictionary or two. Students consult the dictionary in order to check and add other meanings. When they've finished, representatives from each group can add definitions to the board.

Here are suggested answers for 'issue':

✔ **Noun:** A subject for debate/problem; a magazine that comes out at a particular time; a set of items that are made available at a particular time; an official way of giving something that's received by everyone; who belongs to particulara group.

✔ **Verb:** To announce; to make available; to come out of.

St >> St   **8 minutes**

Now challenge students to discuss and rewrite the following sentences without using the word 'issue'. They should use synonyms and similar expressions instead, while maintaining the meanings of the sentences. Dictionaries and thesauruses are allowed.

- ✔ Is there an issue between you and Fiona? You didn't speak to her at all this morning. (a problem)
- ✔ The most important issue to discuss at the conference is world peace. (topic)
- ✔ When will the new coin showing the royal crown be issued? (released, brought out)
- ✔ The police have issued a fog warning to drivers. (announced)
- ✔ The article on men's health should be in the May issue. (edition)

Possible answers are in brackets but students may find other appropriate alternatives. You could give the students a copy each of the sentences, put them on the board or dictate them to throw in some extra listening work.

Do one as an example with the whole class. Elicit suggestions for replacing the verb. For example:

The police chief is **issuing** all his officers with protective clothing.

The police chief is **providing** all his officers with protective clothing.
Group-Group   **2-3 minutes**

Have a brief feedback session. Put two groups together to compare their answers. You have the last word in case of disagreement.

Having a dictionary race

St >> St   **20 minutes**

Prepare questions for the race so that all the students can see them (as a worksheet, on the board, or on screen). The questions are designed to get students searching through sections of the dictionary to confirm their ideas and/or expand their vocabulary.

You write questions 1 to 8 yourself (the answers are in brackets for your reference):

1. Which ten-letter noun begins with AT, ends with T and is a synonym of 'achievement'? (attainment)
2. Which musical expression is a five-letter noun that begins with C, ends with D and refers to playing more than one note at once? (chord)

3. Which seven-letter noun beginning with F and ending with R describes a person who starts an organisation? (founder)

4. Find the adverb and adjective beginning INV that means always, almost always, or not changing. (invariable/invariably)

5. Find a three-letter word beginning with L that has many meanings including a written record of something that has happened or part of a cut tree. (log)

6. Which word has two identical syllables beginning with M and has several meanings connected with a quiet or soft noise? (murmur)

7. Find two meanings of *realm.* How do you pronounce it and is it an adjective? (/relm/ – noun meaning a kingdom, or a field of study)

8. How do you spell this word, /ɜːdʒ/, which means to advise strongly or to want to do something very much? (urge)

Then the students write questions 9 and 10 themselves. They must not be too obscure. Instruct the groups to be fair by basing their ideas on useful words that can reasonably be found within 90 seconds. Each group swaps questions 9 and 10 with another group.

Now the students work in groups to find the answers. Base the number of groups on the number of dictionaries you have. Ideally, the groups should be able to form their own sub-groups so that the questions can be apportioned five each. All the members of the group need to update each other on the answers they've found, discuss their suggestions for writing questions 9 and 10 and answer another group's version of 9 and 10 before the twenty minute limit ends .

Giving feedback

T >> Sts / **Sts >> Sts**   **4 minutes**

Go through all the answers and allow the groups to reveal the answers to the questions they set.

Doing a cooler activity

St >> T   **5 minutes**

Teach *gizmo, widget, thingy, whatsit,* or your favourite word for something you don't know the name of.

Get students to tell you about things they don't know or can never remember the name for, even in their own language. For example, mine is the thingy you hang round your neck with your work ID on it. Do the students have such useful little words in their languages?

Extension activities

The following sections offer a variety of extension activities using dictionaries.

Listing abbreviations

Most dictionaries have a page at the front explaining useful abbreviations in English and often more technical abbreviations that are used in the main pages of the dictionary too. Get students to research these abbreviations and create a guide to using them that you can stick on the wall. For example, students may include: e.g., etc., i.e., N.B., sic, circa., B.C., A.D., et al. and lb.

Creating quizzes

Ask students to complete a list of new words they learn over a period of a week. Then they can go to www.wordsmyth.com to create quizzes and glossaries so they can teach the vocabulary to classmates.

Nominating a word of the day

Students can take control of the warmer stage of lessons by teaching each other new words and phrases. Appoint students to present a new word or expression to the class each day.

Extending synonyms

Prepare a deliberately boring story in which you use the same vocabulary repeatedly. Set the students the task of improving the text by finding the widest choice of appropriate synonyms. For example, the teacher's text may read:

> A man walked down the city street. The street was almost deserted, so the man decided to ask another man who was selling fast food on the street what was going on.

Then the student's text may be as follows:

> A man walked down the city street. The road was almost deserted, so the confused male decided to ask another guy who was selling fast food on the pavement there what was going on.

Chapter 19

Technology: Interactive Websites

• •

In This Chapter

▶ Considering reasons to use interactive websites in class

▶ Using a variety of websites with classes at different levels

▶ Using video messaging as a lesson task

• •

*I*n this chapter, I cover the benefits of using *interactive websites* in the classroom, I suggest a number of sites to get you started and activities to try with your students.

I include various ways for students to post work on the Internet for public viewing, from blogs to social media forums. But don't worry, you don't need to be an IT geek to use technology of this kind. In fact, you're likely to find that the students are using tools such as blogs anyway, so all you need to do is point them in the right direction so that they use them for a linguistic purpose.

For all of these lesson ideas I assume that you use the Internet on a large screen in the classroom, and that students are used to accessing the Internet on their own devices.

Some websites restrict under-18s from posting online or registering, so do check the terms and conditions of websites with your particular students in mind.

Using Interactive Websites as a Lesson Resource

If you're wondering whether technology in the classroom is really for you, think about the advantages of interactive websites for both you and your students:

✔ Creating and uploading work online has become increasingly easy with the rapid development of the Internet.

✔ The Internet gives students a much wider audience for their work instead of just you and their classmates.

✔ Students can use English to communicate with people anywhere in the world.

✔ The open nature of uploaded work on many websites facilitates peer correction. Students can all look and comment at the same time.

✔ Class bonding takes place because the students work together on a project that will be visible to the outside world.

✔ Timid students are sometimes able to post online what they'd never say in real life because of the relative anonymity the Internet affords them.

✔ These lessons are likely to be less teacher-centred.

✔ Students feel more motivated to be accurate when work is shown on public forum.

✔ Posting work online is an exciting way of recording students' progress, for them and you.

✔ Expanding literacy in IT is an important life skill for students to take beyond their language learning.

✔ Resources created by your students are available to other language learners and vice versa.

✔ When the teacher encourages the students to use the Internet students often go on to access other websites in English. This makes the English language even more relevant to them.

✔ Using interactive websites is fun!

Incorporating Interactive Websites at All Levels

Websites exist to assist any age group in their language learning. Young learners take to the Internet naturally, and older ones enjoy the experience of using modern methods. So consider all levels of proficiency and types of classes you teach. Get all students on the Internet.

Beginner and elementary

With Beginner and Elementary classes, try the following:

✔ Start a lesson with Wordle (www.wordle.net). Instead of brainstorming words on the board, small groups of students can create a word cloud using any vocabulary they know about a particular subject. They can then compare the clouds and teach each other about words they didn't previously know. Print the word clouds or save them so that they're still available when you've finished teaching the topic.

✔ Students can register and use Animoto (`www.animoto.com`) to create a short video about one of their travel experiences by loading their own photos or video clips and writing some text to accompany the film. After watching each other's videos, the students can then interview each other using the past simple: *When did you go there? Did you have a good time?* and so on.

✔ Use Class Tools (`www.classtools.net`) to create a quiz using a QR code (squares like barcodes that a scanner on your mobile device reads). This site allows you to input the quiz questions your students come up with and create the QR codes. It makes for a wonderful treasure hunt as students design the questions, get a code for each one, put each code up in a secret location and challenge their classmates to find the questions, scan, and answer them. So if you want to do some effective revision, you could set each group a different topic to write questions about. For example, one group can ask questions about food, another group about clothes, and another group items in the house.

The majority of students these days have scores of images stored on their computers or a website. However, you need to advise those who use technology less beforehand that they need a few photographs for this lesson. Perhaps the school has some memory sticks students can borrow. If all else fails, they can use images from the Internet.

Pre-intermediate

Try these suggestions with your pre-intermediate students:

✔ To motivate extended reading, show some student-made trailers for books on School Tube (`www.schooltube.com`). Then get groups to read and discuss a graded reader before creating their own trailer video to post on the website. See what they can do to pique the curiosity of other potential readers.

✔ A great website for people not used to the sophistications of the Internet is Penzu (`www.penzu.com`). It looks like the page of an exercise book with the date written at the top. The idea is to use it as an online journal. Get the students to complete the journal at the end of each lesson or each week. In this way the students can record what they've learnt from their perspective, which is sometimes surprising to you, the teacher. Also, if one student has been absent, when he returns peers can refer back to the journal for the previous days to explain what you taught them. Over a period of time the journal becomes an excellent revision tool, a collaborative work, and a record of achievement. Students can also have fun with this journal by uploading photographs and describing unusual or interesting events around the school.

Intermediate

Have a go at these activities with your intermediate classes:

- ✔ Introduce your students to Toondoo (www.toondoo.com), which is a website for creating your own cartoon strips. Teach students vocabulary for physical descriptions such as *wrinkled*, *toned*, and so on. The students create a character according to the detailed description you give them, including new vocabulary and other words you'd like them to revise (words describing the setting and scenery are useful here). The text for the characters is of the students' own making.

- ✔ Alternatively, you can provide students with beautiful, pre-drawn artwork in the form of an online story book using Storybird (www.storybird.com). The students can then create the story that fits the images and type it into the virtual book. A great deal of vocabulary is generated as students work to express their imaginations.

Upper-intermediate

Browse the Audioboo (www.audioboo.fm) website, where you can listen to audio texts recorded by a wide variety of contributors on many different topics. Choose one that's of interest to your class. After students have listened and discussed the content, they plan their own Audioboo recording on a similar theme. The students register on the site, record their content while speaking as clearly as possible, and then listen to each other's work.

Advanced

The website Flisti (www.flisti.com) allows you to put a simple survey online without the need to register. Students of academic English need to express data and statistics clearly and fluently. With this in mind, learners can create and post a survey question for their own classmates and other classes to respond to. In fact, anyone using the website can join in. After a few days the students prepare a presentation, including slides, explaining the thinking behind their survey question, the results, and their conclusions about the topic. They deliver their presentations to the class and exchange peer feedback which may result in some refining and editing. Finally, they use a site such as authorSTREAM (www.authorstream.com) to post their presentation online.

Upper-intermediate Lesson Plan

This plan features traditional lesson content with a more contemporary twist. Ideally, you spread the plan over two lessons.

Lesson overview

Time: Approximately one hour of initial class time. Time to view the end product depends on how many student videos are made. In addition, some videos may result in students wanting to try activities out in class.

Materials: A pre-prepared video message and student access to the Internet, as well as a webcam and microphone.

Aim: By the end of this lesson, students will have practised describing a process or procedure and the language associated with this function including *furthermore, to begin with, following that, meanwhile* and *as a result.*

Doing a warmer activity

`T >> Sts`   **6 minutes**

Find out what students know about *Mission Impossible*. How do the agents get their instructions? Show a clip on YouTube (the old TV show is a retro novelty for younger students). Then let the students know that today they'll be receiving a mission that they'll listen to twice before it self-destructs!

Recording a student mission video

`T >> St`   **6 minutes**

Pre-record a video message using eyejot (`corp.eyejot.com`), mailVU (`www.mailVU.com`) or a similar website. I do this in the *Mission Impossible* style to give students a little laugh. Your video is an example of what the students themselves are going to produce at the end of this task. See Figure 19-1 for an sample script.

Good afternoon, class. Your mission is to create a 'How to . . .' video explaining how to do an activity you enjoy. It doesn't need to be a complicated activity, but you must explain it very clearly so that anyone could learn how to do it.

Furthermore, your video should be between two and four minutes long. I **therefore** suggest you divide your video into several short stages to make it easier for the viewer to follow. For this task you need to do several things:

To begin with, choose an interesting topic.
Then prepare any props and materials you'll need to demonstrate the activity.
Following that, think about all the stages involved in the activity and list them.
Meanwhile, consider the vocabulary you need to describe each stage.
Next, prepare sequencing expressions.
Another important step is to decide whether you're going to use informal, active sentences or formal, passive sentences.
By the way, if you prefer not to speak in front of the camera, use a more formal style with lots of diagrams and pictures.
As a result of these choices, you then prepare detailed notes.
Rehearse your presentation several times so that **eventually** you won't need to read everything word for word.
Finally, record your video and send it to your teacher.

This is your mission, if you choose to accept it. This message will self-destruct at the end of this lesson.

Figure 19-1:
Script for student 'How to . . .' video task.

Ask the students to watch the recorded message and note the task they have to complete by the date and time you now give them. The timing may be determined by the availability of technology for all the students to use.

St >> T   3 minutes

Give students an opportunity to clarify the task with you. You may allow them to complete this task in pairs or individually. For pair work, mix the nationalities.

Analysing language

St >> St   10 minutes

Students now watch the video again. This time ask them to note useful language for sequencing of the task and linking ideas; for example, *to begin with* and *then*. In the video script I show you in Figure 19-1, the sequencing and linking expressions are shown in bold.

After watching, the students compare their answers. Get a student who believes he has at least ten expressions to list them on the board for everyone to check and copy. Go over the answers and check that the meaning of each vocabulary item is clear.

Next remind students of the grammatical difference between active and passive sentences. This is important to the register (formal or informal language) the students choose to use for their video presentation. For example:

- ✔ **Active:** *He does it this way* – informal, the subject is highlighted.
- ✔ **Passive:** *It is done this way (by him)* – more formal, the object is highlighted.

Practising describing 'How to . . . '

St >> St   15 minutes

Show the class the Howcast website (`www.howcast.com`) briefly and explain that it hosts videos on how to do various things. Ask the students to talk in pairs for a minute and think of three activities that most students in the room know, or can guess, how to do (such as how to make bread). Then, as a class, pool all the ideas to see which is the most popular. Search for a video on this topic using the website. A two-minute video is long enough.

Students must note all the stages they see as you play the video without sound. Then, in small groups, students compare their ideas and talk about the language they'd use to describe each stage. They may use dictionaries to find appropriate vocabulary.

You may repeat the video silently on a loop while the students are discussing. After all, language use is important here rather than memory.

Ask a few students to read out the stages they noted and ask the other classmates for feedback on whether all stages were covered well. Note any significant language errors and go over them using the board when the students have finished speaking. Ensure that the students use the expressions for sequencing and linking sentences.

Now play the video again with the sound on so that the students can compare their versions with the original. Ask whether students have any suggestions on improving or clarifying the video.

Trialling the technology

St >> St   10 minutes

Get the students to build confidence in the video messaging site you're using by recording a very short video for a foreign speaker, showing in their native language how to give greetings for each time of day, or an equally simple task. This allows you and the students to iron out any problems that may otherwise hinder the outcome of the task.

Preparing video ideas

| St | 2 minutes |

Ask students to note down any skills or talents they have that they could teach to another person.

| St >> St | 8 minutes |

Now students compare lists and ask each other questions about their skills, which helps each one to think about what other people want to know. Sometimes an activity is so commonplace to one person that he finds it difficult to imagine another's questions.

Making the videos

Students must now go away and record their videos within the time limit you set.

I suggest that students record their video at home, in the language lab (if the school has one), or during another lesson so that they have adequate time to prepare props and notes. Make yourself available to answer questions and offer students support. For example, give students an email address they can use to contact you.

Watching the videos

Ask each student to inform you when he has posted his video. As the teacher, you should watch all of the students' videos in order to offer constructive feedback.

| St >> T | 4 minutes |

Set a lesson for the students to watch each others' work. However, the students may prefer to watch the videos in small groups, which tends to offer greater opportunity for questions and discussions. In small classes the groups can reconfigure after fifteen minutes so that students present their videos to a different audience. In large classes, students may only see a sample of their classmates' work during the lesson but they can watch the other videos online later.

> Good afternoon, class. Your mission, should you choose to accept it, is to create a 'How to . . . ' video explaining how to do an activity you enjoy. It doesn't need to be a complicated activity, but you must explain it very clearly so that anyone could learn how to do it.

Furthermore, your video should be between two and four minutes long. I **therefore** suggest you divide your video into several short stages to make it easier for the viewer to follow. For this task you need to do several things:

To begin with, choose an interesting topic.

Then prepare any props and materials you'll need to demonstrate the activity.

Following that, think about all the stages involved in the activity and list them.

Meanwhile, consider the vocabulary you need to describe each stage.

Next, prepare sequencing expressions.

Another important step is to decide whether you're going to use informal, active sentences or formal, passive sentences.

By the way, if you prefer not to speak in front of the camera, use a more formal style with lots of diagrams and pictures.

As a result of these choices, you then prepare detailed notes.

Rehearse your presentation several times so that **eventually** you won't need to read everything word for word. **Finally**, record your video and send it to your teacher.

This is your mission, if you choose to accept it. This message will self-destruct at the end of this lesson.

Chapter 20

Read All About It! Focusing on the News

*I*n all corners of the globe, news is available in one form or another. For instance there are 24-hour rolling news channels, radio bulletins, in-depth analyses, and investigations by newspaper journalists. This provides a constant stream of lesson content which is interesting, varied and helps students increase culture awareness. In addition, the same news stories are presented in different ways so there are many opportunities to compare language usage.

In this chapter, I show you how to take advantage of the news and current affairs to create lessons that connect the classroom environment with everyday events in the outside world. I include a lesson plan for advanced students that gets them summarising and discussing several articles from the same newspaper and extending their vocabulary in the process.

Using the News as Lesson Content

There are many reasons to use the news as a resource in lesson planning. However, some teachers shy away from using it because, as they say, 'Today's news is tomorrow's chip paper!' They protest that it isn't easy to re-use a news-based lesson because the story involved ceases to be relevant within a short time. Although this may be true, the advantages of incorporating current news outweigh any drawbacks.

Here are some compelling reasons to explore the news with your students:

- Using news stories involves authentic and current reading/listening material, rather than specially designed EFL resources. This is very motivating for students because they feel they have progressed well when they can use the same resources as native speakers.

- Material is ready to use. If you're in an English-speaking city, you may not even have to photocopy stories. Londoners, for example, have access to at least two free newspapers per weekday and many free magazines, so you only need to grab a pile of them and give them out to students.

- Studying news items increases cultural awareness. It shows what's of concern to a particular nation and reveals public opinion.

- News stories cover a broad range of interests.

- Reading/listening for gist, detail, and inferred meaning are just some of the many important sub-skills you can practise in news-based lessons.

- The news facilitates comparison, which is a great basis for discussion and essays. Students can compare fact and opinion, or tabloid versus broadsheet styles of reporting.

- There are many fascinating photos associated with news stories for students to comment and speculate on, even if the words are rather complicated to understand.

- Listening to newsreaders from different sources provides a good example of clear pronunciation in a range of accents.

Integrating the News at All Levels

You can use news sources to engage all your classes. In this section, I give you ideas on how to do so across the various levels of proficiency.

Beginner and elementary

Try these activities with you beginner and elementary groups:

- Select an interesting photograph from a newspaper and cut it out. Let all the students see it and elicit vocabulary for labelling the objects shown. For example, take a cutting from the sports pages and elicit words like *tennis player*, *ball*, *white t-shirt*, *shorts*, and *trainers*. You can draw in arrows pointing to the objects in the photo you want to highlight (parts of the body perhaps) or give students a completely free rein to identify anything they want. Write the vocabulary you cover on the board. After covering the vocabulary by eliciting, marking stressed syllables and drilling pronunciation, hand out other similar photographs of footballers or cricketers and get pairs of students to label the images.

✔ Teach the word *caption* by showing captions in parts of a newspaper. Ask pairs of students to write a simple caption for each photograph, such as *Rafael Nadal plays in the US Open.*

✔ The weather maps on TV or in the newspaper are excellent for teaching and revising weather vocabulary with *going to.* As a speaking exercise, show students the map and ask the students to deliver the forecast: *It's going to be sunny in the north of England, but it's going to rain in Wales.*

Pre-intermediate

Give these activities a go with pre-intermediate students:

✔ Find a news story with a financial element to it. You can use this story to get students to scan the text for numbers. (*Scanning* means looking through the text for particular information, rather than reading it all carefully. Using this sub-skill makes approaching a longer text less intimidating.)

Start with a general introduction to the news story by discussing the accompanying photograph and explaining the headline. Now give students the numbers mentioned in the text by writing them on the board or preparing a worksheet and ask them to work out what the numbers mean by finding them in the article. I show an example of this kind of activity in Figure 20-1 about the new High Speed 2 train line, which is the kind of story I use with business-minded students. Always do the first number with the class as an example of how to complete the task.

Figure 20-1: Example of activity using numbers in a news article to practise scanning.	Rush-hour commuters will be left stranded if High Speed 2 is scrapped (*Evening Standard*, 5/9/13)	
	Look at the newspaper article and write down what the numbers mean.	
	I.	2024	West Coast mainline will be full by 2024
	II.	32,000,000,000	The government will spend £32 billion on HS2
	III.	4,000	People standing on trains into Euston Station
	IV.	100,000	Extra jobs building it

Intermediate

Try the following with your intermediate students.

Find a recording of an interview with a well-known person in the news on a radio podcast, or by finding a recent video clip of an interview online . Summarise the answers the interviewees give into one sentence per question. Now show the students the answers and ask them to work together in groups to predict the questions that were asked. Make sure that they use the correct grammar for constructing questions.

Tell the students that they must listen carefully as you play the interview. Each group receives two points if they get the question right, and one point if their question wasn't correct but stills fits the answer the celebrity gave.

Upper-intermediate

Teach students about the language of newspaper headlines and the typical words that are used in them. For example, Figure 20-2 shows how you can teach the meaning and synonyms of frequently occurring vocabulary by getting students to match words and definitions with the help of a dictionary.

Figure 20-2: Matching exercise to teach the vocabulary of newspaper headlines.

The Vocabulary of Newspaper Headlines	
Match a word on the left with its meaning on the right.	
1) to axe	a) an investigation / to investigate
2) probe (v) (n)	b) a change of mind
3) to call for	c) an argument / to argue
4) U-turn (n)	d) money a government or organisation gives to help a poorer country
5) row (v) (n)	e) a big increase
6) aid (n)	f) to publicly say that you want something to happen
7) boom (n)	g) to stop something from continuing

Separate short news stories from their headlines (you could cut the headlines and stories out). Spread the stories on the floor or desks of the classroom and give each student a headline. Each student then browses the stories until he finds one that matches his headline. He then reads his story again, checking any vocabulary he isn't sure about.

Advanced

Not all countries have a broad spectrum of news reporting that represents differing politic viewpoints, social classes, and state or privately owned broadcasting. For this reason, compare different newspapers, such as a couple of tabloids and a couple of broadsheets. For example, get the students to find out which paper uses more puns, sensational language, phrasal verbs or formal words derived from Latin. Then compare the same story across different news sources for a class discussion. Note which sources seem to focus on facts in a neutral way and which report the matter based on a particular viewpoint. Teach key vocabulary for front pages:

masthead (big title)

logo

splash (main story)

lead (beginning of a story explaining who, what, where, when, why and how)

photo and caption

Ask students to analyse news in the media using questions such as these:

- ✔ What are your first impressions of the news provider? Comment on the style it uses.

- ✔ What kind of reader do you think the news provider is trying to attract? How can you tell?

- ✔ What is this news provider's attitude to the major news of today?

Select two or three major news stories and divide them between different groups of students. Each group covers the same story across different media sources and discusses the attitudes of the reporters. Stories about the monarchy are often good for revealing differences in attitude.

Extension activities

Try these extension activities:

- ✔ As a project, get the students to put together a class/school newsletter with articles of interest to the students themselves. They can take photos, write articles, design puzzles and so on.

- ✔ Listen to the news from BBC World Service or a similar broadcaster and then record students reading the news as a pronunciation and fluency exercise. By listening to their work, the students can identify points they need to work on in the following lessons.

Advanced Lesson Plan

This lesson is not designed around the analysis of one to particular news story, but instead it is more about helping advanced students to get an overview of current events and practise describing news events. It is best suited to students studying in an English-speaking country or those with access to online newspapers in English.

Lesson overview

Time: Approximately 1 hour.

Materials: Several copies of the same newspaper or access to an online newspaper.

Aim: By the end of the lesson the students will be familiar with a range of current news events and will have practised reading and summarising the news. The new vocabulary students learn comes from what is in that day's news articles.

Doing a warmer activity

Whole Class   5 minutes

Play 'Find That Story'. Hand out a few copies of the same newspaper. Read out a headline. In teams, students race to find which page the headline came from. Choose headlines from different sections to subtly get students more familiar with the layout of the newspaper.

Introducing sections of the newspaper

T >> Sts   10 minutes

Brainstorm with students as many different sections of a newspaper as you can and set them out on the board as a list. Your list may include:

international news	localised news	fashion	celebrity gossip
business	entertainment	lifestyle	opinion
politics	technology	sports	classified ads

Make sure students pronounce the names of the sections well and drill any tricky ones.

Give the students two minutes to talk in pairs and ask from their partners:

- ✔ How often do you read the news or a newspaper?
- ✔ Which paper or news source do you prefer?
- ✔ Which sections of the news do you read?

Get feedback from the students, asking one person from each pair to explain their respective reading habits.

Reading the news

St >> St   10 minutes

Ask students to confirm which sections are present in the newspaper you've brought in and used during the warmer activity. Put the class into small groups of three or so students, and give each group a section to work on. You don't need to cover all the sections; just remove the names of the unallocated sections from the board.

Following the feedback you received from the previous speaking activity (see 'Introducing sections of the newspaper'), you can now group students together according to the newspaper section they favour. Doing this tends to ensure that they understand more of the vocabulary that they encounter.

Each group selects a story in their newspaper section, notes the headline and reads the text. They must prepare to explain the headline and story to their classmates. They can use a dictionary as necessary, and you should monitor to give assistance with unclear sentences.

Remind students that for longer stories the lead will supply many of the important facts, so they should make sure that they understand that initial part of the story at least. If there are shorter stories, the group can read more than one, as time permits.

Working together on a news overview

St >> St   15 minutes

After the students have had time to read and discuss their text, ask a representative from each group to note the headline and a very short summary of the story on the board, as I show in Figure 20-3.

When the groups have completed their section, students can highlight on the board a word or phrase they don't understand.

Figure 20-3:
Example
board work
for a news
overview.

Newspaper section	Headline	Story
National/local news	130 VEHICLES IN PILE-UP	Bad weather and careless driving caused a serious crash yesterday.
Celebrity gossip	ROYAL ROMANCE IS THE TALK OF THE TOWN	There are many rumours circulating that Prince Andrew might remarry.
Business	GYM GROUP SNAPPED UP	A chain of businesses called DLGyms has been bought by a major leisure company.

Presenting the news

St >> St   10 minutes

Regroup the students: take one student from each of the previous newspaper section groups and put them all together as a new, larger group. The new group now contains someone who can talk about each section. For example, if the previous groups were organised as AAA, BBB and CCC, they now became ABC, ABC, ABC.

In turn, each person presents their news story, explaining the headline, summarising the story and explaining any new vocabulary that is important to understanding the text. Encourage students to offer opinions about the story and their views of the newspaper's coverage of it. Classmates are free ask the presenter questions.

Giving student feedback

T >> Sts   5 minutes

Having listened carefully to the presentations of each story, correct any significant errors, such as inaccuracies with tenses or poor pronunciation (without identifying the culprits who messed up). If you're doing this on the board, use one section of it but don't erase the news overview chart just yet.

In the rare event that there are no significant errors to feedback on, ask students to explain one of the news stories they didn't read, based on the presentation they heard from a classmate.

Finishing with a board rush activity

Clean the board of everything except the new vocabulary highlighted on the news overview chart. Add all the other new words the students have learnt in the lesson, such as *classified ads* or *splash*. Now have a board rush game: give two students at a time board pens, and challenge them to run to the board and cross off the word that matches the definition you shout out. The first player to cross off the right word wins, but the players can only cross off one word each.

Chapter 21

Dissecting Dictogloss

· ·

In This Chapter

▶ Understanding the benefits of dictogloss activities

▶ Using dictogloss in a range of classes

▶ Planning a dictogloss lesson for a higher-level class

· ·

*I*n this chapter, I discuss *dictogloss*: a kind of dictation activity in which students listen to and reconstruct a text . I explore the benefits, and show you how you can use dictogloss activities with your classes to promote listening, speaking, and writing skills as well as group communication. I also present an advanced lesson showing you how to use a news story as a dictogloss text.

Using Dictogloss as Lesson Content

You've heard of dictation, but perhaps you haven't tried dictogloss. It's somewhat similar to dictation but involves more skills. Here's how it works:

1. **Introduce the topic that's the subject of the text you will read.**

2. **Pre-teach target language that will feature in the text.**

3. **Read or play the text while students listen.**

4. **Read or play the text again while students make detailed notes.**

5. **Get students to review their notes individually.**

6. **Break students into small groups to collaborate, using their notes to reconstruct the text.**

7. **Review the student texts, focusing on the target language.**

8. **Reveal the original text to the students for comparison.**

The dictogloss text needs to be short enough that you can complete the task and analysis within one lesson. Don't use text that contains unknown words or grammar, because this is very disconcerting for the students. The class needn't reconstruct the text word for word; they can use some synonyms. However, they need to understand the overall coherence of the text, rather than just isolated sentences.

Dictogloss activities have many advantages for students:

- ✔ Students can work both individually and as a group (and group work results in less pressure for each individual student).

- ✔ The objective of the activity is clear throughout.

- ✔ Reconstructing the text together results in more learner autonomy. They don't depend on you for continuous feedback.

- ✔ Students teach and correct each other, which reinforces their learning.

- ✔ Students easily notice the difference between what they understand and what they need to say. This in turn highlights the areas of their learning that they need to improve on.

- ✔ You combine teaching and testing in the same activity, which is an effective use of time.

- ✔ Communication between students is authentic in nature: suggesting, confirming and negotiating are frequent aspects of everyday life.

- ✔ Dictogloss tests a broad range of skills including the ability to understand connected speech, instead of isolated words, and to apply syntax.

Incorporating Dictogloss at All Levels

Here are some ideas that you can use for doing dictogloss activities with a variety of classes.

Beginner and elementary

Lower-level students need far more support to both understand the activity and accomplish the reconstruction task. Provide the support by creating a word cloud, an artistic way of showing a lot of vocabulary at once, using the vocabulary of the reading text. The website www.wordle.net enables you to do this very easily, but if you don't have access to the Internet you can write the key vocabulary on the board, or on a worksheet.

You also need to prepare a framework for note-taking to give students a clear idea of what to do. For example, Figure 21-1 shows a worksheet for a dictogloss text describing the teacher's home. A text about 80 words in length is adequate. Following the first question, you revise the meaning of each vocabulary item. Next, students complete the chart during the first reading and then add more details during the second reading.

1. Where do you usually see these things? What do the words mean?

garden kitchen bedroom living-room carpet bookcase cooker bathroom table chair sofa bed cupboard wardrobe curtains

2. Listen to the teacher talk about his/her house. Complete this table.

	Does the teacher talk about this room? Yes/no	What's in this room?
Kitchen		
Living room		
Bathroom		
Bedroom 1		
Bedroom 2		
Office		

Figure 21-1: Worksheet to support elementary-level dictogloss activity.

Pre-intermediate

Use a draw-and-tell approach to your dictogloss text: draw a picture to illustrate each part of the text, adding to the picture as you narrate until you build up a composite picture by the end (see Figure 21-2).

> It was a cloudy Saturday morning.
>
> Richard was at home thinking about his life.

Keep the picture(s) visible to the class during the collaboration stage to help them remember and reconstruct each stage of the story.

Simple pictures along with a simple story serve as a great memory aid and tend to engage students who are visual learners far more than just listening. Unsurprising, children love this form of dictogloss.

Richard Thompson, an author of children's stories, is a master of draw-and-tell storytelling. See an example of his work at `mdfbooks.files.wordpress.com/2012/02/no-pets-allowed.pdf`.

Intermediate

Use a great speech as the source for the dictogloss text. You could choose one from a movie scene or from a real situation, depending on your students' interests. A favourite of mine is from the film *John Q* where the father, John, who believes that he's going to die within minutes, tells his young son everything he needs to know to be a successful man.

It was a cloudy Saturday morning.

Richard was at home thinking about his life.

Figure 21-2:
Example of
a draw-and-
tell method
of storytell-
ing for a
dictogloss.

Upper-intermediate

Incorporate art and literature by combining a famous painting with a text describing its subject matter. For instance, use 'Ophelia' by Sir John Everett Millais, which is a celebrated painting depicting a character in Shakespeare's play *Hamlet*. The painting provokes discussion of students' views on art and speculation on the subject of the painting. You needn't take the reading text directly from the play. Write your own text or use published material.

Tate Modern has a great deal of information about its exhibits online. For example, visit www2.tate.org.uk/ophelia.

To follow up this dictogloss activity, students can prepare a presentation about a paint-ing, write about the artist, or read an extract from the original literature.

Advanced

Get the students reading their own dictogloss texts to each other. First, collect ideas from students about the topics they'd like to discuss. Ask students to each research and copy a short text from a book, magazine or online source about one of the sug-gested topics. Organise the class into groups of four. In each group of four students there are now four short texts. One person in each group is nominated to read their text, while the others take notes. If you then remove the original text that was just read, even the student who read it can join in the reconstruction work of the text along with the other members of the group. Return the original texts to each group so they can check their work at the end of the task. Another student in the group reads her text in the next lesson and so on until all four texts are done.

Advanced Lesson Plan

This lesson serves as an example of how to use dictogloss in your lessons. It's best to choose a text that appeals to your own particular students. I based this lesson on crime following my students' field trip to the law courts.

Lesson overview

Time: Approximately one hour.

Materials: A reading text and a checklist.

Aim: By the end of the lesson students will have practised listening and note-taking. They will also have practised speaking, grammar and syntax through peer discussion.

Doing a warmer activity

Whole Class 5 minutes

Make a list of words that the students have learnt recently and note them down, one each, on slips of paper. Call a few students up to the board one by one. Hand each student a slip of paper and a board marker. Each student must silently draw (not write) a picture on the board within one minute that helps the rest of the class guess their word.

Introducing the topic

T >> St 5 minutes

Draw a stick figure on the board dressed as a thief (mask, striped top, swag bag) and another of the figure in prison looking miserable. Ask the students to brainstorm all the stages between committing the crime and carrying out a prison sentence. They should suggest words like these:

arrested	called a lawyer	questioned by police	charged
went to trial	verdict	guilty	sentenced

Pre-teaching the language

T >> sts   5 minutes

Ask the students whether they know anything about the actress Lindsay Lohan. Elicit information from the class and explain that you're going to read a BBC news article from November 2012 called 'Lindsay Lohan Arrested at New York Night Club'. The article is about 260 words in length and you find it at `http://www.bbc.co.uk/newsbeat/20545971`.

Write on the board the names of any people and places in the article that the students would struggle to recognise or spell. This reduces students' anxiety when they're listening. So you may write the names of the areas in New York that are mentioned and the name of the film writer who features in the text.

Discuss the more difficult words: *probation, allegation,* and *to clip someone with a vehicle.* Put them on the board and elicit examples to clarify the meanings.

Delivering the text

T >> sts   8 minutes

Instruct the students to relax, concentrate and listen to your reading of the text. Read at a slow but normal speed, like a newsreader.

Now instruct the students to get their pens and notebooks ready. They must listen again very carefully and take detailed notes, rather than writing every single word. At the end of this second reading, give students two minutes to read through and edit their notes.

Collaborating in groups

St >> st   15–20 minutes

Put the students into small groups of three or four. They now compare their notes and produce one version of the text per group written on a separate sheet. They should make their text as similar to the original as possible, although you don't expected them to use exactly the same words throughout.

While the students discuss the text, monitor and note any difficulties the students are experiencing in sentence construction or vocabulary. You can address these points in the analysis stage. Make sure all the students are contributing and ask for opinions from anyone who hasn't contributed.

After at least ten minutes of discussion, give the students a checklist so that they can check the content of their text. Table 21-1 shows an example recording all the events in the Lohan text.

Table 21-1	**Checklist Showing Events in the Dictogloss Text**		
Date	*Location*	*Alleged offence*	*Result*
Nov 29 2012	Nightclub on Club Ave, Chelsea, Manhattan	Hit a woman	Charged with assault
Sept 2012	Another N.Y. club	Clipped a man with her car	Charges dropped
May 2012	Hollywood	Hit a manager with her car	Cleared
Oct 2012	Childhood home, Long Island	Fighting with her mother	No evidence
Summer 2012	California	Car crash	Under investigation
2011	Not stated	Stole a necklace	Probation

Analysing students' work

T >> St   12 minutes

As space allows, put the students' texts side by side on the board, wall, or desktop for everyone to see. Gather the students around to compare the texts. Highlight particular language points that students can improve on or learn from. For instance, draw attention to the use of passive constructions in the text that keep Lohan in focus rather than the law enforcers, like this one: 'The star was arrested at 4am.'

Show students the original text and allow them time to read through it.

Doing a cooler activity

T >> St   5 minutes

Make a list of celebrities who have been sent to prison and some who haven't. Go for the celebrities the students will know. Have a true or false quiz. For example, see Table 21-2.

Table 21-2	Example Celebrity Quiz
Quiz Question	*True/False Answer*
Paris Hilton was in jail in 2007.	True
Michael Jackson went to prison in 2005.	False, the verdict was not guilty

Extension activities

Discuss other examples of celebrities who have been on the wrong side of the law. Divide the class into two groups to prepare either side of a debate on the question: 'Is it fair to expect celebrities to be role models for others?' Hold a class debate and then get the students to write an essay on the topic as homework.

Part V
Mixed Classes

In this part . . .

- ✔ Learn how to approach teaching younger children.
- ✔ Keep your teenage students engaged and interested.
- ✔ Find out how to adapt existing resources to the needs of a mixed class.
- ✔ Discover how to put together winning presentations.
- ✔ Explore cultural and linguistic differences through manners and etiquette.
- ✔ Take on the challenge of organising and resourcing field trips.

Chapter 22

Chatting to Children

In This Chapter

▶ Thinking about how children best learn languages

▶ Incorporating fun activities into children's lessons

▶ Teaching children about food with a PowerPoint presentation

They say, 'Never work with animals or children!' But in the case of the latter EFL teachers don't always have a choice, because many parents and educators around the world encourage youngsters to learn English from a very early age. This chapter is for teachers whose students are aged twelve and younger. In *Teaching English as a Foreign Language For Dummies* I wrote about working with younger learners by using games and stories to incorporate grammar. In this chapter, I give you more fun ideas, and I show how to put a whole lesson together with children's needs in mind.

Tailoring Your Lessons to How Children Learn

Here's the good news: teaching children in many ways is easier than teaching adults. Children are less pressed for time, and tend to relax better into their learning. They're less self- conscious and happier to mimic pronunciation because they haven't become used to using their speech organs in a set way. Learning new words is natural for children because they do it every day – plus they don't need to deconstruct grammar or try to match one language to another word for word as adults often try to do.

But working with children does come with some special considerations to keep in mind when you plan your lessons. Remember that children need to learn

- ✔ Chunks of language that serve a particular function; for example, 'Give me it!'
- ✔ Through play, so they thrive on interesting games.
- ✔ Through a variety of activities.
- ✔ While using up some energy through movement – or else they become bored and frustrated (which means naughtier).
- ✔ Progressively – children's activities need to be just slightly more difficult each time to encourage learning without de-motivation.
- ✔ With close support for reading and writing – whereas children can pick up speaking and listening by mere exposure to the language, you have to actively teach most reading and writing skills.
- ✔ With individual attention.
- ✔ In an encouraging environment.
- ✔ Through modelling – with small children you only need to model the correct language point yourself instead of correcting them in detail.

Keep in mind that it's natural for children to be silent while just listening and absorbing; they'll speak when they're ready. But when they do speak, children especially love to learn English that they can recite – such as counting from 1 to 20, reciting the alphabet, or singing a song in English.

Here are some specific tips for your lessons:

- ✔ Give very young students real-life situations as contexts for learning.
- ✔ Personalise activities to match your experiences and your own particular students.
- ✔ Give children another means of responding other than speaking, such as picking up the correct item or drawing a picture.
- ✔ Bring in visual stimuli such as flashcards, pictures, posters, storybooks, models and realia, as well as lively colours.
- ✔ Use lots of actions such as miming and accompanying words with gestures.
- ✔ Incorporate any fun gadgets and technology you can to create interest.
- ✔ Don't worry if children use their native language to speak to you. Continue modelling English as a way to express their ideas.
- ✔ Use creative methods when you're nominating a student to answer a question. Throw a cuddly toy to them, spin a bottle until its neck points at one child, or keep all their names in a hat and pull one out.
- ✔ Don't overload students with grammar labels. Focus on the function of a piece of language or grammar rule so that the children digest the point without being intimidated by jargon.

Working with Young Children at All Levels

Here are ideas for helping children of different ages and levels to develop their English.

Beginner and elementary

Try these ideas with beginner and elementary level students:

✔ Use a puppet as a tool in your lessons. Present the language to the children as a way to communicate with the puppet, who appears during each lesson, from the first day onwards. Teach introductory expressions such as 'Hello!' and 'How are you?' Then get the children to ask the puppet the expressions you taught. An interchange between the puppet and the child in English can then begin.

Make 'English-speaking puppets' in class using socks.

✔ Prepare pictures for words that the children already know and ones you want them to learn. Use internationally recognised words, like *computer,* if you are meeting the students for the first time because they may know some of the words. Put the whole collection of pictures face up on a desk and get everyone to look at them closely. Then all the children close their eyes while you take one picture away. When they turn back they must say which picture is gone, if they know the vocabulary for it. If no one in the class knows the word for the picture that's missing, you teach them the word. Review all the vocabulary at the end of the game. In this way the children learn vocabulary as the need arises rather than sitting through a lengthy presentation stage at the beginning of the lesson. This is one fun way to present vocabulary to children.

Pre-intermediate and intermediate

Try these ideas with pre-intermediate and intermediate students:

✔ **Use children's literature to teach and practise vocabulary.** For example, teach the names of a range of animals, and then use a book like Dear Zoo by Rod Campbell (MacMillan Children's Books 2010) to engage the children. The story is presented in the past simple so that along with the words for the animals the children are introduced to some past simple verbs in a fun context. The repetitive nature of children's books also helps students to get used to sentence structure in English.

✔ **Teach the children to tell the time by playing 'What's the Time, Mr Wolf?'** One person plays the wolf and the others stand at a distance behind her back. When the class ask the time the wolf says four o' clock, for example, and the children take the appropriate number of steps toward her; in this case four. After a few tries at this, the wolf senses the other children are near and when asked the question she shouts 'Dinner time!' and proceeds to chase the children, who are now running back to the safety of their starting line.

✔ **Use picture dictation games.** Describe a simple picture, which the children then draw according to what they hear and understand. See Figure 22-1 for an example that subtly practises the use of prepositions. At the end of the drawing stage, I ask the students to describe the drawings to see whether they produce the language needed.

Figure 22-1:
Example of
an image
and text for
a picture
dictation.

✔ **Get students collaborating on the same large-scale picture.** Use commands such as 'If you are wearing a blue t-shirt, draw two windows upstairs on the house' or 'If you have black hair, draw an apple on the tree'.

You may extend the dictation idea by having a craft session. If appropriate, use materials such as glue, glitter and safety scissors. Give the class instructions about shapes to cut out, decorate and stick on to a larger poster, or a greeting card to take home.

Upper-intermediate and advanced

Activities to try with more advanced students include:

✔ **Prepare team quizzes using questions about antonyms and synonyms.** For example, ask 'What's the opposite of boring?' or 'Which word means big and begins with the letter L?' Award the winning team some stickers. Do this on the first day and later in the course, after the students are used to the question format, get them to prepare their own quiz questions.

✔ **Put on a talent show.** Over a number of lessons the students select, learn and practise a song, speech, or rhyme. Students work individually or in pairs and you can invite the parents or another teacher to watch the show.

✔ **Set up a board games project.** First collect some EFL board games. Many teachers' resource books include photocopiable games for you to print on large paper and laminate where you have to speak for a minute about the topic written in the square you land on after throwing a dice. After the children have played a few of these as examples, get them to design board games of their own, perhaps using questions about English speaking countries – for example, 'Which country are kangaroos from?' The project involves research, creativity and competition, all of which children love.

✔ **Show students how to analyse sentence structure, using visual representation of the various elements of a sentence.** I use coloured blocks to do this. You represent verbs in one colour, nouns in another colour and so on. Get students to physically build sentence structure and then manipulate the structure. Either give them the sentence and let them represent it with blocks, or give them the blocks already organised into a sentence structure and get them to write sentences that match the structure. Figure 22-2 shows you how this works.

Figure 22-2:
Representing
sentence
structure
visually.

I wish I had known

He wishes he had known

Elementary Lesson Plan

For this lesson I show you how to use all those bells and whistles on Microsoft PowerPoint to make an interactive presentation for children, like an electronic version of a pop-up book. This lesson is for the first day of an elementary, but not beginner, course for children aged about seven to nine. I use a food theme because children identify with this topic very easily.

Lesson overview

Time: Approximately one hour.

Materials: Stationery including pens and stickers, a potato or picture of one, a PowerPoint presentation, and a word search.

Aim: By the end of this lesson students will have expressed food preferences through English and art and practised using food-based vocabulary and numbers. I present the words *cake, sweets, fruit, hamburger, chocolate, sandwich* and *potato* but you may prefer to teach other food words.

Doing a warmer activity

`T >> Sts`   8 minutes

Start by making a friendly looking name badge for yourself (with a smiley or cartoon character on it). When the students arrive, introduce yourself, show them your name badge, and give them the necessary materials to make their own (blank stickers, coloured pens and so on). When everybody's ready, gather them together and ask every student *What's your name?* Get everyone to say *I'm [name]* and then greet each child by saying a cheery *Hello!*

Playing 'One Potato, Two Potato'

`Whole Class`   10 minutes

If possible bring a real potato to the lesson, but if not show a picture and elicit from the students what it is. Make a fist and tell students that is also a potato! Get them to make potato fists of both hands and to hold these out in front of them as they stand in a circle. Then begin the game 'One Potato, Two Potato':

1. Touch your fist against each one in the circle successively and say:

   One potato, **two** potato, **three** potato, **four**

   Five potato, **six** potato, **seven** potato, **MORE**

2. The fist touched on the word *more* is put behind the child's back.

3. Start your counting round again.

4. Keep going until children are out of the game due to both fists being counted out.

After the first round or two, encourage the children to say the rhyme instead of you. Finally, ask the children whether or not they like eating potatoes.

If the class is very large, break the children into smaller groups to play the game, when they know what to do. After spending a few minutes showing the children how to play, another of five minutes of the children playing more independently game is enough for one lesson.

Making a PowerPoint presentation

T >> St   **10 minutes**

You need to make six flashcards for key words you want to teach using PowerPoint. The food words you use may be influenced by the local culture. Words and ideas that are familiar to the students are best.

Type in the words for the flashcards one slide at a time and paste in pictures that help explain the meaning (see Figure 22-3 for an example). Then, use the animations feature to have your words and pictures bounce, spin or fly onto the slide. Time animations to move in slowly, which allows you to elicit from the children what the emerging object may be. Then insert audio files from ClipArt or record something interesting yourself. For the food presentation I use munching sounds and also applause to show the children they've done well.

You can choose to make the audio file symbols invisible, but I leave them on the slide to build up the children's anticipation.

Drill the individual words and the sentences on the slides. Ask students for individual responses; for example, *Do you like hamburgers, Yurani?* (said with a beaming smile). Help them say the negative form as necessary; for example, *I don't like fruit* (said with a frown and disgusted expression).

Figure 22-3: PowerPoint presentation showing food vocabulary.

Doing a wordsearch

St >> St   10 minutes

Embed your key words into a wordsearch. You can design it yourself or use an online tool such as the one on the Discovery Education website at `school.discoveryeducation.com/index.html`. Figure 22-4 shows the wordsearch for these words with the first highlighted as an example: *cake, sweets, fruit, hamburgers, chocolate, sandwich, potato.*

Ensure that the students know the rules of the wordsearch. In my example words go forwards, backwards, vertically, horizontally or diagonally, which is fine for children who are already confident readers.

```
h o g u d p b s u s o q u g j
a a s t e e w s a q z o i l r
o k m n v u g n a m c r d y j
h t x b x v d a n n h z d u k
x y a e u w g t a p o o f z v
m u g t i r g q n m c a o l f
u s n c o i g i a o o c r k k
q d h h g p u e b y l i w r b
u m i u t k i q r r a d v p x
n r h k k t y w z s t j p r k
p l p h i j k h p i e w y z o
k a y u h t p l h c n w n k i
x o r c v y b d m s o e t c k
z f o d f f k j a e m o p h w
c a k e i v k j h o n k m p s
```

Figure 22-4:
Example
of a word-
search for
food
vocabulary.

Working from student pictures

St   **15 minutes**

Students now draw pictures in their notebooks of the foods they like and don't like. They can draw any food they like.

Mingle among them and help the students to label each food in English (wherever possible) and to pronounce the words for their pictures.

Round the students' drawings session off after five or six minutes. Encourage a sentence from each child, such as *I like ice-cream*, but don't force anyone. Use yes/no questions for the timid ones; for example, *Do you like pasta?*

Mention any new vocabulary used for the pictures so that the whole class can benefit. Write the words on the board and drill them.

Doing a revision quiz

`T >> St`   **4 minutes**

Go back to the PowerPoint and quickly elicit the vocabulary on the slides as well as any extra words on the board. Ask who likes various food items – throw in a disgusting one for good measure, which checks their understanding and prompts a strong reaction. Finish with a big round of applause for everyone!

Extension activities

Make more PowerPoint slides with the students. Do a survey of the most popular foods and get students to invest in the lesson by helping you choose pictures, effects and sounds for the presentation.

Put food pictures around the room for the children to colour in and label.

Do matching exercises so the children connect pictures of food with the words.

Play the supermarket game, in which each person in the group has to remember and add to an increasingly long shopping list:

> *Student A: I went to the supermarket for some eggs.*

> *Student B: I went to the supermarket for eggs and cheese.*

Chapter 23

Training Teens

In This Chapter

▶ Considering reasons that classes for teens may need extra preparation

▶ Using strategies to hold the interest of younger learners

▶ Teaching teenagers using a task-based approach

*T*eaching teenagers presents a challenge for most teachers. Whether you work in a summer school with kids from a variety of countries, or perhaps in a high school in a non-English-speaking country, you find that teenagers demand more from teachers in the way of adaptability and patience than many other age groups.

In this chapter, I look at the things you need to keep in mind that differentiate a class of teenagers from a class of adults, and I show you how to use a task-based approach to lesson planning for teenage classes of somewhat mixed abilities. For more information on a task-based approach to language learning, refer to Chapter 2.

Understanding Why Teen Classes Need Special Consideration

Many teenagers are, of course, happy and enthusiastic about their English lessons. Still, teenagers generally have a different mindset from other age groups. With this in mind, you're best to prepare for any negative occurrences by considering factors that may affect teenagers in a negative way:

✔ Although they have their own opinions, teenagers are sometimes forced to learn English against their will; for example, some are made to leave home for the summer to practise their English. In such students motivation is low, and they're easily distracted by thoughts of what they'd rather be doing. If they're away from home, they may also struggle with homesickness, which can cover everything in gloom for a young person, even your well-prepared, exciting lessons!

✔ Within the teen category are very different people. There may be a great difference between, for example, a 13-year-old boy, and a 16-year-old girl in their development and maturity. You need to bridge these gaps within the class.

✔ At times language schools keep a whole travelling party of youngsters together for commercial reasons (they're only around for a week and they have a particular schedule) and this results in a mixed-level class. The most and the least capable English speakers in the group both feel frustrated by the level the class is pitched at.

✔ Given the wide variety of countries in which English classes take place, the diverse styles of teaching and parenting create different expectations in students' minds. So many self-conscious teens aren't used to you asking them for an opinion, whereas others fully expect to be heard at all costs.

✔ Language schools test ability in the English language but not cultural knowledge. Different levels of cultural awareness can be an obstacle in generating discussions.

With these factors in mind, here are some tips for classroom management with teenagers:

✔ Learn the names of all the students as soon as possible. It's important to the young people that you recognise them as individuals.

✔ Arrange the room so that you can see everyone clearly (in a horseshoe shape, for example) and make it difficult for anyone to skulk at the back.

✔ Organise where students sit yourself. Mix introverts and extroverts and also the nationalities where possible.

✔ Make sure that you include fun activities such as games, and preferably those where the students can leave their seats, move about and use up some energy. Games are also useful because young people may have shorter attention spans than adults, so they want to intersperse their learning with games instead of sitting quietly doing exercises for long periods of time.

✔ Use the most up-to-date resources you can find, not your old chestnuts! Teens like whatever is cutting-edge.

✔ Distribute questions evenly around the class, but make it clear to the bright sparks in the class that they shouldn't just shout out when someone else is trying to formulate an answer. They need to show patience so that everyone has an equal chance.

✔ Be friendly but authoritative so you maintain control.

✔ Give personal attention to students who lack confidence. For example, if you have an uneven number of students, be the timid student's partner in pair work activities.

- Refer students who aren't coping to the student welfare officer in your school or the tour group leader.

- Let students know why they're doing a particular activity and the aims and objectives of the lesson. Teens have a tendency to ask, 'What's the point?' At the same time they don't usually understand that a methodology they're not used to is still valid and beneficial.

- Offer choices so that the teens feel they have some control.

- Be diligent about your instructions and concept check questions (I discuss these types of questions in Chapter 3). Make sure that students understand exactly what to do and how long they have in which to do it, because they won't necessarily ask you when they're unsure. They'll just play on their mobile phones instead.

- Do plenty of group work so that you can mix the personalities and levels of proficiency together. Divide the tasks within the group activity into easier and more difficult parts and *productive* (writing and speaking) or *receptive* (reading and listening) skills so that everyone can contribute.

- Find a modern and youthful context for all language points. For example, demonstrate how to use comparative adjectives by asking: 'Is Emma Watson prettier / more beautiful than Miley Cyrus?'

Teaching Teens at All Levels

While some classes are of mixed abilities, others are geared towards one particular level. In this section, I give you ideas for teaching teens at particular levels of proficiency.

Elementary

Problem-solving is fun, competitive and holds the attention. So after your students have learnt some adjectives and how to use them, present them with some riddles. For example:

> *I am small but long. I come to school with you. I am sometimes in your hand. I am black inside but colourful outside. (Answer: pencil.)*

Then get pairs of students to write some riddles about things in the classroom or at home. They can then swap their riddles and see how many they get right.

Role plays are also popular. Survey the class on hobbies and interests, and then help students to devise role plays based on the things they enjoy. For example, have a role play set in a videogame store and use it to teach shopping vocabulary such as *Do you have the new . . . ?* and *How much is that?*

In general, you can still follow the course book syllabus, but exchange the book's settings for more relevant and youthful ones.

Pre-intermediate

Make cultural comparisons of teenagers around the world. Get 16- to 19-year- old students to make a list of the differences they note between your culture and theirs, for instance.

Select some clips from the TV show *The World's Strictest Parents* (being careful to avoid the more offensive opening scenes). There are many clips showing families around the world on Youtube. Tell students which countries are involved in your clips. Then get the class to predict the problems one pair of teens will find when they travel to another country, using the future simple. For example:

> The new parents won't like the teen's fashion style.
>
> The teen will sleep less there because there is a lot of work to do in the house.

Finally, show the clips to check whether the students guessed correctly.

Intermediate

Use a new movie trailer to generate discussions. Trailers for action movies like *Iron Man* (perhaps the latest sequel or prequel) make a great impact in just two minutes or so.

To pre-teach some interesting vocabulary, give the students a checklist of things that do and don't appear in the trailer. Play the trailer without sound for the first watching task. For example, use the trailer for the film *Iron Man 3*. You can find it on Youtube (`www.youtube.com/watch?v=muIsc5lIEyQ`). Your checklist may require students to tick if they see the following: a red carpet, a microphone, a sword, a cliff, a villain.

After the students have compared their answers, play the trailer again with the sound on. Ask students to discuss their ideas about the plot based on what they've seen. Follow up by setting research questions for actors' biographies, and ask the class to design movie posters.

Upper-intermediate

Set the class a project about youth subcultures past or present. Each group can research and create a presentation on a different subculture, such as hip-hop, punk, emo and so on. They can all answer the same questions, such as:

- ✔ How can you identify a member of this subculture? Comment on music, fashion, and general behaviour.
- ✔ How did this subculture begin?
- ✔ In which countries mainly do you find this subculture?
- ✔ Are there any celebrities who belong to this subculture?

Advanced

Introduce students to Ernest Hemingway's challenge of writing a story in six words. Use www.sixwordstories.net for scores of examples that students can speculate on. Then bring the idea up to date by comparing the restricted characters on social media sites (it's 140 characters for Twitter feeds).

Challenge the teens to condense the entire plots of famous films, books, or plays into a set number of words, or a maximum number of characters. Other classmates can guess which story is being described.

Lesson Plan for a Mixed Ability Class of Teenagers

In this lesson, I take the popular topic of music and use it to present a task-based approach to planning a lesson for teens.

Lesson overview

Time: Approximately one hour.

Materials: A list of recording artists.

Aim: To practise the language of popular music and parties in a communicative way. New vocabulary includes *play* list, *lyrics, beat, catchy, hit, instruments, vocals* and *track.* I also include expressions for expressing choice and preferences. However, in a task-based lesson plan you are guided by the language the students need to complete the activity well and this may vary.

Doing a warmer activity

T >> St   5 minutes

Start the lesson with some music to set the scene. Play part of a song or video clip and challenge the students to identify the artist. Do they like the song? Which other tracks from the artist do they know? How many enjoy this music genre?

Preparing with a pre-task activity

T >> St   10 minutes

To prepare students to discuss their preferred playlists, elicit or pre-teach this useful language:

> a playlist
>
> the lyrics
>
> a beat
>
> to be catchy
>
> a hit instruments
>
> the vocals
>
> a track

Go over the meaning, part of speech (they're all nouns except *catchy)*, and pronunciation of each word. Refer back to the opening song in the warmer activity to concept-check. For example, ask the class:

- ✔ Was that song a hit in your country?
- ✔ Why do people like it? Is it the beat or the catchy lyrics?

Setting the party playlist task

St >> St   10 minutes

Explain the task to students. In pairs or small groups they must imagine that they're organising a party for friends, their classmates perhaps, and they must choose five music artists from the list you supply. From the tracks of these artists they're going to make the party playlist. Your selection list should include around 20 artists, and you can simply put it on the board or show it on the computer screen (see Figure 23-1 for an example).

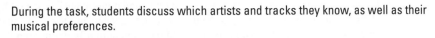

Figure 23-1:
Example
of the
selection list
for the party
playlist task.

Top UK Recording Artists

Choose just five of these artists for your party playlist:

Emeli Sande Coldplay Adele Muse

One Direction Robbie Williams Leona Lewis Take That

Jessie J Professor Green Labyrinth Little Mix

During the task, students discuss which artists and tracks they know, as well as their musical preferences.

If the students aren't too familiar with British music, allow the use of the Internet for research, but offer a reduced list – ten artists perhaps.

Planning the task report

St >> St   10 minutes

The students plan to report their artist selection to the rest of the class. They prepare a reason for each of their choices. Encourage students to make notes and practise what they want to say (they can nominate one spokesperson or share the responsibility). Each report should last two to three minutes.

Delivering the report

Whole Class   10 minutes

Invite the representative(s) from each group to deliver the report explaining their choices. Listen carefully as they speak and note language points (errors or particularly good language use) that you can address during the next stage of the lesson.

If you have a large class, making students sit through more than three or four reports of very similar content is unfair. In that case, put several pairs or groups together to present their reports to each other. When all the presentations are finished, ask a few students to summarise the main differences between the presentations they heard for the whole class.

Analysing the lesson

T >> St   10 minutes

During the reporting stage, you probably noted various language points to review with the students. There may have been several examples of poor pronunciation or grammatical errors. You can now use the board to highlight the problems and elicit corrections.

On the other hand, you might feel that students need general assistance with reporting skills. Students may take the easy option of continually saying *I like this one because. . ..* However, this expression soon sounds repetitive and boring.To encourage the use of alternative expressions when reporting preferences, put these gapped sentences on the board for students to note down:

We chose. . . . . .because. . . . .

The reason we like. . . . . .is. . . .

This one is better due to . . . .

We selected. . . . . .thanks to. . . . .

Practising the language point

St >> St   10 minutes

Give students the opportunity to practise the language point you've just analysed. Depending on what you highlighted, you could ask students to write sentences using the language point and then discuss their sentences with a partner. For example, following the alternative expressions for reporting preferences I show in the preceding section, ask students to go back into their pairs or small groups and decide on the food for the party with a budget of £50. This allows the students to use the new vocabulary in a practical way. After five minutes they can again report their choices to a wider group of students. So this time they can present sentences such as:

> The reason we like buying pizza is we can eat it hot or cold. And we chose crisps because you get different flavours and they are easy to serve.

Doing a cooler activity

T >> St   5 minutes

Play a game like the old TV show *Name That Tune*. Play just five seconds of the year's biggest hits and get groups of students to name the song and artist. If they're bold enough, one group can hum a tune for the rest of the class to guess.

Extension activity

You've covered party music and food. In groups, students now design and conduct class surveys about party experiences, including the different kinds of parties they've attended and which ones they enjoyed most. From the results, they report back on the recipe for the perfect party.

Here's an example of some survey questions:

1. In hot weather, which do you prefer (a) a pool party? (b) a beach party?

2. Do you think it's better to have a party at: (a) your house? (b) at a rented place?

3. What is the perfect number of guests at a party: (a) 20? (b) 50? (c) 100?

Introduce the Jona Lewie song 'You'll Always Find Me in the Kitchen at Parties'. Type out the lyrics and then cut each copy into sections: verses and chorus. As students listen to the track, they re-order the lyrics by moving the cut-out pieces into place on their desks. After that, students make a note of the vocabulary they don't understand. Assign different groups of students to look up a few words each in the dictionary before you review all the new words. Naturally, a follow-up question is: 'Where do you like to be at a party?'

Chapter 24

Making Use of Readers

In This Chapter

▶ Seeing how readers can support learning

▶ Drawing inspiration from readers to motivate students of all levels

▶ Linking reading activities with other media to stimulate interest in reading skills

Graded *readers* are small books, mostly fictional, that are written to suit a particular level of proficiency in English. They're self-study resources and some are original stories, whereas others are adaptations from other works. Many schools keep a library of graded readers for students to borrow and take home.

In this chapter, I show why bringing readers into the classroom as lesson content is a great idea, and how you can best do so. Some schools purchase a class set of the same book (many copies of the same reader), which is ideal for classroom work. In other cases all the students have a different reader. I show you a lesson that presents the same story in two formats, a graded reader and a Hollywood movie, to teach a language point in a memorable way.

Using Readers as a Lesson Resource

Reading in English is a skill to encourage because as it enables students to access far more vocabulary, grammar and cultural input than you could ever teach during the course. And, of course, good reading skills generally translate to better writing skills.

If you have a library of readers in your school, don't just leave them for students to study by themselves. Without your input, students may not be motivated to take English-language books out and develop their reading skills. So bring books into the lesson to raise awareness of how advantageous they are to language learners.

Using readers is great because

✔ Reading these tailor-made books gives students the confidence to read English in general. At first they are too intimidated by the new language to read stories, but when they manage a short, reader and find it enjoyable they begin to read other material in English too.

✔ Readers are graded to make the reading experience more pleasurable. So each book is labelled to show how difficult it is based on the grammar and vocabulary content. That's why students don't have to keep stopping to consult the dictionary as long they're reading at the right level.

✔ Many readers come with an audio CD in which the receptive skills (listening and reading) are linked together. The student also has access to a good pronunciation model.

✔ Building vocabulary is important for increasing language proficiency. Readers enable students to find new vocabulary within a clear and interesting context.

✔ Preparing to study a particular reader prompts research for background information about the author and the setting. In the example I use in the lesson plan, the Amistad account presented in the reader tends to generate interest in slavery, the actor Djimon Hounsou and American history. Students therefore expand their general knowledge and so have more material to discuss with classmates and write essays about.

✔ Extended reading, as provided by readers, allows students to consolidate what they have been learning in class by seeing it reinforced in black and white.

Incorporating Readers at All Levels

Most reader collections go from level one to level six, which covers all students from elementary to advanced. That's why there is no excuse for leaving readers out of your courses. In this section, I show you ways to use these books in your lessons.

Elementary

Use a couple of pages from a reader as material for a role-play (for more on role-plays, head to Chapter 9). Students can find examples of direct speech in the text, work out how many characters are involved, and then act out the scene. If the direct speech is patchy you can also assign one stronger student to be a narrator and read the other parts of the text. So, with all the parts allocated, the students read the text aloud in an animated fashion (and maybe even with actions).

You can also use the audio CD to prepare the students for their role-play. Focus on imitating intonation patterns.

After reading a few different books outside the classroom, student groups can collaborate to prepare posters in class that review the stories. According to the number of copies you have of each publication, put students into reading groups with a time limit to complete the reading of the book and produce the poster review, as well as a short oral presentation. This exercise serves to motivate students to read even more books.

Pre-intermediate

Get the students to work in small groups and produce a cartoon strip based on a chapter of a reader they have all read. This exercise will involve discussion work, summarising of language, and a large amount of creativity. Younger learners should enjoy this activity.

Assign the students a portion of reading as homework. Then, in class, play the next part of the story on the audio CD. The students have to listen, answer comprehension questions, and then predict what happens next. When they read the next part, they can compare it with their own predictions and share the results with classmates.

Intermediate

Have a 'Literacy Time' segment in your lessons. If you're teaching an intensive course of 15 hours or so per week, why not dedicate three slots of 20 minutes each to quiet reading using the school's library of graded readers? The students can choose any title to match their level and ability.

Literacy Time may allow you to do private tutorials with one or two students while others read, not to mention catching up on your course administration.

You can create a Literacy Time template using the 'Wh–' questions, in order to focus students' minds and give them a structure for feedback with other students at the end. Figure 24-1 shows an example of a small worksheet for a graded reader, including a student's answers, based on one of the Penguin readers adapted from the *No.1 Ladies' Detective Agency* series.

Book Title	The Kalahari Typing School For Men, Chapter 1	
Questions	Answers	Useful language
What is happening in the story?	The heroine, Precious, agreed to marry a man but now he is ill	Fortunate = lucky Orphan children = their parents died He <u>was thought to be</u> the best mechanic (passive) Dull = not interesting
Where/when is the action set?	Gaborone, Botswana	
Which characters are involved?	1. Precious Ramotswe 2. JLB Matekone	
What do you learn about each character from the latest events?	Precious: was married to an exciting man before and owns a detective agency. JLB: fixes cars; seems depressed.	

Figure 24-1:
A worksheet for students to summarise their reading during Literacy Time.

Upper-intermediate

Reading ahead of the students is useful because you can then help the class anticipate particular language points.

For instance, find words in the text that you know have more than one meaning. Get the students to look at the various meanings in a dictionary, or set them out yourself as a multiple choice exercise. Then the students select the particular meaning for the context of the story, as they read the relevant section.

Here's an example using the word *allotment*. You challenge students to deduce the correct meaning by using the clues in the text about digging and planting:

> **allotment** (n) a) an amount of something that is given to a particular person b) a small area of land inside a larger garden that the local community use

Extract from text:

> Tanyeem arrived exhausted from her afternoon of digging and planting, but pleased with the vegetables from her allotment, which she planned to cook for her guests that night.

For stories that exist as both a graded reader and a film, students could watch the video clip and then write their version of the scene as they think it will appear in the book. They then read and compare their version with the text from the reader.

Advanced

Encourage the students to get inside the minds of the characters of a book the whole class is reading. Students should communicate with the character by sending messages of advice, support, or warning. Use a notice board as a place to post students' messages to the character or the students could post their messages into a box you set up in the classroom. You may let a student prepare replies in the voice of the character too. This is a particularly effective technique if you're reading an historical tale that you want to bring to life. .

Intermediate to Upper-Intermediate Lesson Plan

This lesson is designed to give you ideas about combining graded readers with other media to provide context for a language point. It also whets the students' appetites for further reading of the book in question or of background information.

Lesson overview

Time: Approximately 1 hour.

Materials: *Amistad* (Penguin Graded Reader) by Joyce Annette Barnes. Stephen Spielberg's *Amistad* on DVD or just a clip of the relevant scene. Sentence prompts for students, written on the board, or on a worksheet.

Aim: By the end of this lesson students will have used the Amistad story (in print and film) to practise using modal perfect forms and adverbs.

Doing a warmer activity

| T >> Sts | 5 minutes

Find out from students what they know about two of the principal actors in the film they'll later view: Djimon Hounsou (starred in *Gladiator and Blood Diamond*) and Matthew McConaughey (starred in *The Wedding Planner* and *A Time to Kill*). Show pictures and provide some background information about the actors. Explain that the two men starred in Spielberg's film *Amistad* about Mende people from Africa who, in 1839, broke free from their captors while on a slave ship to America, but then faced a huge legal struggle for the right to return home.

Hounsou's story is an interesting rags-to-riches tale. He was homeless in France when he was discovered, and he became a fashion model and later a Hollywood actor. Use his story as a springboard. Students can give presentations about a similarly dramatic rise to fame of a celebrity from their own country.

Introducing the modal perfect

| T >> St | 7 minutes

Write a list of modal verbs on the board and ask students how to use them to talk about the past. Draw a chart like the one in Table 24-1 and elicit the information to fill it in.

Table 24-1   Structure and Use of Modal Perfect Forms: Board Work

Modal Verb	+ Have	+ Past Participle:	Usage
must	have	done	70–90% sure it was
might	have	thought	50% sure it was
can't	have	been	70–90% sure it was not
should	have	gone	Advice and opinions about something that already happened

St >> St   8 minutes

Now get students to construct five or six sentences about the Amistad story using the modal perfect form. Provide prompts for their sentences in this way:

Use the verb in brackets to complete the sentence in the modal perfect form. Write your own opinion.

> 1. Spielberg [to choose] Asian actors for this film.
>
> Spielberg can't have chosen Asian actors for this film because it's set in Africa and the USA
>
> 2. After reading the story the filmmakers [to go] to Africa for advice.
>
> After reading the story the filmmakers might have gone to Africa for advice.
>
> 3. The people in the real Amistad story [to be] really happy to win their freedom.
>
> The people in the real Amistad story must have been happy to win their freedom.

After students have compared their answers, go through the exercise with the class, paying attention to their use of grammar.

Working with the graded reader

T >> Sts   5 minutes

The same scene is portrayed in the Penguin graded reader *Amistad* and in Spielberg's film. First students read a scene in the book.

Explain the background to this scene: After weeks of struggle, a court has granted the Africans in America their freedom. Baldwin, the lawyer, and Covey, the interpreter, speak to Cinque, a brave African who was celebrating in prison.

Give students a minute or two to read the scene in the book by themselves. Here is an extract from the graded reader (page 31):

They sat down at a table outside the prison. Baldwin began to speak. Covey repeated his words.

'Our president, our "big man" wants your case to go to a higher court'.

'What does that mean?' asked Cinque.

'It means' said Baldwin, 'that a different judge will have to decide the case again.'

'No!' shouted Cinque. 'We had a decision. We're free!'

'That's almost true . . . ' began Baldwin.

'Almost?' Cinque asked.' Almost? What sort of place is this? Where you almost mean what you say? Where people are almost free?'

Predicting

St >> St   10 minutes

Ask the students to work in threes and predict how they think the actors, Hounsou, McConaughey and Chiwetel Ejiofor (who plays the interpreter), will portray this scene in the film.

Write a list of adverbs on the board, like *worriedly*, *desperately*, *angrily*, *cautiously*, *suspiciously*, and *apologetically*. Students can use these adverbs to describe each action that takes place, or they can use their own ideas. Dictionaries are allowed.

For example:

Student A: I think the lawyer sits down cautiously because he knows he has bad news to give them.

Student B: Maybe Cinque sits suspiciously because he can see that Baldwin wants to say something bad.

Role-playing the scene

St >> St   5 minutes

In groups of three, students act out the short scene. Instead of the Mende language, if some of your students share the same first language and are in the same group, they can take the parts of Covey and Cinque, translating from English into their own tongue such as Spanish or Chinese. As each group acts, the group members must try to convey the emotions of the various characters.

Linking the graded reader to the film clip

St >> St   16 minutes

Now the students watch the dramatic film clip to see whether their predictions were actually right. After watching, they discuss in pairs the appropriate adverbs to describe the actors' portrayal. Find out whether they're surprised by Spielberg's version.

Next students watch the scene again and complete the gapped text of the film script shown in Figure 24-2. It highlights the problem posed by translating modal verbs. The gaps in the text are mainly in Baldwin's words, which are repeated frequently. Let the students know that this is the reason why numbers for the gaps are also repeated in the text. You see in the script that number one, for example, appears twice. I have filled in gap one as an example for the students to follow.

Play the scene straight through once, but if the students still have gaps, play it a second time. Students compare their answers, and then you give general class feedback.

Amistad   **Scene 16**   1:46.30–1:49:49

There are seven words or phrases missing from the film script. Many are repeated. Watch the film and complete the text. The first one has been done for you.

Baldwin: Our President, our big, big man has appealed the decision to our Supreme Court.

Covey: What does that mean?

Baldwin: We have to try the case again. I know it's hard to understand Cinque. I don't understand for that matter.

Covey: You said there would be a . . . (1) . . . . . . [judgement] and if we won the (1) . . . . . . [judgement] we would go (2) . . . . . .

Baldwin: No, no what I said was that we won it at the state level. What I said was that we won it at the state level and we would then go on.

Covey: That's what you said.

Baldwin: No what I said was that we won it at the state level. Yes, that's what I said but I 3) . . . . . . , I 3) . . . . . . Now what I should have (4) . . . . . . , what I should have (4) . . . . . .

Covey: No I can't translate that.

Baldwin: You can't translate what?

Covey: I can't translate 'should'.

Baldwin: You're saying there's no word in Mende for 'should'?

Covey: No, either you do something or you don't do it.

Baldwin: What I (5) . . . . . . say, what I (5) . . . . . . say?

Covey: No not in the way you mean it.

Baldwin: Cinque try and understand.

Covey: It's the same as 'should'. You're misunderstanding the language.

Baldwin: Cinque listen to me! Understand what I'm saying. What I said to you before the judgement is 6) . . . . . . how it works here. (6) . . . . . . ! Yes Cinque but not (7) . . . . . . , and that's what's happened here.

Cinque: What kind of place is this where you almost mean what you say? Where laws almost work? How can you live like that?

Figure 24-2: Fill the gaps worksheet for Amistad film listening and watching activity.

Answers: 1. Judgement; 2. Free; 3. shouldn't have; 4. Said; 5. meant to; 6. Almost; 7. Always;

Discussing issues raised in the book

St >> St   9 minutes

In pairs or small groups students discuss the following questions related to the scene:

- ✔ Do you think the lawyer should have explained more about the court system before the case first went to trial? Why or why not?
- ✔ Is it fair that you can win your case in one court but then lose it in another?
- ✔ Cinque seems to find America a very strange place. What do you find strange about British/American culture?
- ✔ Which word from your language has no direct translation into English? How would you try to explain the word to an English speaker?

Ask a few students to summarise the opinions expressed in their pair/group to the whole class.

Extension activities

At this point students are usually anxious to know what happens to Cinque and the others. Set the students more reading work from the book to do at home. You can then discuss the importance of freedom and human rights during class time.

Ask the students to research and tell the story of someone who fought for something that's considered important in their country. This information can then also be used as an essay topic.

Chapter 25

Developing Presentation Skills

- -

In This Chapter

▶ Teaching the kind of language that students' need to give a good presentation

▶ Helping students structure effective presentations

▶ Organising two lessons on presentations

- -

*P*resentations are a part of many university courses and professions these days. For those developing a career that makes use of the English language, getting a foothold on presentation skills in English is vital. This chapter features the structure and lexis students need to speak effectively and professionally in front of others.

Using Presentation Skills as Language Context

When you set your class the task of giving presentations, you provide them with an opportunity to practise various skills. In addition, you have an ideal setting to assess your students' abilities individually.

Consider these advantages of teaching presentation skills:

- ✔ You bring the productive skills of writing and speaking into play in a freer way than in practice activities, and the students are able to show off the language skills they have developed so far.

- ✔ The students are likely to research the set topic in English using the Internet and printed resources, which encourages independent learning and authentic use of the language.

- ✔ A level of differentiation takes place because all students are able to put their own slant on the set topic.

- ✔ Even if they are used to giving presentations in their own language, students are now able to explore what people in the English-speaking world are likely to expect. Students can note cultural differences.

- Students practise the transferrable skill of signposting – using key expressions to move from one stage of a verbal/written presentation to another.

- Giving a successful presentation can really boost a student's confidence.

- In the preparation and delivery of a presentation session, students play a more active role, which gives them variety and motivation.

- Presentation lessons allow you to embrace a number of approaches and methodologies (referred to in Part 1 of this book) such as task-based learning and CALL (computer assisted language learning).

Incorporating Presentation Skills at All Levels

Here are some ways you can bring presentation skills into lessons for students of all abilities.

Beginner and elementary

The roots of good presentations lie in making notes and thinking about information before speaking. For example, if you want students to talk about music, get them thinking about different aspects of the topic first, so that they give a comprehensive answer. Write instructions and questions like these on the board:

- Name three kinds of music you like.

- Which artists do you prefer?

- When do you listen to the music you like?

As the teacher, you should give your own answers to these questions as a structured example of what you expect from the students. Put examples like this one on the board, highlighting the structure by adding in labels in brackets and underlining basic connecting words such as ordinal numbers:

> (Intro) I like three kinds of music. (Body) <u>First</u>, I like jazz, and my favourite artist is Natalie Cole. Usually, I listen to jazz when I drive my car. <u>Next</u>, I like some pop music. I listen to Take That at home in the evening. And <u>also</u>, at parties I like salsa music because I can dance to Paulo FG. (Conc) I prefer those three kinds of music but I have lots of different CDs at home.

In this brief example, I show students a basic introduction, body, and conclusion. By extending this idea, you can build students up to an answer of one minute or two, instead of just '*I like jazz, pop, and salsa.*'

REMEMBER

Students always give a more extended answer if you offer clues and examples on what to say.

Pre-intermediate and intermediate

Teach signposting expressions and connectors like the following, which form the skeleton of a short presentation.

Intro	*I would like to tell you about . . .*
	My presentation today is about . . .
Body	*Point 1*
	To begin with . . .
	First of all . . .
	To start. . .
	Point 2
	We'll move on to . . .
	Now let's look at. . .
	Point 3
	My final area is. . .
	Other useful expressions
	For example . . .
	That's why . . .
	In addition . . .
	This image/clip shows . . .
Conclusion	*In conclusion . . .*
	To sum up . . .

Upper intermediate and advanced

Teach students how to handle quotes and references using active and passive expressions such as:

According to (someone)

(Someone) stated/believed

(Someone) reported that. . .

It is said/ thought/ believed/ reported (by someone) that. . .

Moving on from basic language, get students using more interest-arousing expressions such as opening questions and requests for audience participation. Notice how expressions like these draw the audience in:

How many of you have ever . . . ?

This is my opinion but what do you think?

This point is of particular interest to students like us because . . .

Intermediate (and Above) Lesson Plan

There are two stages to this plan. The first lesson involves preparation, and the other is the actual delivery on the part of the students.

Use this plan only for students who are of intermediate level and above, because those students will embellish their presentation according to confidence and ability.

Overview for Lesson 1

Here I present the first lesson which prepares students to give a presentation. This lesson gives the students some advice and practice.

Time: Approximately one hour.

Materials: A worksheet about presentations.

Aims: By the end of this first stage plan students will have learnt how to prepare and deliver a presentation on a given topic. They will have co-operated as a team and practised all four language skills. Vocabulary to help students connect ideas during the presentation is covered by means of the worksheet.

Doing a warmer activity

T >> St   **5 minutes**

Play Fortunately/Unfortunately, a game in which you begin a sentence and then nominate a student to complete it by saying 'Fortunately . . .' or 'Unfortunately . . .' in order to build up the story. For example:

> T: I saw a famous singer on Oxford Street. Unfortunately . . .
>
> St 1: Unfortunately, I didn't have my camera.
>
> St 2: Fortunately, my friend had her phone which has a camera in it.

I first found this warmer on the www.busyteacher.org website. Just search there for other warmers.

Choosing the topic

T >> St   10 minutes

Explain that students will be giving a short presentation each on a specified day and that as a class they must agree on how the presentations will be organised. Set out the criteria, including:

- ✔ **Audience:** Explain whether students will present to the whole class or to a smaller group.
- ✔ **Time limit:** Give a minimum and maximum time; for example, five to eight minutes.
- ✔ **Topic:** Agree the topic of the presentations with the class.
- ✔ **Visual aids:** State whether students should use presentation software, the board, props, and so on.

For larger classes, sitting through presentation after presentation can be somewhat of a strain, even if they're pretty good. In this case, divide the class into groups of six or so and give each group access to a laptop, flipchart, or similar presentation aid. They can now present to their own group and perhaps nominate one student from each group to present to the entire class, so the students get an interesting sample of the presentations they haven't heard previously.

This is an opportunity for a class discussion, during which you can step back and let the students negotiate in English. You may take a Community Language Learning approach here (refer to Chapter 2 for details about CLL discussions). You could also offer an example or two of presentation topics to get students started. Here are some suggestions:

- ✔ A hobby or interest I enjoy
- ✔ Important sites and landmarks in my hometown
- ✔ Inspirational people
- ✔ Ways I can improve my community
- ✔ My favourite artist

Setting your students up to succeed

Now that the students have set the criteria for the presentation day, help them to work out the language and structure they need. I put this information into a worksheet to make it easier for the students to discuss and store the language points and tips.

St >> St   15 minutes

Prepare a worksheet like that in Figure 25-1 or put the information from the figure on the board/screen. Put students in pairs to discuss the answers. Give examples based on each box in the figure so that the students are clear on how to proceed.

Giving Presentations

Structure How do you organise a short presentation? i) Introduction ii) .... iii) .... iv) .... v)	**Synonyms** What is the overall topic of your presentation? Find three synonyms for each key word.
Connecting words Find an other way to say these words or phrases: i) and ii) for example iii) so iv) in fact v) but vi) of course vii) then	**True or false** 1. It's best to write down everything you want to say and read from your notes. 2. If you speak slowly you sound boring. 3. You should get your computer/board ready before you start speaking. 4. You can ask your teacher for help while you're doing the presentation. 5. You can read through your notes while another person is giving their presentation. 6. What's important is speaking about something interesting, so organising all the information doesn't matter. 7. The audience might ask you some questions. 8. In your presentation you can read sentences you've found on the Internet or in books.

Figure 25-1: Worksheet to prepare students for giving a presentation.

Giving student feedback

T >> St   **8 minutes**

Go over the answers to the worksheet in a feedback session.

The answers to Worksheet in Figure 25-1 are:

- ✓ **Structure**: Introduction/3 main points/conclusion
- ✓ **Synonyms**: Answers depend on the topic. For example, in a presentation entitled 'Ways we can improve our community', synonyms for key words could be

    - *Community*: society, neighbourhood, locality, the public
    - *Improve*: advance, develop, correct, boost

✔ **Connecting Words** i) in addition, also   ii) or instance   iii) therefore
iv) actually   v) however   vi) naturally   vii) following/after that

✔ **True or False:**

1. F. The notes should be really reminders and not word for word.

2. F. Slow speech is clearer.

3. T.

4. F. Ask before the presentation.

5. F- it's rude not to pay attention.

6. F- you should always organise your ideas so you remember your key points and the audience can follow you more easily.

7. T

8. T, but only if you actually understand them.

Giving mini presentations

St >> St   **15 minutes**

The students are going to give some mini-presentations to each other as practice. They need some easy topics to present on so that they can concentrate on structure and language instead of content. Try these:

✔ My family

✔ My favourite films/books

✔ My favourite possessions

✔ My holidays

✔ My house

✔ My job/school

Ask a student to pick a topic for you to speak on. Spend a short time making notes on the board in a structured way. Now give a mini-presentation of about three minutes. Another student can time you so that you stop on time.

Now the students take turns to pick a topic, prepare, and speak for three minutes.

Giving feedback

St >> T   **5 minutes**

As a feedback and cooler activity, elicit from students the most interesting facts they learnt about each other during the presentations.

Advice for technology use

When students use presentation software and the Internet in their presentations, give them some advice:

- Don't copy long passages into bullet points. Short points are best.

- Don't include long video clips leaving little time left to speak.

- Make sure all visual images are clear and relevant.

- Check the spelling and use of English on anything that the audience will be reading (teachers can help).

Overview for Lesson 2: Presenting

This lesson is very student-centred because the students deliver their presentations so they don't need you to teach them. On the actual presentation day make sure that the students have the necessary equipment and that it's in good working order. Give some consideration to room layout too and ensure that the audience can see the presenters clearly.

Time: Variable depending on the number of students you have

Materials: Sufficient and appropriate equipment for students to deliver their presentations well, for example a computers and internet access, or flipcharts.

Aims: By the end of this lesson the students will have delivered their own presentations, listened to their classmates' presentations and offered each other feedback.

Doing a warmer activity

St >> St   5 minutes

Start with a warmer so that everyone has time to arrive and settle down. Set up 'proxy interviews', in which students pretend to be someone else in the room. One student conducts an interview with another student who is now in character as someone else. The interviewer tries to guess who the other student is pretending to be.

Giving the presentations

St >> Class   **Most of the lesson**

As each student gives their presentation, the audience must take notes. This focuses the mind on listening and consequently prompts interesting follow-up questions. Give out a worksheet or ask students to write down headings. Students should note:

✔ Topic

✔ Main points

✔ What they liked best about the presentation

✔ Any tips/advice for the student who spoke

Depending on your time constraints, students can offer their feedback after each presentation or save it up for the next session.

Extension activities

Students give each other feedback about their presentations. You may make time for one-to-one feedback between you and individual students too.

Discuss with students how the presentations went and together make a checklist of things to remember for the next presentation session.

Before the next presentations, have a lesson on body language. Get students practising these points:

✔ Ensure good eye contact with the audience.

✔ Maintain good posture (no slouching, leaning or hands kept in pockets).

✔ Remove barriers such as folded arms.

✔ Use hands for meaningful gestures.

Chapter 26

Focusing on Manners and Etiquette

....

In This Chapter

▶ Considering reasons why students need cultural awareness

▶ Using activities with different levels that help students to be polite when they speak English

▶ Teaching a lesson plan that incorporates both UK culture and the students' own cultural etiquette

....

*N*o matter how accurate your grammar is or how wide ranging your vocabulary, people just don't enjoy speaking to you unless you observe the basics of cultural etiquette. And the converse is also true. People go out of their way to assist someone who's polite and well-mannered.

In this chapter, I show you how to train students so that they're more aware of courteous customs. Depending on your own background and the needs of your students, you may familiarise them with another English-speaking community. However, here I use UK culture as the point of reference.

The chapter isn't about presenting manners and etiquette in the UK as being superior in any way. It's about what people expect others to do in the UK. Whether or not the students choose to act according to these customs, or maintain their own, is entirely up to them.

Using Manners and Etiquette as Lesson Content

You have a responsibility to smooth your students' passage into the English-speaking world, especially when you're one of the few native speakers students have access to. With your assistance, students benefit greatly from lessons on manners and etiquette for these reasons:

✔ Courtesy makes the speaker more approachable and likeable.

✔ Good manners help students avoid causing offence.

✔ People are more likely to meet students' requests if they ask in an appropriate way.

✔ Foreign students are as much convinced that their way of doing things is correct as Brits are with regard to their own customs. So, it will not be obvious to foreign students that certain behaviour is unacceptable in the UK.

✔ It's easier to understand the language if you understand the customs.

✔ Students are fascinated by cultural comparisons, so generating discussions is easy.

Incorporating Manners and Etiquette at All Levels

You can start teaching polite language from beginner stage upwards and through role-plays you can demonstrate acceptable behaviour too.

Beginner and elementary

Integrate polite vocabulary into all the new expressions you cover and into your general classroom language also by saying

(Yes) please   (No) thanks   Excuse me   Sorry

Show your classes how to address people correctly, so teach the pronunciation and usage of

Mr/mɪstə/   Mrs/mɪsɪz/   Miss/mɪs/   Ms /mz/

And for those who are planning to use English at work, teach *Sir/Madam* for formal situations.

Pre-intermediate

Highlight to students polite and impolite topics to discuss when starting conversations. For example:

- ✔ **Impolite:** Age, weight, gossip, jokes about race and nationality, sex, religion, politics, earnings.
- ✔ **Polite:** Weather, present surroundings, general news topics, sport, work, and studies.

Intermediate

Compare and contrast local and foreign customs with regard to these matters in shops and restaurants:

- ✔ Complaining
- ✔ Getting attention/service
- ✔ Haggling
- ✔ Queuing
- ✔ Refunds
- ✔ Tipping

Set up role-plays or give out a multiple choice questionnaire to teach the best ways to handle these situations.

Upper intermediate

At this level students are able to debate with a fair level of fluency. Teach them expressions for agreeing, disagreeing and interrupting appropriately, as well as the etiquette surrounding such discussions. In some cultures people are used to speaking over others and expressing opinions quite freely, whereas in others listeners are more likely to let speakers finish and they may think it impolite to disagree. Teach debating skills with lexis like this:

That's a good point, but . . .

It may seem that way. However . . .

No way!

I'm totally against that.

Spot on!

That's a fair point!

Can I jump in here?

May I just add that . . .

Advanced

Students at this level aren't to be so easily forgiven if their speech comes across as abrupt. For this reason, teach the grammar of polite indirect questions. For example:

~~Tell me the time!~~   Could I ask what the time is, please?

~~Can I come in?~~   Would you mind if I came in?

~~Did he like it?~~   Do you mind if I ask whether he liked it?

Students tend not to notice that the word order here is more like a sentence than a question, so they may attempt to say, *Could I ask what is the time please?*

You may like to use The Smiths' song 'Please, Please, Please, Let Me Get What I Want' to introduce polite requests.

For students who aim to work using English, teach telephone language. Workers using the wrong expressions in professional situations create a very bad impression. Here are some of the most useful phrases:

Speaking!

Hold the line, please!

I'll put you through.

May I ask who's calling, please?

What is it regarding?

He/she is unavailable, I'm afraid.

I'll ask him/her to return your call.

I'll let him/her know.

Teaching food and drink customs

Table manners are important for students from different cultures who are travelling to stay with UK host families. For instance, some may be surprised by TV dinners, which are common in the UK, and others may wonder which fork/spoon to use for each food or even when it's okay to use fingers. Show some pictures as examples of typical family mealtimes and bring in some cutlery and crockery as props (plastic will do) to role play with if the eating culture is markedly different.

Make sure students know those little idioms such as

✔ Say when!

✔ Help yourself!

✔ I'm full/peckish!

✔ That's tasty.

✔ Would you like a second helping?

✔ Could you pass the . . . , please?

✔ It's not my cup of tea, I'm afraid!

Of course, the pub requires a different form of etiquette again. Students are never sure who pays for what, how to get the attention of the barperson and so on. Teach the basics, perhaps with a clip of The Rovers Return from *Coronation Street*, and teach a few vital expressions such as *It's my round*. Remember that the word 'invite' often translates into other languages as an offer to pay rather than just a request for the person to come along! *It's on me* is a useful phrase to listen out for instead.

Intermediate Lesson Plan

This lesson gives students the opportunity to discuss what British people generally regard as acceptable behaviour in aspects of UK culture and also encourages students to write about their own cultural norms.

Lesson overview

Time: Approximately one hour

Aim: By the end of the lesson students will have discussed examples of manners and etiquette in UK culture in conjunction with modal verbs for explaining rules. They will also have reflected on their own cultures in order to design a poster.

Materials: A set of vocabulary cards and a worksheet. You may prepare poster templates and stationery such as coloured pens and large paper to design posters.

Doing a warmer activity

Whole class   8 minutes

Do a 'board rush' activity. Here's how:

1. Prepare a set of cards showing expressions for offering rules and advice. Put the categories A–F on the board which I show in Figure 26-1 where you can also see the vocabulary cards.

2. Put the cards a little distance away from the board.

3. Choose one student to pick a card and give her ten seconds or so to run to the board and stick the card up under the correct category. The other students can help by shouting out.

4. Review the vocabulary, making sure that students know how to use it well in sentences.

Keep the game visible for later use.

You can play this game on the floor too. Or you can set out the categories on two A3 sheets so that groups compete against each other using separate sets of vocabulary cards. The first team to have filled in the chart correctly, as judged by you, wins.

_A_	_B_	_C_	_D_	_E_	_F_
Good idea	**Bad idea**	**Necessary**	**Not necessary**	**Never do this**	**Possible**
should	*it's best not to*	*have to*		*mustn't*	*can*
ought to	*shouldn't*	*must*	*don't have to*	*don't*	
it's best to				*can't*	

Figure 26-1: Example of the rush game showing lexical categories for rules and advice.

Working through a UK manners worksheet

The next activities relate to the worksheet shown in Figure 26-2.

Vocabulary Match the vocabulary on the left with the definitions on the right.

I.	To shake hands	a) It bends your arm.
II.	To stare	b) A set of clothes that look good together
III.	Elbow (n)	c) Move your head up and down.
IV.	To nod	d) Look for a long time (negative)
V.	Parallel (adj)	e) Put your index finger straight out.
VI.	To point	f) Hold someone's hand and move it up and down
VII.	An outfit	g) Two straight lines lying in the same direction.

UK Manners and Etiquette

Complete the rules of UK manners and etiquette using an appropriate expression.

1) Don't/You can't/You mustn't **speak with your mouth full of food.**
2) Shake hands the first time you meet someone, but .... kiss her.
3) You .... stare at someone you don't know.
4) If someone invites you for dinner in their house, you .... take a gift such as chocolates.
5) When you receive a gift, ... open it immediately.
6) You .... be up to ten minutes late for dinner at someone's house.
7) You .... keep your elbows off the table during a meal.
8) When you've finished eating, ... show that you've finished by putting your knife and fork together parallel on your plate.
9) Men .... stand up and give their seat to a woman on the bus/train.
10) You .... point at someone with your finger.
11) If a driver stops to let you go, you .... nod or lift your hand to say thanks.
12) You .... chat in your language in front of a friend who doesn't understand you.
13) If someone is old enough to be your parent, you .... call them by their first name.
14) You .... stand at arm's length (about 1 metre away) when you are talking to a Brit you don't know very well.
15) If your friend's wearing an outfit you don't like, you .... tell them.

Figure 26-2: Intermediate worksheet for UK manners and etiquette.

T >> St   **7 minutes**

Copy the worksheet in Figure 26-2 or prepare a similar one.

Hand out the worksheet to the class. Introduce the vocabulary section and allow students to use a dictionary to help them as they match each word with its definition in preparation for the discussion on UK manners. Get students in pairs to compare words with definitions and tell them to ask you for input if they disagree.

St >> st   **15 minutes**

Ask students to listen carefully as you read the 15 sentences in the 'UK Manners and Etiquette' section on the worksheet. They should underline any words they don't understand and ask you to explain them when you finish that sentence.

Make a funny noise every time you come to a gap in the text. This introduces humour, which helps to hold students' attention.

Now divide students into small groups to discuss the sentences in the worksheet and put in the correct expressions. They should choose from the vocabulary used in the warmer activity such as *ought to* and *don't* to complete the sentences. Let them know that different expressions are possible. Their answers must be about UK culture, not their own opinions, and if they aren't sure, they should guess. Do the first sentence with the whole class as an example.

Giving feedback

Whole class   **10 minutes**

Go over the answers to the UK Manners and Etiquette section of the worksheet. Get each student to read a completed answer. Discuss the answers as a class and explain any unfamiliar practices that are common in UK culture.

Here are suggested answers for the worksheet.

1. Don't/ You can't/ You mustn't

2. You don't have to

3. Mustn't /can't

4. Should/ ought to

5. You can/ you don't have to

6. Can

7. It's best to/ You ought to/ you should/ you must

8. It's best to/ You ought to/ you should/ you must

9. Don't have to/ can

10. Shouldn't

11. Ought to/should

12. Shouldn't/ mustn't/can't

13. Can

14. Should/ ought to

15. Don't have to

Making an alien information poster

St >> St   **15 minutes**

In this activity students describe their own cultures. They work in small groups to complete information posters. You can prepare templates like the one in Figure 26-3, or give students a free rein. In multi-lingual classes you may group students by country or continent.

The Alien Information Service

Do's

Don'ts

And always remember.........

Figure 26-3:
Template
for alien
information
cultural
rules poster.

Tell the class that alien visitors are going to live in the students' home towns or regions for a while. The aliens will stay in the homes of local families and do normal activities. Students need to write the most important rules of culture as advice for the extra-terrestrial tourists. Tell the students to choose from one of these topics and write cultural advice about it on their poster:

- ✔ Dating

- ✔ Dressing

- ✔ Eating

- ✔ Socialising

- ✔ Working

Use UK culture to provide examples of what students might write.

Giving feedback

Whole class mingle   **5 minutes**

Stick up a gallery of posters around the class so that students can look at the work of each group. If there're different nationalities and cultures represented in the class, the students from each background can explain the various rules further to other members of the class.

Extension activities

Set a class project on UK culture. You can have a feature wall in the room that you gradually build up with pictures and facts following students' research. Allow class or homework time for research on UK designers, architecture, music, recipes, history, law, education and so on.

Chapter 27

Team Work: Going on Field Trips

---

*H*opefully, you're fortunate enough to work for a school that allows and encourages field trips for students. Taking students out of the classroom brings a wide range of advantages. However, you need good preparation and planning to ensure that the students get some real benefit out of the visit.

In this chapter, I show you how to get the best out of field trips, and avoid the pitfalls, so that they have real educational value. I show how to use trips to build some strong lessons, and then offer a pre-intermediate lesson plan spanning three sessions.

Using Field Trips for EFL Lessons

A field is when you take the students outside the school to experience learning in a natural setting. So for us TEFL teachers, it means taking the students to a location, in any country, where English is the language of communication. When you mention going out on a trip to your students their first thought might be, 'Hooray! We're going to have some fun.' That's not unreasonable. After all, who doesn't like to enjoy themselves? And field trips should, indeed, be fun – students having fun learn better. But as the teacher you need to put most of the emphasis on the pedagogic value of the visit.

With that in mind, consider some great reasons to take your students out:

- **Authenticity:** Often after teaching a particular point of grammar in the classroom students ask, 'But do people actually say that?' Taking them out into the real world provides opportunities to see how people use language in authentic settings. At the same time, they pick up new words or phrases in real context.

- **Control:** Well-prepared visits facilitate controlled interactions because students know where they're going, what they need to say, and the nature of the responses they'll get.

- **Culture:** Trips away provide students the opportunity to learn about traditions, customs, and heritage, which inevitably influence language itself.

- **Immediacy:** You can help learners make sense of everyday experiences in English right there on the spot. The outside world of the English language speakers becomes more accessible as a consequence.

- **Life skills:** You can help students build skills in the outside world, such as using public transport in a foreign country.

- **Linking the outside world and the classroom:** The classroom is a comfort zone for students, yet the reality is that they're learning English to handle aspects of life in the outside world. When you bring the two worlds together students are reminded of their purpose and spurred on to more progress.

- **Material:** A trip isn't just a self-contained event. In the preparation stage you can inspire discussion and vocabulary input. Likewise after the visit you can use the trip for analysis, project work, essays, and so on.

- **Variety:** Even the best of activities can seem tedious if done relentlessly. Diversifying learning activities keeps students enthusiastic about their studies. New challenges also provide new perspectives on why particular learning strategies are important.

You may find that some students are rather reluctant to go out and about. Likely they haven't thought about the positive aspects I outline in the preceding bullet points and so don't think that trips are a useful part of the course. You need to highlight the benefits from the outset.

Some students may have particular concerns that you need to address. A private conversation with a reluctant student helps you get to the bottom of the situation. The concern may relate to

- **Accessibility:** Check on access for students with mobility difficulties.

- **Convenience:** Remember that some learners are already hard pushed to attend lessons, alongside work and other commitments so energy levels may vary considerably. If you float the idea early on, the students can raise concerns, which helps you plan.

- ✔ **Cost:** Those on a tight budget may not have the fare to and from the location, or the entrance fee to a place of interest. I find that if you discuss the idea of going on trips with the class well in advance of preparing a specific event, you can gauge where to take them (free event, local challenge, and so on).

- ✔ **Social anxiety:** Some students are very shy and would scarcely talk to a stranger in their own language, let alone undertake a conversation in another language in an unfamiliar setting. So if you're setting a task that involves asking for information, you may need to provide the reassurance of group work. Mix the personalities and roles so perhaps the shy types can do the note-taking while the more extrovert types speak.

Running Field Trips at All Levels

Because many variables exist in the teaching situations you face, I offer suggestions here for low- to high-level students, in their home country or overseas.

Elementary

Try the following with your elementary students:

- ✔ In English-speaking countries get students to navigate the shopping areas. You can give them a series of tasks, such as listing two products in the supermarket confectionery aisle, or the most expensive item in the stationery section.

- ✔ In non-English speaking countries, think about areas frequently visited by foreigners in your city. Are any signs translated into English? Is information by the public presented in both languages? If so, set students the task of surveying an area and writing down as many signs and notices in English as possible.

Intermediate

Give these activities a go with your intermediate students:

- ✔ In English-speaking countries visit a museum, art gallery or a place that has free exhibits of any kind. Set the specific task of comparing and contrasting two exhibits of particular interest. The students have to make notes and then prepare an essay or oral presentation based on the two that they've chosen.

- ✔ In non-English speaking countries make a 'How to' guide for tourists. The students come up with an activity in the locality that would be interesting or useful for a visitor, such as finding the best restaurant and ordering a meal, a day's sightseeing, or using a form of public transport. Take the students out to the location of the activity they choose where they observe and list all the stages of the activity a visitor may need to prepare for. Back in the classroom write up all the stages in English and perhaps post them online.

✔ *National Geographic* has a great online section called 'I Heart My City'. Not only does it provide inspiration for selling your home town to others but there is also a great writing template to fill in. See `intelligenttravel.nationalgeographic.com/author/iheartmycity`.

Advanced

Some activities for advanced students can include:

✔ In English-speaking countries take students to the magistrate's court to listen to a case. You can prepare by looking at the language of crime and punishment, and after the visit the students can write their own newspaper article about the case.

To prepare for a trip to the courts try the UK website called You Be the Judge (`www.ybtj.justice.gov.uk`). You can follow along with a simulated case, looking at the aggravating and mitigating circumstances, before discussing the appropriate sentence.

✔ In non-English speaking countries design interview questions and surveys that students can use to speak to tourists and visitors in the area. The survey can be about practically anything that students are interested in as long as it doesn't take too long and it won't bore the visitors. Collate the responses into graphs and charts with a summarising report of student findings.

Pre-intermediate Lesson Plan (for Three Sessions)

You can use this lesson plan in many ways. Ideally, you spread the ideas here over three sessions:

1. **Prepare for the visit.**

2. **Enjoy the day out.**

3. **Follow up with class discussion.**

I've written this plan mainly for students who are already in an English-speaking country or are planning a visit to one.

Using one lesson to set up further work gives the class a sense of continuity, which builds anticipation for the next lesson.

Lesson overview

Time: Approximately one hour for the first session, two or three hours for second session and about thirty minutes for the third session.

Materials: A map showing the route from the school to the place of interest. A written template showing students how to prepare a report.

Aims and objectives: To use students' desire to visit places of interest to practise many language skills. By the end of this lesson students will have practised pronunciation, writing, listening, grammar of questions, and perhaps reading.

Session One: Preparing

In the first session you build up anticipation for the trip and help students prepare language that is useful for travelling there and also recording information while there.

Doing a warmer activity

`St >> Sts`   6 minutes

In pairs the students tell each other about three places of interest in their hometown that they'd recommend to tourists. Have a class feedback session in which the students tell you which places sound the most interesting.

If all your students are from the same place, get them to draft a short list of the five best places to visit. Together they can compare their lists and try to reach an agreement.

Planning the journey

`T >> Sts` **3 minutes**

Show pictures of places of interest the class may be able to visit. Either get them to choose one or tell them which one you've decided upon, and why. Find out what they know about the place.

`St >> St` **10 minutes**

The next step is to plan the route. Make sure that all the students can see a map of the area covering the route from the school to their place of interest. It may be a road map or a local transport map. In small groups, ask students to note down the route from the school to the location. Start them off by noting the first couple of places on the board; for example, train stations, bus stops, or villages that they'll probably go through.

A representative of one group then shows the route on the board as a list. Ask whether the other students agree or not. Some may choose to come up to the board and adjust the route.

`T >> Sts` **5 minutes**

At this point you should have a list of place names from the route. Drill the names of these places, highlighting pronunciation features such as the use of the schwa, which is /ə/ on the phonemic chart, in typical endings. I write about the schwa in Teaching English as Foreign Language For Dummies in Chapter 12. You usually find a smattering of syllables like these in English language place names:

–ford	/fəd/
–bury	/brɪ/
–shire	/ʃə/
–wich	/ɪdʒ/ or /ɪtʃ/
–burgh/borough	/brə/
–ham	/əm/ or /həm/

The advantage of teaching the pronunciation of place names is that students have something to focus on en route to the place of interest. For example, they can listen to the announcements on public transport, which will confirm the pronunciation previously drilled in class. They can also pick off the various places mentioned on the map as they travel along the route.

If there happen to be no interesting place names to work on, instruct your students to write down some directions to the location instead.

Considering the place

St >> St   10 minutes

Together pairs of students write down eight to ten things they'd like to find out about while visiting the chosen destination. For example, students visiting Tate Modern in London may ask:

✔ What time does it close?

✔ Can I take photographs there?

✔ Which is the most expensive painting?

✔ Is it similar to a place in my country?

Start students off with an example or two on the board.

Writing questions in English is always tricky for students, especially at lower levels. In particular you need to remind them about using the auxiliary verb as well as the main verb in the infinitive form (unless the main verb is 'to be'). So, not 'What you see in this gallery?' but 'What *can* you *see* in this gallery?'

Monitor the progress of each group for accuracy and content.

St >> St   10 minutes

Now take one person from each of the previous pairs to form new groups. In this way they can compare their ideas.

Ask one student to read out all of his questions to the whole class. Other students note down good questions they don't have.The other studentsrs can read out any individual question they think is particularly good. The class can note these too. As a result, all the students should have interesting questions to work with.

While the students are at the place of interest they must find the answers to as many of these questions as possible. This task stops them from just wandering around, messing about, or missing the point of the visit.

St >> St   10 minutes

The next challenge is to find out what the visitors to this place of interest think about it. Many students have a camera phone or voice recorder they can use for this purpose. Students will use their gadgets to interview other tourists and get their opinions on what they liked or disliked about their visit.

Make sure students know how to speak politely when interviewing others. Go over a little script like this, putting it on the board:

> Excuse me, please. We are studying English. We would like to ask you two questions and record your answers. Is that okay?

What did you like most about this place? What did you not like?

Thank you very much.

Elicit from the students the reasons why recording the answers is useful: namely, that understanding everything that people say at the time may be difficult and that it will be interesting to listen to the responses in class and get the help of the other students as well as the teacher in understanding the comments.

Pick two or three pairs of students to perform a role-play for the class. So some students act as tourists and the other students interview them using the script on the board. It's a good idea to practise recording the 'tourists' answers too to iron out any technical issues.

Organising homework

T >> St   6 minutes

Make sure that the students understand the meaning of each part of the report and that they know what kind of information to write there. They can use the template as a framework for note taking while on the trip.

Session two: Going on the trip

When you go off on the trip, take the route map and remind the students of the place names. Elicit the pronunciation from them and get them to follow the route on the map as you go.

At the place of interest, move around among the various groups and help them to complete their questions.

Look after any shy students and, if necessary, introduce them personally to tourists to make it easier for your students to interview them.

Session three: Feeding back to the class

This session gives the class the opportunity to review the trip and go over the data they recorded.

Doing a warmer

T >> st   5 minutes

Ask students some general knowledge questions about the place you visited. Put students into teams and make the activity into a quiz. Keep score on the board and see which team is victorious.

Reporting Back

St >> st   10 minutes

Now ask students to take out the notes they made during the trip. They must compare the answers to the eight to ten questions they decided upon in session one. Then check as a class, that all the students know the answers.

Whole Class   15 minutes

Ask students to share their recordings with the class. After playing them aloud, see whether the class can transcribe what the tourists said. Help them where necessary.

T >> Sts   5 minutes

Set the students homework to write a report based on the notes they made in your template (see Figure 27-1). Give them plenty of time to complete and hand in homework.

Report: Visiting a Place of Interest

Introduction

Where did you go and when?

....

....……..

How did you get there?

....

....

....

Findings

What interesting information do you know about this place?

....

....

....

....

....

What did other tourists think about this place?

....

....

....

....

Conclusion

Is it a good place to visit?

....

....

....

Figure 27-1:
A template
for writing
a report as
homework.

Extension activities

Get students to research other places to visit and make suggestions to the class by writing their ideas on the weekly plan (I mention this in Chapter 3).

How about breakfast out? A colleague of mine, Steve, arranges outings to a traditional café for a full English (and usually manages to get his own meal on the house, in view of all the custom he brings in!). It's great for food and menu lexis as well as British customs.

Finally, following the drilling of place names, have a session on pronouncing typical surnames such as Smith, Robinson and Jones. You could highlight the 'th' sounds, and pronunciation of vowel sounds.

Part VI

The Part of Tens

Visit www.dummies.com/extras/tefllessonplans for free online lesson plan ideas and outlines.

In this part . . .

✔ Improve your teaching skills by reflecting on what goes well (and not so well).

✔ Learn how to get valuable pointers from your colleagues.

✔ Gather and use feedback from your students.

✔ Discover how to make your own feedback really valuable.

✔ Find out the value of educational games.

✔ Make the best possible use of online resources.

Chapter 28

Ten Ways to Improve Your Teaching Skills

*P*erhaps by now you've already taught your first lessons, maybe even a whole course. Whether you intend to spend a single gap year on the job, or you can see yourself having a lifelong career in the world of TEFL, you should work towards being a conscientious teacher who knows her craft. It is your responsibility to give students value for money and a good education.

In this chapter, I show you ten ways to up-skill, to your students' delight.

Get the Right Job

Many different types of teaching establishments exist around the world. Some basically entertain students on a study trip, and others run evening courses year round. There are those that have continuous enrolment programmes so students come and go all the time, and others run alongside university degrees to support non-native speakers.

If you want to be taken seriously as a TEFL teacher, you need a serious job in a decent school or teaching establishment. Frankly, an employer who shows little regard for the progress and welfare of the students is unlikely to invest in developing you.

There are a few points to look out for when you are looking for a good employer. Schools that are accredited by a professional body are obliged to conform to certain professional standards and this provides protection for students and employees. Either speak to (former) students in the area to gauge whether a school has a good reputation or search online for students' comments. It is very important that students receive exactly what they are promised and, in addition, schools must base their courses on sound pedagogy. Find out what you can about the premises too. The resources available to students and teachers tell you a lot about the school's budget and what it considers important.

Be realistic! If you realise that your job has no long-term prospects, get onto TEFL.com (www.TEFL.com), Tefl-jobs.co.uk (www.tefl-jobs.co.uk), or an agency and look for an accredited school with a rate of pay that attracts more serious teachers.

At a job interview:

- ✔ Bring up the subject of continuing professional development and ask how this happens at the school.
- ✔ Find out which courses are taught in the school and whether you will be trained to teach each of them over time.

Be a Reflective Teacher

Being a reflective teacher means that you note (in your own teaching journal or at the bottom of a lesson plan you just used) what went well and what didn't during each lesson.

Every teacher must bear her own load of responsibility with regard to teaching. It's your job to give the good valuef by covering the syllabus in a practical and hopefully enjoyable way. So if your students tend to look apathetic at the end of each lesson, find out why.

If something went badly, consider how you could prevent a recurrence, even if it wasn't your fault. Did you go through the activities too quickly? Did you choose enjoyable subject matter? Can you manage your students differently so that rowdy ones cause less disruption? And so on. It's up to you. And if you don't know how to make improvements through your own research, ask for help.

If possible, record yourself teaching once in a while. You can assess yourself more objectively that way.

Learn from Your Boss

Your Director of Studies (DOS) is a teacher. Okay, so many end up locked in an office planning courses and fighting fires, but the DOS probably got the job based on her experience and fine teaching skills. Therefore, she can offer some useful pointers.

Most good schools set up a programme of observations so that the DOS, or ADOS (the assistant), can ensure that you're on track regarding your teaching. If this isn't the case, you can always ask for a visit.

An observation by your manager can be nerve wracking, but it's highly beneficial at the same time. You see, sometimes your students are fond of you just because you have a nice personality, regardless of your teaching ability, and this can result in complacency on your part. Your boss's objective view of your lessons can really sharpen you up.

Whether or not you agree with the feedback you get, the act of preparing a thorough plan that the observer reads reminds you of good habits you may have lost. You can also ask that the observer look out for any aspect of your lesson that you may be concerned about. This shows that you really want to benefit from the experience and narrows the advice you receive to something you're really interested in.

Getting Input from Peers

Less scary than the DOS (see the preceding section) but often just as effective is observation by a peer. This is when teachers agree to watch each other's lessons and give feedback. Friendly colleagues generally concentrate on giving praise and suggestions, and rarely criticism. But peer observations do help you develop as a teacher. As an open-minded, reflective teacher, when you see your colleagues' excellent habits your own conscience will be pricked and you are likely to resolve in yourself to remove any bad habits that have crept in.

In a staff meeting or appraisal, ask the management of your school to allow paid time for teachers to watch each other, even if it's just for 15 or 20 minutes each. The DOS may agree to step into your classroom and hold the fort while you do this, and in so doing she gets a rare chance to connect with the students too.

Gathering Student Feedback

As a rule, consumers make more effort to tell a service provider when things go badly than when everything goes perfectly well. Our learners are no different, but when you encourage feedback (good or bad) you're able to make appropriate adjustments to your lessons before the complaint arrives on the DOS's desk. Furthermore, if the feedback informs you that a particular lesson went well, you can repeat the model with other classes too.

So make sure that students have a range of formats for expressing their opinions. Speak to them individually face to face, have class discussions, allow for anonymous written feedback, pin a feedback sheet on a notice board or whatever other means is suitable for them.

Don't automatically take offence if students complain. Students have the right to do so. Although I accept that not all complaints are valid. I've had some very spurious ones myself, including, 'I know I got only 17 per cent in my progress test, but I think the lessons are too easy for me!'

Check Out Teachers' Clubs

I am very fortunate to teach in Central London where some of the well-established schools run special events and clubs for teachers. For example, Saint Giles International has its longstanding Tuesday night club and Oxford House College often has visiting speakers who are authors of TEFL resources. Clubs like these aim to raise teaching standards and keep colleagues abreast of new developments in the industry.

Find out whether any such clubs run in your area and whether your managers will provide funding for you to attend (but do go along even if they don't). Adding any activities like these to your CV impresses prospective employers because it shows that you take the time to further your knowledge.

No doubt some of you are working in remote places where attending such a club sounds rather implausible. However, if you have access to the Internet, you have access to other teachers. Subscribe to the *EL Gazette* (www.elgazette.com), the *International TESL Journal* (www.iteslj.org), and *HLT Magazine* (www.hltmag.co.uk) for starters, and make use of teachers' blogs or forums (you could always start one). Regular input of this kind helps you keep your teaching fresh and innovative.

Attend Conferences and Seminars

Depending on where in the world you teach, major annual conferences for English language teaching are likely to take place in the country. These are opportunities for people in and around the TEFL industry to talk to each other and promote what they do. For example, I enjoy the IATEFL conference, which changes location each year, and the Language Show at London's Olympia too. Exhibitors are very happy to talk to you, offer freebies and swap contact details so you can find out about products, jobs, techniques, and so on.

Some such events last for days and cost a fair amount, so you may not attend the whole thing. In this case, ask your employer to obtain membership and sponsor one member of staff to go who'll feed the information back to the rest of the team. In addition, many plenaries are available as videos online and information sheets are downloadable, so it's worth visiting conference websites.

Reading through all the educational research presented at conferences is quite time consuming. Start by looking for sessions that teach only classroom applications.

The British Council lists upcoming conferences worldwide on their website. Check out www.teachingenglish.org.uk/conferences. The English UK website also has a training section that gives information about training days and conferences: www.englishuk.com/en/training.

Set New Challenges

If you want to move forward, set yourself professional aims and objectives. These may be

- ✔ **In-house:** For example, learning to teach exam, business, EAP (English for Academic Purposes), or one-to-one courses. Perhaps you're prepared to take on a senior teacher or ADOS role, or maybe you want to learn how to use technology such as moodles and interactive whiteboards.

- ✔ **External:** You may gain your CELTA and DELTA qualifications. These are the certificate and diploma in English language teaching.

You need to avoid being frozen in time. Some teachers get off to a blistering start by designing a bunch of lesson plans, but they've been using them ever since, even 15 years later. Big mistake! In this technological age, you've no excuse for not keeping up with the times. Access to information is unprecedented and the students know it. So by all means hold on to your lesson ideas, but keep adapting and updating them.

Make the Most of What You've Got

Have you had a good look around your teachers' room at work? Perhaps it houses a library of resource books. Even if they're a little dusty and look unloved, take a look through them, because they indicate that someone took enough interest in lesson quality to provide you with a bit of back-up. Root through whatever your school provides and try out something different as a result.

It's not just about books either. Is there a games shelf or a file with some prepared worksheets? And how about those books and hand-outs you got on your initial TEFL course? Review all resources. Doing so will inspire you.

Keep an Eye on Useful Websites

Throughout this book I refer to a vast number of websites, but here are a select few for professional development, jobs and lesson plans:

✔ www.Britishcouncil.org: Offers jobs, information and lesson plans.

✔ www.busyteacher.org: Get worksheets and flashcards here.

✔ www.eslcafe.com: Try this one for advice on jobs abroad.

✔ www.etprofessional.com: A useful resource for professional development.

✔ www.iteslj.org: Read articles on academic findings related to EFL.

✔ www.onestopenglish.com: Run by MacMillan books, this site provides endless information about lesson planning.

✔ www.tefl.net: A general resource network for TEFL.

✔ www.usingenglish.com: This is a good general resource for advice and information.

Chapter 29

Ten Ways to Make Your Students Happy

In This Chapter

▶ Being prepared with the students' needs in minds

▶ Offering praise, constructive criticism, and helpful corrections

▶ Making lessons fun with games and humour

*S*tudents of English come in all shapes and sizes, not to mention demeanours. Obviously, you can't please all of the people all of the time, but you can do some things to create a happy teaching environment for your students and you. Your job is far easier if your students are content. And, of course, lessons are more motivating for students if they feel you're serious about doing a good job.

In this chapter, I show you various ways to keep your courses running smoothly that will inevitably put a smile on your students' faces.

Put Your Students at the Heart of Planning

Ask your students about topics they'd like to cover and try, where possible, to fit them in. (Flick to Chapter 3 for more details on creating weekly plans that allow room for student input.)

Sometimes your course is just one part of the students' overall educational programme. In this case, find out more about the other classes they're taking. Perhaps their other teachers can you give you some basic information that allows you to make your lesson content more relevant to your students' needs and interests. Likewise, pick up a brochure about the company if you're running a business English course. Ask questions about your students' jobs from the students themselves or the human resources department, and then work related points into your lessons.

Also, consider timing. Could you carry out that test at a more appropriate time? Can you find out what kind of schedule the students have before setting a detailed homework assignment? Showing consideration often produces better results from students in the long run.

Prepare Solidly

Although some of the best lessons go in a direction you least expect, you still need to be well prepared. As your career develops you become more skilful at planning, and consequently spend less time doing so than when you started. However, in order to achieve the best quality lessons, you must always prepare with your particular students in mind.

Even if you're using a course book that has a teachers' book to accompany it, you still need to make the material your own. You may decide to change the order of play (the Presentation, Practice, and Production approach can become Engage, Study, Activate, for example – see Chapter 3) and adjust the examples so that they fit your class. Get your materials ready, with any CDs that you use in place, and any supplementary references on hand.

Be reflective (see Chapter 28), offer variety, and listen to what your students want.

Give One-to-One Tutorials

A *tutorial* is a private conversation with a student, designed to discuss his educational progress or any matters concerning it. They are best done by arrangement so that both of you are prepared and know what you want to discuss. Some schools may insist on tutorials, but as the teacher, you can also take the initiative to arrange them.

The advantages of these little one-to-one sessions are many:

- ✔ Shy students speak more frankly in this kind of setting.
- ✔ You demonstrate that you're genuinely interested in your students' individual progress, which is in itself motivating for them.

✔ You can address the particular needs of one student that the class as a whole doesn't share.

✔ You can handle sensitive issues with less embarrassment for students.

✔ You prevent issues from escalating.

Unfortunately, tutorials are pretty time consuming, but the good news is that you don't have to do them all in one go. One appointment a week for less than ten minutes may work. So, for example, you get a group activity going and then withdraw one student. I tend to give my class a TV programme to watch online along with some comprehension questions or conversation points, and then step outside the room with one learner for the tutorial.

Find out what the student is doing outside of the lessons to improve his English. You may choose to recommend particular books, films, or websites to give further practice.

Use Educational Games

Games play an important role in EFL lessons because, as many approaches and methods acknowledge (see Chapter 2), relaxed students acquire language better. (Though that doesn't mean you can fall into the trap of playing games simply to kill time or to raise a laugh.) Have a good selection of TEFL games up your sleeve and be aware of the skills your games develop in students and what you aim to accomplish by using them.

Convert traditional games by incorporating a language-based challenge in order for the players to win the advantage. For example:

✔ **Noughts and crosses:** Fill the squares with grammar/vocabulary topics. When students want to claim a square, they have to answer a question on that topic first. For example, a question about adjectives could be 'Name three adjectives beginning with L.' With reference to register, which means choosing the right degree of formality in your of expression, you might ask 'What is an informal word for "man"?'

The same principle applies to snakes and ladders; just have a question for each square.

✔ **Twenty questions:** Get the students to guess which celebrity you are, but refuse to answer unless the question asked is grammatically correct. This game inspires great peer correction.

✔ **Board rushes:** Divide students into teams. One member from each team has to run to the board in order to write something or rub something off. For example, I put recently learnt vocabulary on the board and students rush to cross off the word that matches the definition I shout out.

Help with Revision and Testing

For most people the best way to remember information is to repeat it. Great lessons can disappear into the ether if you don't reiterate the main points. Some ways to use revision tactics are

- ✔ Have a brief review at the end of the lesson.
- ✔ Set a homework assignment based on the lesson content.
- ✔ Begin a new lesson by reviewing the last session.
- ✔ If you have to write lesson notes after each lesson, get the students to tell you what to put down.

Most tests are mandatory in schools but don't exactly have students leaping for joy. Have class revision sessions in which the students scan their notes and prepare quizzes to test each other. And if you get to design the test yourself, incorporate variety (essays, oral presentations, listening questions that lead to diagrams, and so on) so that students with different learning styles have a chance to shine.

Encourage and Praise

Never underestimate the value of praise! Everyone enjoys a pat on the back and recognition of a job well done. So do the same for your students by always finding something to praise them on, even if correction or criticism follows.

When you have a feedback session after an activity, don't feel that you have nothing to say if everything went well. Tell the students why they accomplished their task successfully so that they know how to use their strengths. You'll certainly motivate your students by doing so.

This guidance applies to written work too. Instead of just highlighting errors, write notes such as 'Good point!' or 'Nice use of synonyms!' in the margin.

Give Constructive Criticism

In the TEFL classroom students must understand where they went wrong and develop the skills to minimise their errors. With this in mind, it isn't enough to say that a student's utterance is wrong or 'just doesn't sound right'. Make sure that your students understand why, or else they feel frustrated. For example, a student says this:

I been to cinema last night!

There are two possible areas for criticism here: the tense construction and the lack of article. So you may offer constructive criticism like this:

> That's interesting! So tell me, which tense do we use with 'last night', 'last week' or 'yesterday'? What is the past simple of 'to go'? And where is the article in this sentence?

Questions of this kind remind the students of rules they've learnt and lead them to self-correction, which boosts their confidence.

There is nothing constructive about 'You can't say that!' unless you explain why. Rules and patterns exist for most expressions in English, so learn them!

Correct Effectively

Students benefit greatly from correction. They find out which areas they need to work on, and knowing that you're analysing their activities provides reassurance that you're able to help them.

If you correct too much or too intrusively, you dishearten your students. Choose errors that will improve communication the most.

Make a distinction between fluency- and accuracy-based activities. So if you're working on fluency, let the students get into the flow of speech. As long as communication is effective, correction can wait. Make a note of a few points you can bring up as feedback, not an exhaustive list.

You don't need to say who the made the error in front of the whole class. Just put the erroneous sentence on the board and ask for suggestions from the class on how to correct it.

Stick to the Syllabus

Use the syllabus to orient learners. It tells everyone concerned where the course is headed and what it will include. That is not to say that you can't depart from the syllabus at all. It might be invigorating if you do, from time to time. Input from students is valuable. But as a general rule, stick to the syllabus because then

- ✔ Both teacher and students are aware of what the course covers.
- ✔ Students understand the difference between each level and course.
- ✔ Students can prepare.

For more on the syllabus, see Chapter 3.

Keep a Sense of Humour

The good thing about a sense of humour is that it helps you acknowledge the mistakes you'll inevitably make and deal with them. Trying to be the perfect authority on the English language is pointless when everyone makes the odd typo and board error and has the occasional mental block.

If you laugh at yourself, students feel more comfortable about making errors too. And an injection of humour into the lesson itself is excellent for relaxing the students, which enables better language acquisition.

Index

Notes

Notes

About the Author

Michelle Maxom began teaching part-time in 1997 after doing an intensive Trinity TESOL certificate. She later moved to Italy where she furthered her studies in EFL and honed her skills working with students of all ages and from a wide variety of backgrounds. She toured secondary schools and gave seminars in Caribbean literature and Britain's multi-ethnic culture showing how the English language can open doors and minds. On returning to the UK she took on the post of Director of Studies at a central London EFL school, bringing it to accreditation by the British Council for the first time and learning how to work behind the scenes in the industry. She has made an instructional film for Thomson ELT and become a specialist in one-to-one courses. After becoming a freelance teacher/trainer Michelle delivered a work experience programme, taught on intensive TEFL courses in London and Paris, and tutored those studying EFL by distance learning. These days she can be found teaching at the University of the Arts, London.

Author's Acknowledgments

Many thanks to those who supported me during the writing of this book. In particular, I would like to thank The Language Centre staff at UAL for being flexible and providing many wonderful colleagues to learn from. Thanks to Rashida for helping me hit my dealine and to all my students who inspire amazing ideas with their enthusiasm. Lorraine and Letitia you egged me on all the way. As usual, my family have been supportive at every turn, especiallly Myrtle May. I appreciate you all.

Publisher's Acknowledgments

We're proud of this book; please send us your comments at http://dummies.custhelp.com. For other comments, please contact our Customer Care Department within the U.S. at 877-762-2974, outside the U.S. at (001) 317-572-3993, or fax 317-572-4002.

Some of the people who helped bring this book to market include the following:

Acquisitions, Editorial, and Vertical Websites

Project Editor: Simon Bell

Commissioning Editor: Mike Baker

Assistant Editor: Ben Kemble

Development Editor: Charlie Wilson

Copy Editor: Martin Key

Publisher: Miles Kendall

Vertical Websites: Rich Graves

Cover Photos: ©iStockphoto.com/egal

Project Coordinator: Melissa Cossell

Take Dummies with you everywhere you go!

Whether you're excited about e-books, want more from the web, must have your mobile apps, or swept up in social media, Dummies makes everything easier.

Visit Us

Like Us

Follow Us

Watch Us

Join Us

Pin Us

Circle Us

Shop Us

FOR DUMMIES®

A Wiley Brand

BUSINESS

978-1-118-73077-5

978-1-118-44349-1

978-1-119-97527-4

MUSIC

978-1-119-94276-4

978-0-470-97799-6

978-0-470-49644-2

DIGITAL PHOTOGRAPHY

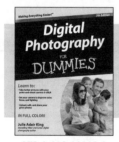

978-1-118-09203-3

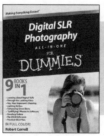

978-0-470-76878-5

978-1-118-00472-2

Algebra I For Dummies
978-0-470-55964-2

Anatomy & Physiology For Dummies, 2nd Edition
978-0-470-92326-9

Asperger's Syndrome For Dummies
978-0-470-66087-4

Basic Maths For Dummies
978-1-119-97452-9

Body Language For Dummies, 2nd Edition
978-1-119-95351-7

Bookkeeping For Dummies, 3rd Edition
978-1-118-34689-1

British Sign Language For Dummies
978-0-470-69477-0

Cricket for Dummies, 2nd Edition
978-1-118-48032-8

Currency Trading For Dummies, 2nd Edition
978-1-118-01851-4

Cycling For Dummies
978-1-118-36435-2

Diabetes For Dummies, 3rd Edition
978-0-470-97711-8

eBay For Dummies, 3rd Edition
978-1-119-94122-4

Electronics For Dummies All-in-One For Dummies
978-1-118-58973-1

English Grammar For Dummies
978-0-470-05752-0

French For Dummies, 2nd Edition
978-1-118-00464-7

Guitar For Dummies, 3rd Edition
978-1-118-11554-1

IBS For Dummies
978-0-470-51737-6

Keeping Chickens For Dummies
978-1-119-99417-6

Knitting For Dummies, 3rd Edition
978-1-118-66151-2

FOR DUMMIES®
A Wiley Brand

SELF-HELP

978-0-470-66541-1

978-1-119-99264-6

978-0-470-66086-7

LANGUAGES

978-0-470-68815-1

978-1-119-97959-3

978-0-470-69477-0

HISTORY

978-0-470-68792-5

978-0-470-74783-4

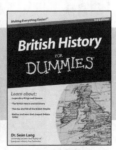
978-0-470-97819-1

Laptops For Dummies 5th Edition
978-1-118-11533-6

Management For Dummies,
2nd Edition
978-0-470-97769-9

Nutrition For Dummies, 2nd Edition
978-0-470-97276-2

Office 2013 For Dummies
978-1-118-49715-9

Organic Gardening For Dummies
978-1-119-97706-3

Origami Kit For Dummies
978-0-470-75857-1

Overcoming Depression For Dummies
978-0-470-69430-5

Physics I For Dummies
978-0-470-90324-7

Project Management For Dummies
978-0-470-71119-4

Psychology Statistics For Dummies
978-1-119-95287-9

Renting Out Your Property For Dummies,
3rd Edition
978-1-119-97640-0

Rugby Union For Dummies, 3rd Edition
978-1-119-99092-5

Stargazing For Dummies
978-1-118-41156-8

Teaching English as a Foreign Language
For Dummies
978-0-470-74576-2

Time Management For Dummies
978-0-470-77765-7

Training Your Brain For Dummies
978-0-470-97449-0

Voice and Speaking Skills For Dummies
978-1-119-94512-3

Wedding Planning For Dummies
978-1-118-69951-5

WordPress For Dummies, 5th Edition
978-1-118-38318-6